38TH CONGRESS, 1st Session.	HOUSE OF REPRESENTATIVES.	REPORT No. 65.

FORT PILLOW MASSACRE.

MAY 6, 1864.—*Resolved*, That forty thousand extra copies of the Report of the Joint Committee on the Conduct of the War, &c., with the accompanying testimony, in relation to the late massacre at Fort Pillow, be printed for the use of the members of this house.

JOINT RESOLUTION directing the Committee on the Conduct of the War to examine into the recent attack on Fort Pillow.

Resolved by the Senate and House of Representatives of the United States of America in Congress assembled, That the Joint Committee on the Conduct of the War be, and they are hereby, instructed to inquire into the truth of the rumored slaughter of the Union troops, after their surrender, at the recent attack of the rebel forces upon Fort Pillow, Tennessee; as, also, whether Fort Pillow could have been sufficiently re-enforced or evacuated, and if so, why it was not done; and that they report the facts to Congress as soon as possible.

Approved April 21, 1864.

Mr. GOOCH, from the Joint Select Committee on the Conduct of the War, made the following

REPORT.

The Joint Committee on the Conduct and Expenditures of the War, to whom was referred the resolution of Congress instructing them to investigate the late massacre at Fort Pillow, designated two members of the committee—Messrs. Wade and Gooch—to proceed forthwith to such places as they might deem necessary, and take testimony. That sub-committee having discharged that duty, returned to this city, and submitted to the joint committee a report, with accompanying papers and testimony. The report was read and adopted by the committee, whose chairman was instructed to submit the same, with the testimony, to the Senate, and Mr. Gooch to the House, and ask that the same be printed.

REPORT OF SUB-COMMITTEE.

Messrs. WADE and GOOCH, the sub-committee appointed by the Joint Committee on the Conduct and Expenditures of the War, with instructions to proceed to such points as they might deem necessary for the purpose of taking testimony in regard to the massacre at Fort Pillow, submitted the following report to the joint committee, together with the accompanying testimony and papers:

In obedience to the instructions of this joint committee adopted on the 18th ultimo, your committee left Washington on the morning of the 19th, taking with them the stenographer of this committee, and proceeded to Cairo and Mound City, Illinois; Columbus, Kentucky; and Fort Pillow and Memphis, Tennessee; at each of which places they proceeded to take testimony.

Although your committee were instructed to inquire only in reference to the attack, capture, and massacre of Fort Pillow, they have deemed it proper to take some testimony in reference to the operations of Forrest and his command immediately preceding and subsequent to that horrible transaction. It will appear, from the testimony thus taken, that the atrocities committed at Fort

Pillow were not the result of passions excited by the heat of conflict, but were the results of a policy deliberately decided upon and unhesitatingly announced. Even if the uncertainty of the fate of those officers and men belonging to colored regiments who have heretofore been taken prisoners by the rebels has failed to convince the authorities of our government of this fact, the testimony herewith submitted must convince even the most skeptical that it is the intention of the rebel authorities not to recognize the officers and men of our colored regiments as entitled to the treatment accorded by all civilized nations to prisoners of war. The declarations of Forrest and his officers, both before and after the capture of Fort Pillow, as testified to by such of our men as have escaped after being taken by him; the threats contained in the various demands for surrender made at Paducah, Columbus, and other places; the renewal of the massacre the morning after the capture of Fort Pillow; the statements made by the rebel officers to the officers of our gunboats who received the few survivors at Fort Pillow—all this proves most conclusively the policy they have determined to adopt.

The first operation of any importance was the attack upon Union city, Tennessee, by a portion of Forrest's command. The attack was made on the 24th of March. The post was occupied by a force of about 500 men under Colonel Hawkins, of the 7th Tennessee Union cavalry. The attacking force was superior in numbers, but was repulsed several times by our forces. For the particulars of the attack, and the circumstances attending the surrender, your committee would refer to the testimony herewith submitted. They would state, however, that it would appear from the testimony that the surrender was opposed by nearly if not quite all the officers of Colonel Hawkins's command. Your committee think that the circumstances connected with the surrender are such that they demand the most searching investigation by the military authorities, as, at the time of the surrender, but one man on our side had been injured.

On the 25th of March, the enemy, under the rebel Generals Forrest, Buford, Harris, and Thompson, estimated at over 6,000 men, made an attack on Paducah, Kentucky, which post was occupied by Colonel S. G. Hicks, 40th Illinois regiment, with 655 men. Our forces retired into Fort Anderson, and there made their stand—assisted by some gunboats belonging to the command of Captain Shirk of the navy—successfully repelling the attacks of the enemy. Failing to make any impression upon our forces, Forrest then demanded an unconditional surrender, closing his communication to Colonel Hicks in these words: "If you surrender you shall be treated as prisoners of war, but if I have to storm your works you may expect no quarter." This demand and threat was met by a refusal on the part of Colonel Hicks to surrender, he stating that he had been placed there by his government to defend that post, and he should do so. The rebels made three other assaults that same day, but were repulsed with heavy loss each time, the rebel General Thompson being killed in the last assault. The enemy retired the next day, having suffered a loss estimated at three hundred killed, and from 1,000 to 1,200 wounded. The loss on our side was 14 killed and 46 wounded.

The operations of the enemy at Paducah were characterized by the same bad faith and treachery that seem to have become the settled policy of Forrest and his command. The flag of truce was taken advantage of there, as elsewhere, to secure desirable positions which the rebels were unable to obtain by fair and honorable means; and also to afford opportunities for plundering private stores as well as government property. At Paducah the rebels were guilty of acts more cowardly, if possible, than any they have practiced elsewhere. When the attack was made the officers of the fort and of the gunboats advised the women and children to go down to the river for the purpose of being taken across out of danger. As they were leaving the town for that purpose, the rebel sharpshooters mingled with them, and, shielded by their presence, advanced and fired upon the gunboats, wounding some of our officers and men.

Our forces could not return the fire without endangering the lives of the women and children. The rebels also placed women in front of their lines as they moved on the fort, or were proceeding to take positions while the flag of truce was at the fort, in order to compel our men to withhold their fire, out of regard for the lives of the women who were made use of in this most cowardly manner. For more full details of the attack, and the treacherous and cowardly practices of the rebels there, your committee refer to the testimony herewith submitted.

On the 13th of April, the day after the capture of Fort Pillow, the rebel General Buford appeared before Columbus, Kentucky, and demanded its unconditional surrender. He coupled with that demand a threat that if the place was not surrendered, and he should be compelled to attack it, "no quarter whatever should be shown to the negro troops." To this Colonel Lawrence, in command of the post, replied, that "surrender was out of the question," as he had been placed there by his government to hold and defend the place, and should do so. No attack was made, but the enemy retired, having taken advantage of the flag of truce to seize some horses of Union citizens which had been brought in there for security.

It was at Fort Pillow, however, that the brutality and cruelty of the rebels were most fearfully exhibited. The garrison there, according to the last returns received at headquarters, amounted to 19 officers and 538 enlisted men, of whom 262 were colored troops, comprising one battalion of the 6th United States heavy artillery, (formerly called the 1st Alabama artillery,) of colored troops, under command of Major L. F. Booth; one section of the 2d United States light artillery, colored, and one battalion of the 13th Tennessee cavalry, white, commanded by Major W. F. Bradford. Major Booth was the ranking officer, and was in command of the post.

On Tuesday, the 12th of April, (the anniversary of the attack on Fort Sumter, in April, 1861,) the pickets of the garrison were driven in just before sunrise, that being the first intimation our forces there had of any intention on the part of the enemy to attack that place. Fighting soon became general, and about 9 o'clock Major Booth was killed. Major Bradford succeeded to the command, and withdrew all the forces within the fort. They had previously occupied some intrenchments at some distance from the fort, and further from the river.

This fort was situated on a high bluff, which descended precipitately to the river's edge, the side of the bluff on the river side being covered with trees, bushes, and fallen timber. Extending back from the river, on either side of the fort, was a ravine or hollow—the one below the fort containing several private stores and some dwellings, constituting what was called the town. At the mouth of that ravine, and on the river bank, were some government buildings containing commissary and quartermaster's stores. The ravine above the fort was known as Cold Creek ravine, the sides being covered with trees and bushes. To the right, or below and a little to the front of the fort, was a level piece of ground, not quite so elevated as the fort itself, on which had been erected some log huts or shanties, which were occupied by the white troops, and also used for hospital and other purposes. Within the fort tents had been erected, with board floors, for the use of the colored troops. There were six pieces of artillery in the fort, consisting of two 6-pounders, two 12-pounder howitzers, and two 10-pounder Parrots.

The rebels continued their attack, but, up to two or three o'clock in the afternoon, they had not gained any decisive success. Our troops, both white and black, fought most bravely, and were in good spirits. The gunboat No. 7, (New Era,) Captain Marshall, took part in the conflict, shelling the enemy as opportunity offered. Signals had been agreed upon by which the officers in the fort could indicate where the guns of the boat could be most effective. There being but one gunboat there, no permanent impression appears to have been produced upon the enemy; for as they were shelled out of one ravine, they would make their appearance in the other. They would thus appear and retire as the gunboat moved from one point to the other. About one o'clock the fire on both sides slackened somewhat, and the gunboat moved out in the river, to cool and clean its guns, having fired 282 rounds of shell, shrapnell, and canister, which nearly exhausted its supply of ammunition.

The rebels having thus far failed in their attack, now resorted to their customary use of flags of truce. The first flag of truce conveyed a demand from Forrest for the unconditional surrender of the fort. To this Major Bradford replied, asking to be allowed one hour to consult with his officers and the officers of the gunboat. In a short time a second flag of truce appeared, with a communication from Forrest, that he would allow Major Bradford twenty minutes in which to move his troops out of the fort, and if it was not done within that time an assault would be ordered. To this Major Bradford returned the reply that he would not surrender.

During the time these flags of truce were flying, the rebels were moving down the ravine and taking positions from which the more readily to charge upon the fort. Parties of them were also engaged in plundering the government buildings of commissary and quartermaster's stores, in full view of the gunboat. Captain Marshall states that he refrained from firing upon the rebels, although they were thus violating the flag of truce, for fear that, should they finally succeed in capturing the fort, they would justify any atrocities they might commit by saying that they were in retaliation for his firing while the flag of truce was flying. He says, however, that when he saw the rebels coming down the ravine above the fort, and taking positions there, he got under way and stood for the fort, determined to use what little ammunition he had left in shelling them out of the ravine; but he did not get up within effective range before the final assault was made.

Immediately after the second flag of truce retired, the rebels made a rush from the positions they had so treacherously gained and obtained possession of the fort, raising the cry of "No quarter!" But little opportunity was allowed for resistance. Our troops, black and white, threw down their arms, and sought to escape by running down the steep bluff near the fort, and secreting themselves behind trees and logs, in the bushes, and under the brush—some even jumping into the river, leaving only their heads above the water, as they crouched down under the bank.

Then followed a scene of cruelty and murder without a parallel in civilized warfare, which needed but the tomahawk and scalping-knife to exceed the worst atrocities ever committed by savages. The rebels commenced an indiscriminate slaughter, sparing neither age nor sex, white or black, soldier or civilian. The officers and men seemed to vie with each other in the devilish work; men, women, and even children, wherever found, were deliberately shot down, beaten, and hacked with sabres; some of the children not more than ten years old were forced to stand up and face their murderers while being shot; the sick and the wounded were butchered without mercy, the rebels even entering the hospital building and dragging them out to be shot, or killing them as they lay there unable to offer the least resistance. All over the hillside the work of murder was going on; numbers of our men were collected together in lines or groups and deliberately shot; some were shot while in the river, while others on the bank were shot and their bodies kicked into the water, many of them still living but unable to make any exertions to save themselves from drowning. Some of the rebels stood on the top of the hill or a short distance down its side, and called to our soldiers to come up to them, and as they approached, shot them down in cold blood; if their guns or pistols missed fire, forcing them to stand there until they were again prepared to fire. All around were heard cries of "No quarter!" "No quarter!" "Kill the damned niggers; shoot them down!" All who asked for mercy were answered by the most cruel taunts and sneers. Some were spared for a time, only to be murdered under circumstances of greater cruelty. No cruelty which the most fiendish malignity could devise was omitted by these murderers. One white soldier who was wounded in one leg so as to be unable to walk, was made to stand up while his tormentors shot him; others who were wounded and unable to stand were held up and again shot. One negro who had been ordered by a rebel officer to hold his horse, was killed by him when he remounted; another, a mere child, whom an officer had taken up behind him on his horse, was seen by Chalmers, who at once ordered the officer to put him down and shoot him, which was done. The huts and tents in which many of the wounded had sought shelter were set on fire, both that night and the next morning, while the wounded were still in them—those only escaping who were able to get themselves out, or who could prevail on others less injured than themselves to help them out; and even some of those thus seeking to escape the flames were met by those ruffians and brutally shot down, or had their brains beaten out. One man was deliberately fastened down to the floor of a tent, face upwards, by means of nails driven through his clothing and into the boards under him, so that he could not possibly escape, and then the tent set on fire; another was nailed to the side of a building outside of the fort, and then the building set on fire and burned. The charred remains of five or six bodies were afterwards found, all but one so much disfigured and consumed by the flames that they could not be identified, and the identification of that one is not absolutely certain, although there can hardly be a doubt that it was the body of Lieutenant Akerstrom, quartermaster of the 13th Tennessee cavalry, and a native Tennesseean; several witnesses who saw the remains, and who were personally acquainted with him while living, have testified that it is their firm belief that it was his body that was thus treated.

These deeds of murder and cruelty ceased when night came on, only to be renewed the next morning, when the demons carefully sought among the dead lying about in all directions for any of the wounded yet alive, and those they found were deliberately shot. Scores of the dead and wounded were found there the day after the massacre by the men from some of our gunboats who were permitted to go on shore and collect the wounded and bury the dead. The rebels themselves had made a pretence of burying a great many of their victims, but they had merely thrown them, without the least regard to care or decency, into the trenches and ditches about the fort, or the little hollows and ravines on the hill-side, covering them but partially with earth. Portions of heads and faces, hands and feet, were found protruding through the earth in every direction. The testimony also establishes the fact that the rebels buried some of the living with the dead, a few of whom succeeded afterwards in digging themselves out, or were dug out by others, one of whom your committee found in Mound City hospital, and there examined. And even when your committee visited the spot, two weeks afterwards, although parties of men had been sent on shore from time to time to bury the bodies unburied and rebury the others, and were even then engaged in the same work, we found the evidences of this murder and cruelty still most painfully apparent; we saw bodies still unburied (at some distance from the fort) of some sick men who had been met fleeing from the hospital and beaten down and brutally murdered, and their bodies left where they had fallen. We could still see the faces, hands, and feet of men, white and black, protruding out of the ground, whose graves had not been reached by those engaged in re-interring the victims of the massacre; and although a great deal of rain had fallen within the preceding two weeks, the ground, more especially on the side and at the foot of the bluff where the most of the murders had been committed, was still discolored by the blood of our brave but unfortunate men, and the logs and trees showed but too plainly the evidences of the atrocities perpetrated there.

Many other instances of equally atrocious cruelty might be enumerated, but your committee feel compelled to refrain from giving here more of the heart-sickening details, and refer to the statements contained in the voluminous testimony herewith submitted. Those statements were obtained by them from eye-witnesses and sufferers; many of them, as they were examined by your committee, were lying upon beds of pain and suffering, some so feeble that their lips could with difficulty frame the words by which they endeavored to convey some idea of the cruelties which had been inflicted on them, and which they had seen inflicted on others.

How many of our troops thus fell victims to the malignity and barbarity of Forrest and his followers cannot yet be definitely ascertained. Two officers belonging to the garrison were absent at the time of the capture and massacre. Of the remaining officers but two are known to be living, and they are wounded and now in the hospital at Mound City. One of them, Captain Potter, may even now be dead, as the surgeons, when your committee were there, expressed no hope of his recovery. Of the men, from 300 to 400 are known to have been killed at Fort Pillow, of whom, at least, 300 were murdered in cold blood after the post was in possession of the rebels, and our men had thrown down their arms and ceased to offer resistance. Of the survivors, except the wounded in the hospital at Mound City, and the few who succeeded in making their escape unhurt, nothing definite is known; and it is to be feared that many have been murdered after being taken away from the fort.

In reference to the fate of Major Bradford, who was in command of the fort when it was captured, and who had up to that time received no injury, there seems to be no doubt. The general understanding everywhere seemed to be that he had been brutally murdered the day after he was taken prisoner.

There is some discrepancy in the testimony, but your committee do not see how the one who professed to have been an eye-witness of his death could have been mistaken. There may be some uncertainty in regard to his fate.

When your committee arrived at Memphis, Tennessee, they found and examined a man (Mr. McLagan) who had been conscripted by some of Forrest's forces, but who, with other conscripts, had succeeded in making his escape. He testifies that while two companies of rebel troops, with Major Bradford and many other prisoners, were on their march from Brownsville to Jackson, Tennessee, Major Bradford was taken by five rebels—one an officer—led about fifty yards from the line of march, and deliberately murdered in view of all there assembled. He fell—killed instantly by three musket balls, even while asking that his life might be spared, as he had fought them manfully, and was deserving of a better fate. The motive for the murder of Major Bradford seems to have been the simple fact that, although a native of the south, he remained loyal to his government. The testimony herewith submitted contains many statements made by the rebels that they did not intend to treat "home-made Yankees," as they termed loyal southerners, any better than negro troops.

There is one circumstance connected with the events herein narrated which your committee cannot permit to pass unnoticed. The testimony herewith submitted discloses this most astounding and shameful fact: On the morning of the day succeeding the capture of Fort Pillow, the gunboat Silver Cloud, (No. 28,) the transport Platte Valley, and the gunboat New Era, (No. 7,) landed at Fort Pillow under flag of truce, for the purpose of receving the few wounded there and burying the dead. While they were lying there, the rebel General Chalmers and other rebel officers came down to the landing, and some of them went on the boats. Notwithstanding the evidences of rebel atrocity and barbarity with which the ground was covered, there were some of our army officers on board the Platte Valley so lost to every feeling of decency, honor, and self-respect, as to make themselves disgracefully conspicuous in bestowing civilities and attention upon the rebel officers, even while they were boasting of the murders they had there committed. Your committee were unable to ascertain the names of the officers who have thus inflicted so foul a stain upon the honor of our army. They are assured, however, by the military authorities that every effort will be made to ascertain their names and bring them to the punishment they so richly merit.

In relation to the re-enforcement or evacuation of Fort Pillow, it would appear from the testimony that the troops there stationed were withdrawn on the 25th of January last, in order to accompany the Meridian expedition under General Sherman. General Hurlbut testifies that he never received any instructions to permanently vacate the post, and deeming it important to occupy it, so that the rebels should not interrupt the navigation of the Mississippi by planting artillery there, he sent some troops there about the middle of February, increasing their number afterwards until the garrison amounted to nearly 600 men. He also states that as soon as he learned that the place was attacked, he immediately took measures to send up re-enforcements from Memphis, and they were actually embarking when he received information of the capture of the fort.

Your committee cannot close this report without expressing their obligations to the officers of the army and navy, with whom they were brought in contact, for the assistance they rendered. It is true your committee were furnished by the Secretary of War with the fullest authority to call upon any one in the army for such services as they might require, to enable them to make the investigation devolved upon them by Congress, but they found that no such authority was needed. The army and navy officers at every point they visited evinced a desire to aid the committee in every way in their power; and all expressed the highest satisfaction that Congress had so promptly taken steps to ascertain the facts connected with this fearful and bloody transaction, and the hope that the investigation would lead to prompt and decisive measures on the part of the government. Your committee would mention more particularly the names of General Mason Brayman, military commandant at Cairo; Captain J. H. Odlin, his chief of staff; Captain Alexander M. Pennock, United States navy, fleet captain of Mississippi squadron; Captain James W. Shirk, United States navy, commanding 7th district Mississippi squadron; Surgeon Horace Wardner, in charge of Mound City general hospital; Captain Thomas M. Farrell, United States navy, in command of gunboat Hastings, (furnished by Captain Pennock to convey the committee to Fort Pillow and Memphis;) Captain Thomas Pattison, naval commandant at Memphis; General C. C. Washburne, and the officers of their commands, as among those to whom they are indebted for assistance and attention.

All of which is respectfully submitted.

B. F. WADE.
D. W. GOOCH.

Adopted by the committee as their report.

B. F. WADE, *Chairman.*

TESTIMONY.

CAIRO, ILLINOIS, *April* 22, 1864.

Brigadier General Mason Brayman sworn and examined by the chairman.

Question. What is your rank and position in the service?

Answer. Brigadier General of volunteers; have been in command of the district of Cairo since March 19, 1864.

Question. What was the extent of your district when you assumed command, and what your available force?

Answer. The river, from Paducah to Island No. Ten, inclusive, about 160 miles, and adjacent portions of Tennessee and Kentucky. My available force for duty, as appears from tri-monthly report of March 20, as follows:

Paducah, officers and men	408
Cairo ......do	231
Columbus ...... do	998
Hickman ....do	51
Island No. Ten..do	162
Union City. ....do	479
Aggregate	2,329

Question. What was the character of your force and the condition of your command at that time?

Answer. Three-fourths of the men were colored, a portion of them not mustered into service, and commanded by officers temporarily assigned, awaiting commission. Of the white troops about one-half at the posts on the river were on duty as provost marshals' guards and similar detached duties, leaving but a small number in condition for movement. The fortifications were in an unfinished condition, that at Cairo rendered almost useless by long neglect. Many of the guns were dismounted, or otherwise unfit for service, and the supply of ammunition deficient and defective. A body of cavalry at Paducah were not mounted, and only part of those at Union City. I had not enough mounted men within my reach for orderlies.

Question. What is the character of the public property and interests intrusted to your care?

Answer. Paducah commands the Ohio. In hostile hands, the Tennessee and Cumberland rivers are no longer ours. Mound City, eight miles above Cairo, is the great naval depot for the western fleet. Gunboats there receive their armaments, crews, and supplies. An average of probably $5,000,000 of public property is constantly at that point; I found it guarded by, perhaps, fifty men of the veteran reserve corps, not referring to gunboats lying there. Cairo, at the confluence of the great rivers, is the narrow gateway through which all military and naval operations of the Mississippi valley must be made. I cannot compute the amount or value of shipping and property at all times at this point. The committee must observe that the loss of Mound City and Cairo would paralyze the western army and navy. The points below Columbus and Island Ten are fortified places; while holding them, the rebels had control of the river. It required a prodigious effort to dislodge them. To concede to them any point on the river, even for a week, would bring disaster. Furthermore, the rebels now control western Kentucky; they are murdering, robbing, and driving out the loyal men ; they avow their determination to permit the loyal men to take no part in the approaching elections. Unless protected in their effort to protect themselves, the Union men must give way, and the country remain under insurrectionary control.

Question. Did you consider your force, as stated, adequate to the protection of your district?

Answer. Wholly inadequate, considering the interests at stake, and the hostile forces within attacking distance.

Question. When did you first hear that Forrest was advancing?

Answer. On March 23, four days after I took command, Colonel Hicks, at Paducah, and Colonel Hawkins at Union City, advised me by telegraph of the presence in their neighborhood of armed bands, both fearing an attack. At night of the same day, Colonel Hawkins reported Forrest at Jackson, 61 miles south, with 7,000 men; and again that he expected an attack within 24 hours. He wanted re-enforcements.

Question. Had you the means of re-enforcing him?

Answer. Of my own command, I had not 150 available men; however, some regiments and detachments of General Veatch's division had arrived and awaited the arrival of boats from St. Louis to carry them up the Tennessee. General Veatch had gone to Evansville, Indiana. Simultaneously with the reports from Hicks and Hawkins, I received from General Sherman, then at Nashville, this despatch: "Has General Veatch and command started up the Tennessee? If not, start them up at once." Down to this time it was uncertain whether Union City or Paducah was the real object of attack. Late in the evening I applied to Captain Fox, General Veatch's assistant adjutant general, to have 2,000 men in readiness to move during the night, if wanted, promising to have them back in time to embark, on arrival of their transports. I telegraphed Hawkins that he would receive aid, directing him to "fortify and keep well prepared." About 4½ o'clock of the morning of of the 24th, I was satisfied that Union City was the point of attack. Boats were impressed, four regiments were embarked, and I left at ten; disembarked at Columbus, and arriving within six miles of Union City at four p. m., where I learned that a surrender had taken place at 11 a. m., and the garrison marched off. I turned back, and at three the next morning turned over General Veatch's men, ready to go up the Tennessee.

Question Why did you not pursue Forrest?

Answer. For three reasons: *First*, his force was all cavalry; mine all infantry. *Second*, he was moving on Paducah, and, while I could not overtake him by land, I could head him by the rivers. *Third*, another despatch from General Sherman reached me as I was going out from Columbus, prohibiting me from diverting the troops bound up the Tennessee from that movement on account of the presence of Forrest. My purpose was to save Union City, bring in its garrison, and have General Veatch's men back in time for their boats. While I was willing to risk much to secure a garrison supposed to be yet engaged in gallant defence, I could do nothing to mitigate the accomplished misfortune of a surrender.

Question. Do you think the surrender premature?

Answer. The garrison was within fortifications; the enemy had no artillery. A loss of one man killed and two or three wounded does not indicate a desperate case. The rebels were three times repulsed A flag of truce followed, and a surrender.

Question. How large was the attacking party?

Answer. I judge fifteen hundred, the largest portion of Forrest's force being evidently on the way to Paducah.

Question. How large was his entire force?

Answer. Apparently 6,500.

Question. When was Paducah attacked?

Answer. About 3 p. m. the next day, March 25.

Question. Was Paducah re-enforced previous to the attack?

Answer. It was not. I had no men to send, but sent supplies.

Question. Where was General Veatch's command?

Answer. Embarking for the Tennessee.

Question. Was Paducah well defended?

Answer. Most gallantly, and with success. The conduct of Colonel Hicks and his entire command was noble in the highest degree.

Question. How did his colored troops behave?

Answer. As well as the rest. Colonel Hicks thus refers to them in his official report: "I have been one of those men who never had much confidence in colored troops fighting, but those doubts are now all removed, for they fought as bravely as any troops in the fort."

Question. Why was the city shelled and set on fire?

Answer. Our small force retired within the fort; the rebels took possession of the town, and from adjacent buildings their sharpshooters fired upon us. It was necessary to dislodge them. The gunboats Peosta, Captain Smith, and Paw Paw, Captain O'Neal, and the fort drove them out, necessarily destroying property. Most of the inhabitants being still rebel sympathizers, there was less than the usual regret in performing the duty.

Question. What became of the enemy after the repulse?

Answer. They went south, and on the 26th I was notified by Colonel Hicks and by Colonel Lawrence that they were approaching Columbus.

Question. What was done?

Answer. I went to Columbus again, with such men as could be withdrawn from Cairo, and awaited an attack, but none was made. We were too strong, of which rebels in our midst had probably advised them.

Question. Do you permit rebels to remain within your lines?

Answer. Of course; after they have taken the oath.

Question. What is done in case they violate, by acting as spies, for instance?

Answer. I don't like to acknowledge that we swear them over again, but that is about what it amounts to.

Question. What became of your garrison at Hickman?

Answer. It was but 14 miles from Union City; too weak for defence, and unimportant. Having no re-enforcements to spare, I brought away the garrison.

Question. Was Union City important as a military post?

Answer. I think not, except to keep the peace and drive out guerillas. The railroad was operated to that point at the expense of the government, being used in carrying out supplies, which went mostly into disloyal hands, or were seized by Forrest. The road from Paducah to Mayfield was used by its owners. Enormous quantities of supplies needed by the rebel army were carried to Mayfield and other convenient points, and passed into the hands of the rebel army. I found this abuse so flagrant and dangerous that I made a stringent order stopping all trade. I furnish a copy herewith, making it part of my answer, (Exhibit A.)

Question. What, in your opinion, is the effect of free trade in western Kentucky and Tennessee?

Answer. Pernicious beyond measure; corrupting those in the public service, and furnishing needed supplies to enemies. I am in possession of intercepted correspondence, showing that while the trader who has taken the oath and does business at Paducah gets permits to send out supplies, several wagons at a time, his partner is receiving them within the rebel lines under permits issued by Forrest. A public officer is now under arrest and held for trial for covering up smuggling of contraband goods under permits, and sharing the profits. Pretended loyal men and open enemies thus combined, and the rebel army gets the benefit. We are supplying our enemies with the means of resistance.

Question. Could not the rebels have been sooner driven out of your neighborhood?

Answer. They could by withdrawing men from duties which are presumed to be of greater importance. That point was settled by my superior officers Forrest's force was near Mayfield, about equidistant from Paducah, Cairo, and Columbus, only a few hours from either. He was at the centre, I going round the edge of a circle. I could only watch the coming blow and help each weak point in turn. One evening, for instance, I sent 400 men to Columbus, expecting trouble there, and the next morning had them at Paducah, 75 miles distant

Question. Had you instructions as to the presence of that force so near you?

Answer. Not specific. General Sherman, on the 23d of March, telegraphed that he was willing that Forrest should remain in that neighborhood if the people did not manifest friendship, and on April 13 he expressed a desire that Forrest should prolong his visit until certain measures could be accomplished. I think General Sherman did not purpose to withdraw a heavy force to pursue Forrest, having better use for them elsewhere, and feeling that we had force enough to hold the important points on the river. It may be that the strength of the enemy and the scattered condition of our small detachments was not fully understood. We ran too great a risk at Paducah. Nothing but great gallantry and fortitude saved it from the fate of Fort Pillow.

Question. What information had you of the attack of Fort Pillow.

Answer. Fort Pillow is 170 miles below here, not in my district, but Memphis. On April 13, at 6 p. m., I telegraphed General Sherman as follows:

"The surrender of Columbus was demanded and refused at six this morning. Women and children brought away. Heavy artillery firing this afternoon. I have sent re-enforcements. Paducah also threatened. No danger of either, but I think that Fort Pillow, in the Memphis district, is taken. General Shepley passed yesterday and saw the flag go down and thinks it a surrender. I have enough troops now from below, and will go down if necessary to that point. Captain Pennock will send gunboats. If lost, it will be retaken immediately."

I was informed, in reply, that Fort Pillow had no guns or garrison; had been evacuated; that General Hurlbut had force for its defence, &c. I understand that Fort Pillow had been evacuated and reoccupied, General Sherman not being aware of it. On the 14th he again instructed me as follows:

"What news from Columbus? Don't send men from Paris to Fort Pillow. Let General Hurlbut take care of that quarter. The Cairo troops may re-enforce temporarily at Paducah and Columbus, but should be held ready to come up the Tennessee. One object that Forrest has is to induce us to make these detachments and prevent our concentrating in this quarter."

Question. Did you have any conversation with General Shepley in relation to the condition of the garrison at Fort Pillow when he passed by that point? If so, state what he said. What force did General Shepley have with him? Did he assign any reason for not rendering assistance to that garrison? if so, what was it?

Answer. General Shepley called on me. He stated that as he approached Fort Pillow, fighting was going on; he saw the flag come down "by the run," but could not tell whether it was lowered by the garrison, or by having the halliards shot away; that soon after another flag went up in another place. He could not distinguish its character, but feared that it was a surrender, though firing continued. I think he gave the force on the boat as two batteries and two or three hundred infantry. When he came away the firing was kept up, but not as heavily as at first. He was not certain how the fight was terminating. In answer to a question of mine, he said the batteries on board could not have been used, as the bluff was too steep for ascent or to admit of firing from the water's edge, and the enemy above might have captured them. This was about the substance of our conversation.

Question. What information have you relative to the battle and massacre at Fort Pillow, particularly what transpired after the surrender?

Answer. That place not being in my district, official reports did not come to me. However, under instructions from General Sherman, I detailed officers, and collected reports and sworn proofs for transmission to him, also to the Secretary of War. Having furnished the Secretary of War with a duplicate copy for the use of your committee if he so desired, I refer to that for the information I have on the subject.

Question. Do you consider the testimony thus furnished entirely reliable?

Answer. "In the mouth of two or three witnesses shall every work be established." Here are scores of them living and dying. There are doubtless errors as to time and place, and scenes witnessed from different points of observation, but in the main I regard the witnesses honest and their accounts true.

Question. What did you learn concerning violations of the flag of truce?

Answer. I learn from official sources that at Paducah, Columbus, Union City, and Fort Pillow, the rebels moved troops, placed batteries, formed new lines, advanced, robbed stores and private houses, stole horses and other property while protected by flags of truce. J. W. McCord and Mrs. Hannah Hammond state, in writing, that at Paducah they forced five women nurses at the hospital out in front of their line, and kept them there for an hour, thus silencing our guns. Mrs. Hammond was one of the five. Reference is made to testimony furnished on the subject, and to official reports when transmitted to the War Department.

Question. What information have you as to the intention of the enemy to perpetrate such acts as the massacre at Fort Pillow?

Answer. I furnish the correspondence growing out of demands to surrender at Union City, Paducah, and Columbus, showing premeditation on the part of officers in command of the rebel army.

[Take in from reports of Lieutenant Gray, Colonel Hicks and Colonel Lawrence, with which the committee is furnished.—See Appendix.]

Question. Has there been co-operation and harmony among commanders since these troubles began?

Answer. Entire and in every respect, so far as I know. Officers of the army in charge of troops temporarily here gave all the aid possible. They were under orders which prevented their going out in pursuit of Forrest, but they gave me detachments to guard our river posts when threatened.

Question. What have been the relations existing generally between you and Captain Pennock, of the navy, fleet captain of the Mississippi squadron?

Answer. Captain Pennock is commandant of the naval station at Cairo and Mound City, and I understand represents Admiral Porter in his absence. Our relations have been cordial, and we have co-operated in all movements. The aid given by his gunboats has been prompt, ample, and very efficient. His admirable judgment and ready resources have always been available.

Question. During the operations consequent upon the movements of Forrest, did you or did you not receive cordial co-operation and support from Lieutenant Commander Shirk, commanding the 7th division Mississippi squadron?

Answer. I can only repeat my answer to the last question. Lieutenant Shirk is an admirable officer, vigilant, brave, and of exceeeingly safe judgment.

MOUND CITY, ILLINOIS, *April* 22, 1864.

Surgeon Horace Wardner sworn and examined.

By the chairman:

Question. Have you been in charge of this hospital, Mound City hospital?

Answer. I have been in charge of this hospital continually since the 25th of April, 1863.

Question. Will you state, if you please, what you know about the persons who escaped from Fort Pillow? And how many have been under your charge?

Answer. I have received thirty-four whites, twenty-seven colored men, and one colored woman, and seven corpses of those who died on their way here.

Question. Did any of those you have mentioned escape from Fort Pillow?

Answer. There were eight or nine men, I forget the number, who did escape and come here, the others were paroled. I learned the following facts about that: The day after the battle a gunboat was coming up and commenced shelling the place; the rebels sent a flag of truce for the purpose of giving over into our hands what wounded remained alive; a transport then landed and sent out details to look about the grounds and pick up the wounded there, and bring them on the boat. They had no previous attention.

Question. They were then brought under your charge?

Answer. They were brought immediately to this hospital.

Question. Who commanded that boat?

Answer. I forget the naval officer's name.

Question. How long after the capture of the place did he come along?

Answer. That was the next day after the capture.

Question. Did all who were paroled in this way come under your charge, or did any of them go to other hospitals?

Answer. None went to other hospitals that I am aware of.

Question. Please state their condition.

Answer. They were the worst butchered men I have ever seen. I have been in several hard battles, but I have never seen men so mangled as they were; and nearly all of them concur in stating that they received all their wounds after they had thrown down their arms, surrendered, and asked for quarters. They state that they ran out of the fort, threw down their arms, and ran down the bank to the edge of the river, and were pursued to the top of the bank and fired on from above.

Question. Were there any females there?

Answer. I have one wounded woman from there.

Question. Were there any children or young persons there?

Answer. I have no wounded children or young persons from there.

Question. Those you have received were mostly combatants, or had been?

Answer. Yes, sir, soldiers, white or colored.

Question. Were any of the wounded here in the hospital in the fort, and wounded while in the hospital?

Answer. I so understand them.

Question. How many in that condition did you understand?

Answer. I learned from those who came here that nearly all who were in the hospital were killed. I received a young negro boy, probably sixteen years old, who was in the hospital there sick with fever, and unable to get away. The rebels entered the hospital, and with a sabre hacked his head, no doubt with the intention of splitting it open. The boy put up his hand to protect his head, and they cut off one or two of his fingers. He was brought here insensible, and died yesterday. I made a post-mortem examination, and found that the outer table of the skull was incised, the inner table was fractured, and a piece driven into the brain.

Question. This was done while he was sick in the hospital?

Answer. Yes, sir, unable to get off his bed.

Question. Have you any means of knowing how many were murdered in that way?

Answer. No positive means, except the statement of the men.

Question. How many do you suppose from the information you have received?

Answer. I suppose there were about four hundred massacred—murdered there.

Question. What proportion white, and what proportion colored, as near as you could ascertain?

Answer. The impression I have, from what I can learn, is, that all the negroes were massacred except about eighty, and all the white soldiers were killed except about one hundred or one hundred and ten.

Question. We have heard rumors that some of these persons were buried alive; did you hear anything about that?

Answer. I have two in the hospital here who were buried alive.

Question. Both colored men?

Answer. Yes, sir.

Question. How did they escape?

Answer. One of them I have not conversed with personally, the other I have. He was thrown into a pit, as he states, with a great many others, white and black, several of whom were alive; they were all buried up together. He lay on the outer edge, but his head was nearer the surface; he had one well hand, and with that hand he was able to work a place through which he could breathe, and in that way he got his head out; he lay there for some twenty-four hours, and was finally taken out by somebody. The others, next to him, were buried so deep that they could not get out, and died.

Question. Did you hear anything about any of them having been thrown into the flames and burned?

Answer. I do not know anything about that myself. These men did not say much, and in fact I did not myself have time to question them very closely.

Question. What is the general condition now of the wounded men from Fort Pillow under your charge?

Answer. They are in as good condition as they can be, probably about one-third of them must die.

Question. Is your hospital divided into wards, and can we go through and take the testimony of these men, ward by ward?

Answer. It is divided into wards. The men from Fort Pillow are scattered through the hospital, and isolated to prevent erysipelas. If I should crowd too many badly wounded men in one ward I would be likely to get the erysipelas among them, and lose a great many of them.

By Mr. Gooch:

Question. Are the wounds of these men such as men usually receive in battle?

Answer. The gunshot wounds are; the sabre cuts are the first I have ever seen in the war yet. They seem to have been shot with the intention of hitting the body. There are more body wounds than in an ordinary battle.

Question. Just as if they were close enough to select the parts of the body to be hit?

Answer. Yes, sir; some of them were shot with pistols by the rebels standing from one foot to ten feet of them.

The committee then proceeded to the various wards and took the testimony of such of the wounded as were able to bear the examination.

The testimony of the colored men is written out exactly as given, except that it is rendered in a grammatical form, instead of the broken language some of them used.

MOUND CITY HOSPITAL,
Illinois, April 22, 1864.

Elias Falls, (colored,) private, company A, 6th United States heavy artillery, or 1st Alabama artillery, sworn and examined.

By Mr. Gooch:

Question. Were you at Fort Pillow when the battle took place there, and it was captured by the rebels?

Answer. I was there; I was a cook, and was waiting on the captain and major.

Question. What did you see done there? What did the rebels do after they came into the fort?

Answer. They killed all the men after they surrendered, until orders were given to stop; they killed all they came to, white and black, after they had surrendered.

Question. The one the same as the other?

Answer. Yes, sir, till he gave orders to stop firing.

Question. Till who gave orders?

Answer. They told me his name was Forrest.

Question. Did you see anybody killed or shot there?

Answer. Yes, sir; I was shot after the surrender, as I was marched up the hill by the rebels.

Question. Where were you wounded?

Answer. In the knee.

Question. Was that the day of the fight?

Answer. The same day.

Question. Did you see any men shot the next day?

Answer. I did not.

Question. What did you see done after the place was taken?

Answer. After peace was made some of the secesh soldiers came around cursing the boys that were wounded. They shot one of them about the hand, aimed to shoot him in the head, as he lay on the ground, and hit him in the hand; and an officer told the secesh soldier if he did that again he would arrest him, and he went off then.

Question. Did they burn any buildings?

Answer. Yes, sir.

Question. Was anybody burned in the buildings?

Answer. I did not see anybody burned; I saw them burn the buildings; I was not able to walk about; I staid in a building that night with some three or four white men.

Question. Do you know anything about their going into the hospital and killing those who were there sick in bed?

Answer. We had some three or four of our men there, and some of our men came in and said they had killed two women and two children.

Duncan Harding, (colored,) private, company A, 6th United States heavy artillery, sworn and examined.

By Mr. Gooch:

Question. Were you in Fort Pillow at the time it was captured?

Answer. Yes, sir; I was a gunner No. 2 at the gun.

Question. What did you see there?

Answer. I did not see much until next morning. I was shot in the arm that evening; they picked me up and marched me up the hill, and while they were marching me up the hill they shot me again through the thigh.

Question. Did you see anybody else shot after they had surrendered?
Answer. The next morning I saw them shoot down one corporal in our company.
Question. What was his name?
Answer. Robert Winston.
Question. Did they kill him?
Answer. Yes, sir.
Question. What were you doing at the time?
Answer. I was lying down.
Question. What was the corporal doing?
Answer. When the gunboats commenced firing he was started off with them, but he would not go fast enough and they shot him dead.
Question. When you were shot the last time had you any arms in your hands?
Answer. No, sir.
Question. Had the corporal any arms in his hands?
Answer. No, sir; nothing.

By the chairman:

Question. What do you know about any buildings being burned?
Answer. I saw them burn the buildings; and that morning as I was going to the boat I saw one colored man who was burned in the building.
Question. When was that building burned?
Answer. The next morning.
Question. The morning after the capture?
Answer. Yes, sir.
Question. How did you get away?
Answer. I started off with the rebels; we were all lying in a hollow to keep from the shells; as their backs were turned to me I crawled up in some brush and logs, and they all left; when night come I came back to the river bank, and a gunboat came along.
Question. Were any officers about when you were shot last?
Answer. Yes, sir.
Question. Did you know any of them?
Answer. No, sir.
Question. Did they say anything against it?
Answer. No, sir; only, "Kill the God damned nigger."

Nathan Hunter, (colored,) private, company D, 6th United States heavy artillery, sworn and examined.

By Mr. Gooch:

Question. Were you in Fort Pillow when it was captured?
Answer. Yes, sir.
Question. What did you see done there?
Answer. They went down the hill, and shot all of us they saw; they shot me for dead, and I lay there until the next morning when the gunboat came along. They thought I was dead and pulled my boots off. That is all I know.
Question. Were you shot when they first took the fort?
Answer. I was not shot until we were done fighting.
Question. Had you any arms in your hands when you were shot?
Answer. No, sir.
Question. How long did you lie where you were shot?
Answer. I lay there from three o'clock until after night, and then I went up in the guard-house and staid there until the next morning when the gunboat came along.
Question. Did you see any others shot?
Answer. Yes, sir; they shot down a whole parcel along with me. Their

bodies were lying there along the river bank the next morning. They kicked some of them into the river after they were shot dead.

Question. Did you see that?

Answer. Yes, sir; I thought they were going to throw me in too; I slipped away in the night.

By the chairman:

Question. Did you see any man burned?

Answer. No, sir; I was down under the hill next the river.

Question. They thought you were dead when they pulled your boots off?

Answer. Yes, sir; they pulled my boots off, and rolled me over, and said they had killed me.

Sergeant Benjamin Robinson, (colored,) company D, 6th United States heavy artillery, sworn and examined.

By Mr. Gooch:

Question. Were you at Fort Pillow in the fight there?

Answer. Yes, sir.

Question. What did you see there?

Answer. I saw them shoot two white men right by the side of me after they had laid their guns down. They shot a black man clear over into the river. Then they hallooed to me to come up the hill, and I came up. They said, "Give me your money, you damned nigger." I told them I did not have any. "Give me your money, or I will blow your brains out." Then they told me to lie down, and I laid down, and they stripped everything off me.

Question. This was the day of the fight?

Answer. Yes, sir.

Question. Go on. Did they shoot you?

Answer. Yes, sir. After they stripped me and took my money away from me they dragged me up the hill a little piece, and laid me down flat on my stomach; I laid there till night, and they took me down to an old house, and said they would kill me the next morning. I got up and commenced crawling down the hill; I could not walk.

Question. When were you shot?

Answer. About 3 o'clock.

Question. Before they stripped you?

Answer. Yes, sir. They shot me before they said, "come up."

Question. After you had surrendered?

Answer. Yes, sir; they shot pretty nearly all of them after they surrendered.

Question. Did you see anything of the burning of the men?

Answer. No, sir.

Question. Did you see them bury anybody?

Answer. Yes, sir.

Question. Did they bury anybody who was not dead?

Answer. I saw one of them working his hand after he was buried; he was a black man. They had about a hundred in there, black and white. The major was buried on the bank, right side of me. They took his clothes all off but his drawers; I was lying right there looking at them. They had my captain's coat, too; they did not kill my captain; a lieutenant told him to give him his coat, and then they told him to go down and pick up those old rags and put them on.

Question. Did you see anybody shot the day after the battle?

Answer. No, sir.

Question. How did you get away?

Answer. A few men came up from Memphis, and got a piece of plank and put me on it, and took me down to the boat.

Question. Were any rebel officers around when the rebels were killing our men?

Answer. Yes, sir; lots of them.

Question. Did they try to keep their men from killing our men?

Answer. I never heard them say so. I know General Forrest rode his horse over me three or four times. I did not know him until I heard his men call his name. He said to some negro men there that he knew them; that they had been in his nigger yard in Memphis. He said he was not worth five dollars when he started, and had got rich trading in negroes.

Question. Where were you from?

Answer. I came from South Carolina.

Question. Have you been a slave?

Answer. Yes, sir.

Daniel Tyler, (colored,) private, company B, 6th United States heavy artillery, sworn and examined.

By Mr. Gooch:

Question. Where were you raised?

Answer. In Mississippi.

Question. Have you been a slave?

Answer. Yes, sir.

Question. Were you in Fort Pillow at the time it was captured by the rebels?

Answer. Yes, sir.

Question. When were you wounded?

Answer. I was wounded after we all surrendered; not before.

Question. At what time?

Answer. They shot me when we came up the hill from down by the river.

Question. Why did you go up the hill?

Answer. They called me up.

Question. Did you see who shot you?

Answer. Yes, sir; I did not know him.

Question. One of the rebels?

Answer. Yes, sir.

Question. How near was he to you?

Answer. I was right at him; I had my hand on the end of his gun.

Question. What did he say to you?

Answer. He said, "Whose gun are you holding?" I said, "Nobody's." He said, "God damn you, I will shoot you," and then he shot me. I let go, and then another one shot me.

Question. Were many shot at the same time?

Answer. Yes, sir, lots of them; lying all round like hogs.

Question. Did you see any one burned?

Answer. No, sir.

Question. Did you see anybody buried alive?

Answer. Nobody but me.

Question. Were you buried alive?

Answer. Yes, sir; they thought they had killed me. I lay there till about sundown, when they threw us in a hollow, and commenced throwing dirt on us.

Question. Did you say anything?

Answer. No, sir; I did not want to speak to them. I knew if I said anything they would kill me. They covered me up in a hole; they covered me up, all but one side of my head. I heard them say they ought not to bury a man who was alive. I commenced working the dirt away, and one of the secesh made a young one dig me out. They dug me out, and I was carried not far off to a fire.

Question. How long did you stay there?

Answer. I staid there that night and until the next morning, and then I slipped off. I heard them say the niggers had to go away from there before the gunboat came, and that they would kill the niggers. The gunboat commenced shelling up there, and they commenced moving off. I heard them up there shooting. They wanted me to go with them, but I would not go. I turned around, and came down to the river bank and got on the gunboat.

Question. How did you lose your eye?

Answer. They knocked me down with a carbine, and then they jabbed it out.

Question. Was that before you were shot?

Answer. Yes, sir.

Question. After you had surrendered?

Answer. Yes, sir; I was going up the hill, a man came down and met me; he had his gun in his hand, and whirled it around and knocked me down, and then took the end of his carbine and jabbed it in my eye, and shot me

Question. Were any of their officers about there then?

Answer. I did not see any officers.

Question. Were any white men buried with you?

Answer. Yes, sir.

Question. Were any buried alive?

Answer. I heard that one white man was buried alive; I did not see him.

Question. Who said that?

Answer. A young man; he said they ought not to have done it. He staid in there all night; I do not know as he ever got out.

John Haskins, (colored,) private, company B, 6th United States heavy artillery, sworn and examined.

By Mr. Gooch:

Question. Were you at Fort Pillow when it was captured?

Answer. Yes, sir.

Question. What did you see done there?

Answer. After we had surrendered they shot me in the left arm. I ran down the river and jumped into the water; the water ran over my back; six or seven more men came around there, and the secesh shot them right on the bank. At night I got in a coal-boat and cut it loose, and went down the river.

Question. Did you see anybody else killed after they had surrendered?

Answer. A great many; I could not tell how many.

Question. Did they say why they killed our men after they had surrendered?

Answer. No, sir.

Question. How many did you see killed after they surrendered?

Answer. Six or eight right around me, who could not get into the water as I did; I heard them shooting above, too.

Question. Did they strip and rob those they killed?

Answer. Yes, sir; they ran their hands in my pockets—they thought I was dead—they did all in the same way.

Question. What time were you shot?

Answer. After four o'clock.

Question. How long after you had surrendered?

Answer. Just about the time we ran down the hill.

Question. Did you have any arms in your hands when you were shot?

Answer. No, sir.

Question. Do you know anything about their killing anybody in the hospital

Answer. I could not tell anything about that.

Question. Do you know anything about their burning bnildings?

Answer. Yes, sir; they burned the lieutenant's house, and they said they burned him in the house.

Question. He was a white man?

Answer. Yes, sir; quartermaster of the 13th Tennessee cavalry.

Question. Did you see them kill him?

Answer. No, sir; I did not see them kill him; I saw the house he was in on fire.

Question. Do you know anything about their burying anybody before they were dead?

Answer. No, sir.

Question. Where are you from?

Answer. From Tennessee.

Question. Have you been a slave?

Answer. Yes, sir.

Question. How long have you been in the army?

Answer. About two months.

Thomas Adison, (colored,) private, company C, 6th United States heavy artillery, sworn and examined.

By the chairman:

Question. Where were you raised?

Answer. In South Carolina. I was nineteen years old when I came to Mississippi. I was forty years old last March.

Question. Were you at Fort Pillow when it was captured?

Answer. Yes, sir.

Question. When were you wounded—before or after you surrendered?

Answer. Before.

Question. What happened to you after you were wounded?

Answer. I went down the hill after we surrendered; then they came down and shot me again in my face, breaking my jaw-bone.

Question. How near was the man to you?

Answer. He shot me with a revolver, about ten or fifteen feet off.

Question. What happened to you then?

Answer. I laid down, and a fellow came along and turned me over and searched my pockets and took my money. He said: "God damn his old soul; he is sure dead now; he is a big, old, fat fellow."

Question. How long did you lay there?

Answer. About two hours.

Question. Then what was done with you

Answer. They made some of our men carry me up the hill to a house that was full of white men. They made us lie out doors all night, and said that the next morning they would have the doctor fix us up. I went down to a branch for some water, and a man said to me: "Old man, if you stay here they will kill you, but if you get into the water till the boat comes along they may save you;" and I went off. They shot a great many that evening.

Question. The day of the fight?

Answer. Yes, sir. I heard them shoot little children not more than that high, [holding his hand off about four feet from the floor,] that the officers had to wait upon them.

Question. Did you see them shoot them?

Answer. I did not hold up my head.

Question. How did you know that they shot them then?

Answer. I heard them say, "Turn around so that I can shoot you good;" and then I heard them fire, and then I heard the children fall over.

Question. Do you know that those were the boys that waited upon the officers?

Answer. Yes, sir; one was named Dave, and the other was named Anderson.
Question. Did you see them after they were shot?
Answer. No, sir; they toted them up the hill before me, because they were small. I never saw folks shot down so in my life.

By Mr. Gooch:

Question. Do you know of anybody being buried alive?
Answer. No, sir.
Question. Do you know of any one being burned?
Answer. They had a whole parcel of them in a house, and I think they burned them. The house was burned up, and I think they burned them in it.
Question. Were the men in the house colored men?
Answer. No, sir. The rebels never would have got the advantage of us if it had not been for the houses built there, and which made better breastworks for them than we had. The major would not let us burn the houses in the morning. If they had let us burn the houses in the morning, I do not believe they would ever have whipped us out of that place.

Manuel Nichols, (colored,) private, Company B, 6th United States heavy artillery, sworn and examined.

By Mr. Gooch:

Question. Were you in the late fight at Fort Pillow?
Answer. Yes, sir.
Question. Were you wounded there?
Answer. Yes, sir.
Question. When?
Answer. I was wounded once about a half an hour before we gave up.
Question. Did they do anything to you after you surrendered?
Answer. Yes, sir; they shot me in the head under my left ear, and the morning after the fight they shot me again in the right arm. When they came up and killed the wounded ones, I saw some four or five coming down the hill. I said to one of our boys, "Anderson, I expect if those fellows come here they will kill us." I was lying on my right side, leaning on my elbow. One of the black soldiers went into the house where the white soldiers were. I asked him if there was any water in there, and he said yes; I wanted some, and took a stick and tried to get to the house. I did not get to the house. Some of them came along, and saw a little boy belonging to company D. One of them had his musket on his shoulder, and shot the boy down. He said: "All you damned niggers come out of the house; I am going to shoot you." Some of the white soldiers said, "Boys, it is only death anyhow; if you don't go out they will come in and carry you out." My strength seemed to come to me as if I had never been shot, and I jumped up and ran down the hill. I met one of them coming up the hill; he said "stop!" but I kept on running. As I jumped over the hill, he shot me through the right arm.
Question. How many did you see them kill after they had surrendered?
Answer. After I surrendered I did not go down the hill. A man shot me under the ear, and I fell down and said to myself, "If he don't shoot me any more this won't hurt me." One of their officers came along and hallooed, "Forrest says, no quarter! no quarter!" and the next one hallooed, "Black flag! black flag!"
Question. What did they do then?
Answer. They kept on shouting. I could hear them down the hill.
Question. Did you see them bury anybody?
Answer. Yes, sir; they carried me around right to the corner of the fort, and I saw them pitch men in there.
Question. Was there any alive?

Answer. I did not see them bury anybody alive.
Question. How near to you was the man who shot you under the car?
Answer. Right close to my head. When I was shot in the side, a man turned me over, and took my pocket-knife and pocket-book. I had some of these brass things that looked like cents. They said, "Here's some money; here's some money." I said to myself, "You got fooled that time."

Arthur Edwards, (colored,) private, company C, 6th United States heavy artillery, sworn and examined.

By the chairman:

Question. Where were you raised?
Answer. In Mississippi.
Question. Were you in Fort Pillow when it was taken?
Answer. Yes, sir.
Question. Tell what you saw there.
Answer. I was shot after I surrendered.
Question. When?
Answer. About half past four o'clock.
Question. Where were you when you were shot?
Answer. I was lying down behind a log.
Question. Where were you shot?
Answer. In the head first, then in the shoulder, then in my right wrist; and then in the head again, about half an hour after that.
Question. How many men shot at you?
Answer. One shot at me three times, and then a lieutenant shot at me.
Question. Did they say anything when they shot you?
Answer. No, sir, only I asked them not to shoot me, and they said, "God damn you, you are fighting against your master."
Question. How near was the man to you when he shot you?
Answer. He squatted down, and held his pistol close to my head.
Question. How near was the officer to you when he shot you?
Answer. About five or ten feet off; he was sitting on his horse.
Question. Who said you were fighting against your master?
Answer. The man that shot me.
Question. What did the officer say?
Answer. Nothing, but "you God damned nigger." A captain told him not to do it, but he did not mind him; he shot me, and run off on his horse.
Question. Did you see the captain?
Answer. Yes, sir; he and the captain were side by side.
Question. Did you know the captain?
Answer. No, sir.
Question. How long did you stay there?
Answer. Until next morning about 9 o'clock.
Question. How did you get away?
Answer. When the gunboat commenced shelling I went down the hill, and staid there until they carried down a flag of truce. Then the gunboat came to the bank, and a secesh lieutenant made us go down to such a place, and told us to go no further, or we would get shot again. Then the gunboat men came along to bury the dead, and told us to go on the boat.
Question. Did you see anybody shot after they had surrendered, besides yourself?
Answer. Yes, sir; they shot one right by me, and lots of the 13th Tennessee cavalry.
Question. After they had surrendered?
Answer. Yes, sir.
Question. Do you know whether any were buried alive?

Answer. Not that I saw.
Question. Did you see anybody buried?
Answer. No, sir.
Question. Did you see anybody shot the day after the fight?
Answer. No, sir.

Charles Key, (colored,) private, company D, 6th United States heavy artillery, sworn and examined.

By Mr. Gooch:

Question. Where were you raised?
Answer. In South Carolina.
Question. Have you been a slave?
Answer. Yes, sir.
Question. Where did you enlist?
Answer. In Tennessee.
Question. Were you in the fight at Fort Pillow?
Answer. Yes, sir.
Question. What did you see done there after the fight was over?
Answer. I saw nothing, only the boys run down the hill, and they came down and shot them.
Question. Were you wounded before or after you surrendered?
Answer. After the surrender, about 5 o'clock.
Question. Did you have your gun in your hands when you were wounded?
Answer. No, sir; I threw my gun into the river.
Question. How did they come to shoot you?
Answer. I was in the water, and a man came down and shot me with a revolver.
Question. Did you see anybody else shot?
Answer. Yes, sir; right smart of them, in an old coal boat. I saw one man start up the bank after he was shot in the arm, and then a fellow knocked him back into the river with his carbine, and then shot him. I did not go up the hill after I was shot. I laid in the water like I was dead until night, and then I made up a fire and dried myself, and staid there till the gunboat came along.
Question. Did they shoot you more than once?
Answer. No, sir.

Henry Christian, (colored,) private, company B, 6th United States heavy artillery, sworn and examined.

By Mr. Gooch:

Question. Where were you raised?
Answer. In East Tennessee.
Question. Have you been a slave?
Answer. Yes, sir.
Question. Where did you enlist?
Answer. At Corinth, Mississippi.
Question. Were you in the fight at Fort Pillow?
Answer. Yes, sir.
Question. When were you wounded?
Answer. A little before we surrendered.
Question. What happened to you afterwards?
Answer. Nothing; I got but one shot, and dug right out over the hill to the river, and never was bothered any more.
Question. Did you see any men shot after the place was taken?
Answer. Yes, sir.
Question. Where?

Answer. Down to the river.
Question. How many?
Answer. A good many; I don't know how many.
Question. By whom were they shot?
Answer. By secesh soldiers; secesh officers shot some up on the hill.
Question. Did you see those on the hill shot by the officers?
Answer. I saw two of them shot.
Question. What officers were they?
Answer. I don't know whether he was a lieutenant or captain.
Question. Did the men who were shot after they had surrendered have arms in their hands?
Answer. No, sir; they threw down their arms.
Question. Did you see any shot the next morning?
Answer. I saw two shot; one was shot by an officer—he was standing, holding the officer's horse, and when the officer came and got his horse he shot him dead. The officer was setting fire to the houses.
Question. Do you say the man was holding the officer's horse, and when the officer came and took his horse he shot the man down?
Answer. Yes, sir; I saw that with my own eyes; and then I made away into the river, right off.
Question. Did you see any buried?
Answer. Yes, sir; a great many, black and white.
Question. Did you see any buried alive?
Answer. I did not see any buried alive.

Aaron Fentis, (colored,) company D, 6th United States heavy artillery, sworn and examined.

By the chairman:

Question. Where were you from?
Answer. Tennessee.
Question. Have you been a slave?
Answer. Yes, sir.
Question. Where did you enlist?
Answer. At Corinth.
Question. Who was your captain?
Answer. Captain Carron.
Question. Were you in the fight at Fort Pillow?
Answer. Yes, sir.
Question. What did you see done there?
Answer. I saw them shoot two white men, and two black men, after they had surrendered.
Question. Are you sure they were shot after they had surrendered?
Answer. Yes, sir. Some were in the river swimming out a piece, when they were shot; and they took another man by the arm, and held him up, and shot him in the breast.
Question. Did you see any others shot?
Answer. Yes, sir; I saw two wounded men shot the next morning; they were lying down when the secesh shot them.
Question. Did the rebels say anything when they were shooting our men?
Answer. They said they were going to kill them all; and they would have shot us all if the gunboat had not come along.
Question. Were you shot?
Answer. Yes, sir.
Question. When?
Answer. After the battle, the same evening.

Question. Where were you shot?
Answer. Right through both legs.
Question. How many times were you shot?
Answer. Only once, with a carbine. The man stood right close by me.
Question. Where were you?
Answer. On the river bank.
Question. Had you arms in your hands?
Answer. No, sir.
Question. What did the man say who shot you?
Answer. He said they were going to kill us all.
Question. Did you see any men buried?
Answer. No, sir.
Question. Did you see anybody burned?
Answer. No, sir; I did not see that. Where I was was a good piece off from where they had the battle.
Question. Do you know how many of your company got away?
Answer. I do not think any of my company got away.
Question. How many were killed before they surrendered?
Answer. I don't know how many; a good many, I think.
Question. Would you have surrendered, if you had known what they were going to do to you?
Answer. No, sir.

George Shaw, (colored,) private, company B, 6th United States heavy artillery, sworn and examined.

By Mr. Gooch:

Question. Where were you raised?
Answer. In Tennessee.
Question. Where did you enlist?
Answer. At Fort Pillow.
Question. Were you there at the fight?
Answer. Yes, sir.
Question. When were you shot?
Answer. About four o'clock in the evening.
Question. After you had surrendered?
Answer. Yes, sir.
Question. Where were you at the time?
Answer. About ten feet from the river bank.
Question. Who shot you?
Answer. A rebel soldier.
Question. How near did he come to you?
Answer. About ten feet.
Question. What did he say to you?
Answer. He said, "Damn you, what are you doing here?" I said, "Please don't shoot me." He said, "Damn you, you are fighting against your master." He raised his gun and fired, and the bullet went into my mouth and out the back part of my head. They threw me into the river, and I swam around and hung on there in the water until night.
Question. Did you see anybody else shot?
Answer. Yes, sir; three young boys, lying in the water, with their heads out; they could not swim. They begged them as long as they could, but they shot them right in the forehead.
Question. How near to them were they?
Answer. As close as that stone, (about eight or ten feet.)
Question. How old were the boys?

Answer. Not more than fifteen or sixteen years old. They were not soldiers, but contraband boys, helping us on the breastworks.

Question. Did you see any white men shot?

Answer. No, sir. I saw them shoot three men the next day.

Question. How far from the fort?

Answer. About a mile and a half; after they had taken them back as prisoners.

Question. Who shot them?

Answer. Private soldiers. One officer said, "Boys, I will have you arrested, if you don't quit killing them boys." Another officer said, "Damn it, let them go on; it isn't our law to take any niggers prisoners; kill every one of them." Then a white man took me to wait on him a little, and sent me back to a house about two hundred yards, and told me to stay all night. I went back and staid until about a half an hour by sun. Another man came along and said, "If you will go home with me I will take good care of you, if you will stay and never leave." I did not know what to do, I was so outdone; so I said, "If you will take care of me, I will go." He carried me out about three miles, to a place called Bob Greene's. The one who took me there left me, and two others came up, and said, "Damn you, we will kill you, and not be fooling about any longer." I said, "Don't shoot me." One of them said, "Go out and hold my horse." I made a step or two, and he said, "Turn around; I will hold my horse, and shoot you, too." I no sooner turned around than he shot me in the face. I fell down as if I was dead. He shot me again, and hit my arm, not my head. I laid there until I could hear him no more, and then I started back. I got back into Fort Pillow about sun up, and wandered about there until a gunboat came along, and I came up on that with about ten others.

Major Williams, (colored,) private, company B, 6th United States heavy artillery, sworn and examined.

By the chairman:

Question. Where were you raised?

Answer. In Tennessee and North Mississippi.

Question. Where did you enlist?

Answer. In Memphis.

Question. Who was your captain?

Answer. Captain Lamburg.

Question. Were you in the fight at Fort Pillow?

Answer. Yes, sir.

Question. Was your captain with you?

Answer. No, sir; I think he was in Memphis.

Question. Who commanded your company?

Answer. Lieutenant Hunter and Sergeant Fox were all the officers we had.

Question. What did you see done there?

Answer. We fought them right hard during the battle, and killed some of them. After a time they sent in a flag of truce. They said afterwards that they did it to make us stop firing until their re-enforcements could come up. They said that they never could have got in if they had not done that; that we had whipped them; that they had never seen such a fight.

Question. Did you see the flag of truce?

Answer. Yes, sir.

Question. What did they do when the flag of truce was in?

Answer. They kept coming up nearer and nearer, so that they could charge quick. A heap of them came up after we stopped firing.

Question. When did you surrender?

Answer. I did not surrender until they all run.

Question. Were you wounded then?

Answer. Yes, sir; after the surrender.

Question. At what time of day was that?

Answer. They told me it was about half after one o'clock. I was wounded immediately we retreated.

Question. Did you have any arms in your hands when they shot you?

Answer. No, sir; I was an artillery man, and had no arms.

Question. Did you see the man who shot you?

Answer. No, sir.

Question. Did you hear him say anything?

Answer. No, sir; I heard nothing. He shot me, and it was bleeding pretty free, and I thought to myself, "I will make out it was a dead shot, and may be I will not get another."

Question. Did you see any others shot?

Answer. No, sir.

Question. Was there anything said about giving quarter?

Answer. Major Bradford brought in a black flag, which meant no quarter. I heard some of the rebel officers say: "You damned rascals, if you had not fought us so hard, but had stopped when we sent in a flag of truce, we would not have done anything to you." I heard one of the officers say: "Kill all the niggers;" another one said: "No; Forrest says take them and carry them with him to wait upon him and cook for him, and put them in jail and send them to their masters." Still they kept on shooting. They shot at me after that, but did not hit me; a rebel officer shot at me. He took aim at my side; at the crack of his pistol I fell. He went on and said: "There's another dead nigger."

Question. Was there any one shot in the hospital that day?

Answer. Not that I know of. I think they all came away and made a raft and floated across the mouth of the creek, and got into a flat bottom.

Question. Did you see any buildings burned?

Answer. I staid in the woods all day Wednesday. I was there Thursday and looked at the buildings. I saw a great deal left that they did not have a chance to burn up. I saw a white man burned up who was nailed up against the house.

Question. A private or an officer?

Answer. An officer; I think it was a lieutenant in the Tennessee cavalry.

Question. How was he nailed?

Answer. Through his hands and feet right against the house.

Question. Was his body burned?

Answer. Yes, sir; burned all over—I looked at him good.

Question. When did you see that?

Answer. On the Thursday after the battle.

Question. Where was the man?

Answer. Right in front of the fort.

Question. Did any one else that you know see the body nailed up there?

Answer. There was a black man there who came up on the same boat I was on.

Question. Was he with you then?

Answer. Yes, sir; and there were some five or six white people there, too, from out in the country, who were walking over the place.

Alexander Nayron, (colored,) private, company C, 6th United States heavy artillery, sworn and examined.

By Mr. Gooch:

Question. Where were you raised?

Answer. In Mississippi.

Question. Have you been a slave?
Answer. Yes, sir.
Question. Where did you enlist?
Answer. At Lagrange, last August.
Question. Were you at Fort Pillow at the time of the attack?
Answer. Yes, sir.
Question. When were you wounded?
Answer. After the fight.
Question. About what time?
Answer. About three o'clock, I reckon.
Question. Where were you when you were wounded?
Answer. Down at the river, lying down by the side of a log. They came there and told me to get up, and as I got up they shot me.
Question. Who shot you, an officer or private?
Answer. A private.
Question. How many times were you shot?
Answer. But once; they shot me in my head, and thought they had killed me
Question. Did you see any others shot there?
Answer. Yes, sir; several other black men with me.
Question. Did you see any small boys shot?
Answer. No, sir.
Question. Did you go back from the river after you were shot
Answer. No, sir.
Question. You remained there until you were brought away by the gunboat?
Answer. Yes, sir. I saw several of our boys shot while they were fighting. They said, when they shot me, that they were allowed to kill every damned nigger in the fort—not spare one.
Question. You saw nobody buried or burned?
Answer. No, sir; I saw them throw several in the water.
Question. Were they all dead that were thrown in?
Answer. Yes, sir; about dead.

Eli Carlton, (colored,) private, company B, 6th United States heavy artillery, sworn and examined.

By the chairman:

Question. Where were you raised?
Answer. In East Tennessee.
Question. Have you been a slave?
Answer. Yes, sir.
Question. Who was your master?
Answer. Major Fleming. I was sold once; I have had two masters
Question. Where did you join the army?
Answer. At Corinth, Mississippi, about a year ago.
Question. Were you at Fort Pillow at the time it was taken?
Answer. Yes, sir.
Question. State what happened there.
Answer. I saw 23 men shot after they surrendered; I made 24; 17 of them laid right around me dead, and 6 below me.
Question. Who shot them?
Answer. The rebels; some white men were killed.
Question. How many white men were killed?
Answer. Three or four.
Question. Killed by the privates?
Answer. Yes, sir; I did not see any officers kill any.
Question. Were the white men officers or privates?

Answer. Privates.

Question. Were the men who shot you near to you?

Answer. Yes, sir; ten or fifteen steps off.

Question. Were you shot with a musket or a pistol?

Answer. With a musket. I was shot once on the battle-field before we surrendered. They took me down to a little hospital under the hill. I was in the hospital when they shot me a second time. Some of our privates commenced talking. They said, "Do you fight with these God damned niggers?" they said, "Yes." Then they said, "God damn you, then, we will shoot you," and they shot one of them right down. They said, "I would not kill you, but, God damn you, you fight with these damned niggers, and we will kill you;" and they blew his brains out of his head. They then went around and counted them up; I laid there and made 18 who were there, and there were 6 more below me. I saw them stick a bayonet in the small part of the belly of one of our boys, and break it right off—he had one shot then.

Question. Did you see any of our men shot the next day?

Answer. No, sir; but I heard them shooting. I hid myself in the bushes before the next morning. I left a fellow lying there, and they came down and killed him during the night. I went down there the next morning and he was dead.

Question. Did you see any of our folks buried by the rebels?

Answer. No, sir.

Question. Did you see any buildings burned up?

Answer. Yes, sir; most all were burned up.

Question. Were any persons in them when they were burned?

Answer. I heard so. I went to the quarters and staid about a house there. One of the rebels told me that he should take me out the next morning and kill me. He went out and I slipped out into the bushes, and laid there until the gunboat came. I saw them take the quartermaster; they said, "Here is one of our men; let us take him up and fix him." A white man told me the next day that they burned him.

Question. Was he wounded?

Answer. No, sir; he walked right straight. He had three stripes on his arm. I knew him well; I worked with him. He was a small fellow, weak and puny.

Sandy Cole, (colored,) private, company D, 6th United States heavy artillery, sworn and examined.

By Mr. Gooch:

Question. Where were you born?

Answer. In Tennessee.

Question. Have you been a slave?

Answer. Yes, sir.

Question. Were you at Fort Pillow at the late fight there?

Answer. Yes, sir.

Question. When were you wounded?

Answer. After I started down the hill, after the surrender. They shot me through the thigh and through the arm.

Question. Who shot you?

Answer. A secesh private.

Question. How near was he to you?

Answer. About ten feet.

Question. Did he say anything to you?

Answer. No, sir. I went to the river and kept my body in the water, and my head under some brush.

Question. Did you see anybody else shot?

Answer. Yes, sir; I saw some of them shot right through the head.

Question. How many did you see shot?

Answer. Some seven or eight.

Jacob Thompson, (colored,) sworn and examined.

By Mr. Gooch:

Question. Were you a soldier at Fort Pillow?

Answer. No, sir, I was not a soldier; but I went up in the fort and fought with the rest. I was shot in the hand and the head.

Question. When were you shot?

Answer. After I surrendered.

Question. How many times were you shot?

Answer. I was shot but once; but I threw my hand up, and the shot went through my hand and my head.

Question. Who shot you?

Answer. A private.

Question. What did he say?

Answer. He said, "God damn you, I will shoot you, old friend."

Question. Did you see anybody else shot?

Answer. Yes, sir; they just called them out like dogs, and shot them down. I reckon they shot about fifty, white and black, right there. They nailed some black sergeants to the logs, and set the logs on fire.

Question. When did you see that?

Answer. When I went there in the morning I saw them; they were burning all together.

Question. Did they kill them before they burned them?

Answer. No, sir, they nailed them to the logs; drove the nails right through their hands.

Question. How many did you see in that condition?

Answer. Some four or five; I saw two white men burned.

Question. Was there any one else there who saw that?

Answer. I reckon there was; I could not tell who.

Question. When was it that you saw them?

Answer. I saw them in the morning after the fight; some of them were burned almost in two. I could tell they were white men, because they were whiter than the colored men.

Question. Did you notice how they were nailed?

Answer. I saw one nailed to the side of a house; he looked like he was nailed right through his wrist. I was trying then to get to the boat when I saw it.

Question. Did you see them kill any white men?

Answer. They killed some eight or nine there. I reckon they killed more than twenty after it was all over; called them out from under the hill, and shot them down. They would call out a white man and shoot him down, and call out a colored man and shoot him down; do it just as fast as they could make their guns go off.

Question. Did you see any rebel officers about there when this was going on?

Answer. Yes, sir; old Forrest was one.

Question. Did you know Forrest?

Answer. Yes, sir; he was a little bit of a man. I had seen him before at Jackson.

Question. Are you sure he was there when this was going on?

Answer. Yes, sir.

Question. Did you see any other officers that you knew?

Answer. I did not know any other but him. There were some two or three more officers came up there.

Question. Did you see any buried there?

Answer. Yes, sir; they buried right smart of them. They buried a great many secesh, and a great many of our folks. I think they buried more secesh than our folks.

Question. How did they bury them?

Answer. They buried the secesh over back of the fort, all except those on Fort hill; them they buried up on top of the hill where the gunboats shelled them.

Question. Did they bury any alive?

Answer. I heard the gunboat men say they dug two out who were alive.

Question. You did not see them?

Answer. No, sir.

Question. What company did you fight with?

Answer. I went right into the fort and fought there.

Question. Were you a slave or a free man?

Answer. I was a slave.

Question. Where were you raised?

Answer. In old Virginia.

Question. Who was your master?

Answer. Colonel Hardgrove.

Question. Where did you live?

Answer. I lived three miles the other side of Brown's mills.

Question. How long since you lived with him?

Answer. I went home once and staid with him a while, but he got to cutting up and I came away again.

Question. What did you do before you went into the fight?

Answer. I was cooking for Co. K, of Illinois cavalry; I cooked for that company nearly two years.

Question. What white officers did you know in our army?

Answer. I knew Captain Meltop and Colonel Ransom; and I cooked at the hotel at Fort Pillow, and Mr. Nelson kept it. I and Johnny were cooking together. After they shot me through the hand and head, they beat up all this part of my head (the side of his head) with the breech of their guns.

Ransom Anderson, (colored,) Co. B, 6th United States heavy artillery, sworn and examined.

By Mr. Gooch:

Question Where were you raised?

Answer. In Mississippi.

Question. Were you a slave?

Answer. Yes, sir.

Question. Where did you enlist?

Answer. At Corinth.

Question. Were you in the fight at Fort Pillow?

Answer. Yes, sir.

Question. Describe what you saw done there.

Answer. Most all the men that were killed on our side were killed after the fight was over. They called them out and shot them down. Then they put some in the houses and shut them up, and then burned the houses.

Question. Did you see them burn?

Answer. Yes, sir.

Question. Were any of them alive?

Answer. Yes, sir; they were wounded, and could not walk. They put them in the houses, and then burned the houses down.

Question. Do you know they were in there?

Answer. Yes, sir; I went and looked in there.

Question. Do you know they were in there when the house was burned?

Answer. Yes, sir; I heard them hallooing there when the houses were burning.

Question. Are you sure they were wounded men, and not dead, when they were put in there?

Answer. Yes, sir; they told them they were going to have the doctor see them, and then put them in there and shut them up, and burned them.

Question. Who set the house on fire?

Answer. I saw a rebel soldier take some grass and lay it by the door, and set it on fire. The door was pine plank, and it caught easy.

Question. Was the door fastened up?

Answer. Yes, sir; it was barred with one of those wide bolts.

Sergeant W. P. Walker, (white,) sworn and examined:

By Mr. Gooch:

Question. In what capacity did you serve in the army?

Answer. I was a sergeant in the 13th Tennessee cavalry, company D.

Question. Were you at Fort Pillow at the time of the fight there?

Answer. Yes, sir.

Question. Will you state what took place there?

Answer. In the morning the pickets ran in. We were sent out a piece as skirmishers. They kept us out about a couple of hours, and then we retreated into the fort. The firing kept up pretty regular until about two o'clock, when a flag of truce came in. While the flag of truce was in, the enemy was moving up and taking their positions; they were also pilfering and searching our quarters.

Question. They finally took the fort?

Answer. Yes, sir.

Question. What happened then?

Answer. They just shot us down without showing us any quarter at all. They shot me, for one, after I surrendered; they shot me in the arm, and the shoulder, and the neck, and in the eye.

Question. How many times did they shoot you?

Answer. They shot me in the arm and eye after I surrendered; I do not know when they shot me in the other places.

Question. Who shot you?

Answer. A private shot me with a pistol; there were a great many of us shot.

Question. What reason did he give for shooting you after you had surrendered?

Answer. A man came down the hill and said that General—some one; I could not understand the name—said that they should shoot every one of us, and take no prisoners, and then they shot us down.

Question. How did you escape?

Answer. They thought they had killed me. They searched my pockets half a dozen times, or more, and took my pocket-book from me.

Question. Did you see anybody else shot after they had surrendered?

Answer. Yes, sir; I saw several shot right around me.

Question. Did they shoot all, colored and white?

Answer. They shot all where I was. When they turned in and went to shooting the white men, they scattered and ran, and then they shot them down.

Question. Did you see them do anything besides shooting them?

Answer. I saw some knock them over the heads with muskets, and some stick sabres into them.

Question. Did you see anything of any burning or burying alive?

Answer. No, sir; I did not see that.

Question. Were any of the rebel officers about while this was going on?

Answer. Not where I was; I was down under the hill then. The niggers first ran out of the fort, and then, when they commenced shooting us, we ran down under the hill, and they followed us up and shot us. They came back the next day and shot several wounded negroes.

Question. Did you see that?

Answer. I was lying in a house, but I heard the negroes begging, and heard the guns fired; but I did not see it.

Jason Loudon, sworn and examined.

By the chairman:

Question. To what company and regiment did you belong?

Answer. To company B, 13th Tennessee cavalry.

Question. Were you in the fight at Fort Pillow?

Answer. Yes, sir.

Question. Were you wounded there?

Answer. Yes, sir.

Question. When?

Answer. In the evening, after I surrendered.

Question. Where were you?

Answer. At the fort.

Question. State what happened when you were wounded.

Answer. Nothing; only they were going around shooting the men down. They shot a sergeant by the side of me twice after he had surrendered.

Question. Who shot him?

Answer. A secesh private.

Question. How near was that to you?

Answer. About ten steps off.

Question. Did he say anything to him?

Answer. He commenced cursing, and said they were going to kill every one of us.

Question. How many did you see shot after they had surrendered?

Answer. I saw five or six shot.

James Walls, sworn and examined.

By Mr. Gooch:

Question. To what company did you belong?

Answer. Company E, 13th Tennessee cavalry.

Question. Under what officers did you serve?

Answer. I was under Major Bradford and Captain Potter.

Question. Were you in the fight at Fort Pillow?

Answer. Yes, sir.

Question. State what you saw there of the fight, and what was done after the place was captured.

Answer. We fought them for some six or eight hours in the fort, and when they charged our men scattered and ran under the hill; some turned back and surrendered, and were shot. After the flag of truce came in I went down to get some water. As I was coming back I turned sick, and laid down behind a log. The secesh charged, and after they came over I saw one go a good ways ahead of the others. One of our men made to him and threw down his arms. The bullets were flying so thick there I thought I could not live there, so I threw down my arms and surrendered. He did not shoot me then, but as I turned around he or some other one shot me in the back.

Question. Did they say anything while they were shooting?

Answer. All I heard was, "Shoot him, shoot him!" "Yonder goes one!" "Kill him, kill him!" That is about all I heard.

Question. How many do you suppose you saw shot after they surrendered?

Answer. I did not see but two or three shot around me. One of the boys of our company, named Taylor, ran up there, and I saw him shot and fall. Then another was shot just before me, like—shot down after he threw down his arms.

Question. Those were white men?

Answer. Yes, sir. I saw them make lots of niggers stand up, and then they shot them down like hogs. The next morning I was lying around there waiting for the boat to come up. The secesh would be prying around there, and would come to a nigger and say, "You ain't dead, are you?" They would not say anything, and then the secesh would get down off their horses, prick them in their sides, and say, "Damn you, you ain't dead; get up." Then they would make them get up on their knees, when they would shoot them down like hogs.

Question. Do you know of their burning any buildings?

Answer. I could hear them tell them to stick torches all around, and they fired all the buildings.

Question. Do you know whether any of our men were in the buildings when they were burned?

Answer. Some of our men said some were burned; I did not see it, or know it to be so myself.

Question. How did they bury them—white and black together?

Answer. I don't know about the burying; I did not see any buried.

Question. How many negroes do you suppose were killed after the surrender?

Answer. There were hardly any killed before the surrender. I reckon as many as 200 were killed after the surrender, out of about 300 that were there.

Question. Did you see any rebel officers about while this shooting was going on?

Answer. I do not know as I saw any officers about when they were shooting the negroes. A captain came to me a few minutes after I was shot; he was close by me when I was shot.

Question. Did he try to stop the shooting?

Answer. I did not hear a word of their trying to stop it. After they were shot down, he told them not to shoot them any more. I begged him not to let them shoot me again, and he said they would not. One man, after he was shot down, was shot again. After I was shot down, the man I surrendered to went around the tree I was against and shot a man, and then came around to me again and wanted my pocket-book. I handed it up to him, and he saw my watch-chain and made a grasp at it, and got the watch and about half the chain. He took an old Barlow knife I had in my pocket. It was not worth five cents; was of no account at all, only to cut tobacco with.

William L. McMichael, sworn and examined.

By the chairman:

Question. To what company and regiment did you belong?

Answer. To Company D, 13th Tennessee cavalry.

Question. Were you in the fight at Fort Pillow?

Answer. Yes, sir.

Question. Were you shot after you had surrendered?

Answer. Yes, sir. They shot the most after they had surrendered. They sent in a flag of truce for a surrender, and the major would not surrender. They made a charge and took the fort, and then we threw down our arms; but they just shot us down.

Question. Were you shot after you surrendered, or before?

Answer. Afterwards.

Question. How many times were you shot?

Answer. I was shot four times.
Question. Did you see any others shot?
Answer. I saw some shot; some negroes.

Isaac J. Leadbetter, sworn and examined.

By Mr. Gooch:

Question. To what company and regiment do you belong?
Answer. To company E, 13th Tennessee cavalry.
Question. How long have you been in the army?
Answer. Only about two months.
Question. Were you at Fort Pillow at the time of the fight there?
Answer. Yes, sir.
Question. Will you state what took place after the fort was taken?
Answer. They shot me after I surrendered. I saw them shoot down lots after they surrendered. They would hold up their hands and cry to them not to shoot, but they shot them just the same.
Question. How many do you suppose you saw shot after they had surrendered?
Answer. More than twenty, I reckon.
Question. Did you hear of the rebels doing anything else to them beyond shooting them?
Answer. I heard of their burning some, but I did not see it.
Question. How many times were you shot?
Answer. I was shot twice, and a ball slightly grazed my head.
Question. Were you shot after you had surrendered?
Answer. Yes, sir.
Question. Did you see the man who shot you?
Answer. I saw the man who shot me the last time in the side with a revolver.
Question. Did he say anything to you?
Answer. He did not say anything until he shot me. He then came down to where I was, and finding I was not dead, he cursed me, and said he would shoot me again. He was fixing to shoot me again, when one of the boys standing by told him not to shoot me again.
Question. Did they rob you after they had shot you?
Answer. Yes, sir; they took everything I had, even to my pocket-knife.
Question. You say you heard about the burning?
Answer. Yes, sir, I heard about it; but I did not see it.
Question. Did you see any of the rebel officers about while this shooting was going on?
Answer. None there that I knew. I did not see them until they carried me up on the bluff.
Question. Did they shoot any after they fell wounded?
Answer. I saw them shoot one man in the head after he fell.

D. W. Harrison, sworn and examined.

By the chairman:

Question. To what company and regiment do you belong?
Answer. Company D, 13th Tennessee cavalry.
Question. Were you in the fight at Fort Pillow?
Answer. I had been driving a team and acting as a soldier. I took my gun that morning and went out in line. They then wanted a train to haul some ammunition and provisions in the fort. The rebels were throwing balls around there. I kept hauling, I think five loads. The rest of the wagons would not go back after they had hauled one load; and after I had hauled five loads I

concluded I would not haul any more. I went down under the hill and got with two men there close under a log. It was but a few minutes before the men came over the hill like sheep over a brush fence, when I saw white men and negroes getting shot down. I threw up my hands and said: "Don't shoot me; I surrender." One of them said: "Go on up the hill." I started, but did not get more than two steps before I was shot in the shoulder. I fell, and while I was undertaking to get up again I was hit in the body; and this arm that was hit fell over behind me. A rebel came along with a canteen, and I motioned to him and told him I wanted a little water. He said: "Damn you; I have nothing for you fellows. You Tennesseeans pretend to be men, and you fight side by side with niggers. I have nothing for you." About that time another one came up with his pistol drawn, and asked if I had any money. I told him I had a little, and he told me to give it to him. I told him my shoulder was hurt and he must take it himself. He turned me over and took about $90 and my watch. Another man, who *was* a man, came along and brought me some water.

Question. Did you see any others shot after they had surrendered?

Answer. Yes, sir. One of the two who was under the log with me was killed. I don't know whether the other man was killed or not.

William A. Dickey, sworn and examined.

By the chairman:

Question. Were you at Fort Pillow when it was taken by the rebels?

Answer. Yes, sir.

Question. In what company and regiment?

Answer. Company B, 13th Tennessee cavalry.

Question. Will you state what happened there, especially after the fort was taken?

Answer. After the breastworks were charged I first noticed the colored soldiers throwing down their arms and running down the bluff. After the rebs got inside the white troops saw that there was no mercy shown, and they threw down their arms and ran down the bluff, too; and they were at the same time shot and butchered. I ran myself, but carried my gun with me down the bluff, and hid myself behind a tree close to the edge of the river. I staid there some time, and saw my partner shot, and saw men shot all around me. I saw one man shoot as many as four negroes just as fast as he could load his gun and shoot. After doing this he came to me. As he turned around to me, I begged him not to shoot me. He came to me and I gave him my gun, and he took my caps, saying he wanted them to kill niggers. I begged him to let me go with him, as I would be exposed there; but he said "No, stay there." He made me stay there, and would not let me go with him. Another man came along, and I asked him to spare my life, and he did so. I asked him to let me go with him, but he refused me and ordered me to stay with my wounded partner, who was lying in some brush. I crawled in the brush to him. He was suffering very much, and I unloosed his belt, and took his cartridge-box and put it under his head. Some rebels under the hill spied us moving in the brush and ordered us to come out. My partner could not come out, but I came out. They ordered me to come to them. I started after one of them, begging him at the same time not to shoot me. I went, I suppose, eight or ten steps, when he shot me. I fell there, and saw but little more after that. As I was lying with my face towards the river I saw some swimming and drowning in the river, and I saw them shoot some in the river after that.

Woodford Cooksey, sworn and examined.

By Mr. Gooch:

Question. To what company and regiment do you belong?

Answer. Company A, 13th Tennessee cavalry.

Question. Were you in the fight at Fort Pillow?

Answer. Yes, sir; from 6 o'clock in the morning until about 4 o'clock in the evening.

Question. State what took place after the fort was taken by the rebels.

Answer. There were a great many white men shot down, and a great many negroes.

Question. That you saw?

Answer. That I saw myself.

Question. Were you wounded there?

Answer. Yes, sir.

Question. At what time?

Answer. After 4 o'clock; after we gave up.

Question. How came they to shoot you after you had surrendered?

Answer. I can't tell; it was about like shooting the balance of them.

Question. Do you know who shot you?

Answer. It was a white man. He shot me with a musket loaded with a musket ball and three buck shot.

Question. Did you have any arms in your hands when you were shot?

Answer. No, sir.

Question. Did the one who shot you say anything to you?

Answer. I was lying down. He said, "Hand me up your money, you damned son of a bitch." I only had four bits—two bits in silver and two in paper. I handed it up to him. He said he had damned nigh a notion to hit me in the head on account of staying there and fighting with the niggers. He heard a rally about the bank and went down there. They were shooting and throwing them in the river. A part of that night and the next morning they were burning houses and burying the dead and stealing goods. The next morning they commenced on the negroes again, and killed all they came across, as far as I could see. I saw them kill eight or ten of them the next morning.

Question. Do you know whether any wounded soldiers were burned in any of those buildings?

Answer. I do not. I was not in any of the shanties after they were fired.

Question. Did you see them bury any of the dead?

Answer. No, sir; I was lying outside of the fort.

Question. Did they bury the white and black together, as you understood?

Answer. Yes, sir; they were burying pretty much all night.

Question. How many whites and blacks do you suppose were killed after they had surrendered?

Answer. I had a mighty poor chance of finding out. But I don't think they killed less than 50 or 60, probably more; I cannot say how many. It was an awful time, I know.

Question. How many did you see killed?

Answer. I saw them kill three white men and seven negroes the next morning.

Question. Did you see them shoot any white men the day after the fight?

Answer. No, sir. I saw one of them shoot a black fellow in the head with three buck shot and a musket ball. The man held up his head, and then the fellow took his pistol and fired that at his head. The black man still moved, and then the fellow took his sabre and stuck it in the hole in the negro's head and jammed it way down, and said "Now, God damn you, die!" The negro did not say anything, but he moved, and the fellow took his carbine and beat his head soft with it. That was the next morning after the fight.

Lieutenant McJ. Leming, sworn and examined.

By Mr. Gooch:

Question. Were you in the fight at Fort Pillow?

Answer. Yes, sir.

Question. What is your rank and position?

Answer. I am a first lieutenant and adjutant of the 13th Tennessee cavalry. A short time previous to the fight I was post adjutant at Fort Pillow, and during most of the engagement I was acting as post adjutant. After Major Booth was killed, Major Bradford was in command. The pickets were driven in just before sunrise, which was the first intimation we had that the enemy were approaching. I repaired to the fort, and found that Major Booth was shelling the rebels as they came up towards the outer intrenchments. They kept up a steady fire by sharpshooters behind trees, and logs, and high knolls. The major thought at one time they were planting some artillery, or looking for places to plant it. They began to draw nearer and nearer, up to the time our men were all drawn into the fort. Two companies of the 13th Tennessee cavalry were ordered out as sharpshooters, but were finally ordered in. We were pressed on all sides.

I think Major Booth fell not later than 9 o'clock. His adjutant, who was then acting post adjutant, fell near the same time. Major Bradford then took the command, and I acted as post adjutant. Previous to this, Major Booth had ordered some buildings in front of the fort to be destroyed, as the enemy's sharpshooters were endeavoring to get possession of them. There were four rows of buildings, but only the row nearest the fort was destroyed; the sharpshooters gained possession of the others before they could be destroyed. The fight continued, one almost unceasing fire all the time, until about three o'clock. They threw some shells, but they did not do much damage with their shells.

I think it was about three o'clock that a flag of truce approached. I went out, accompanied by Captain Young, the provost marshal of the post. There was another officer, I think, but I do not recollect now particularly who it was, and some four mounted men. The rebels announced that they had a communication from General Forrest. One of their officers there, I think, from his dress, was a colonel. I received the communication, and they said they would wait for an answer. As near as I remember, the communication was as follows:

"HEADQUARTERS CONFEDERATE CAVALRY,
"*Near Fort Pillow, April* 12, 1864.

"As your gallant defence of the fort has entitled you to the treatment of brave men, (or something to that effect,) I now demand an unconditional surrender of your force, at the same time assuring you that they will be treated as prisoners of war. I have received a fresh supply of ammunition, and can easily take your position.

"N. B. FORREST.

"Major L. F. BOOTH,
"*Commanding United States Forces.*"

I took this message back to the fort. Major Bradford replied that he desired an hour for consultation and consideration with his officers, and the officers of the gunboat. I took out this communication to them, and they carried it back to General Forrest. In a few minutes another flag of truce appeared, and I went out to meet it. Some one said, when they handed the communication to me, "That gives you 20 minutes to surrender; I am General Forrest." I took it back. The substance of it was: "Twenty minutes will be given you to take your men outside of the fort. If in that time they are not out, I will immediately proceed to assault your works," or something of that kind. To this Major Bradford replied: "I will not surrender." I took it out in a sealed envelope, and gave it to him. The general opened it and read it. Nothing was said; we simply saluted, and they went their way, and I returned back into the fort.

Almost instantly the firing began again. We mistrusted, while this flag of truce was going on, that they were taking horses out at a camp we had. It was mentioned to them, the last time that this and other movements excited our suspicion, that they were moving their troops. They said that they had noticed it themselves, and had it stopped; that it was unintentional on their part, and that it should not be repeated.

It was not long after the last flag of truce had retired, that they made their grand charge. We kept them back for several minutes. What was called —— brigade or battalion attacked the centre of the fort where several companies of colored troops were stationed. They finally gave way, and, before we could fill up the breach, the enemy got inside the fort, and then they came in on the other two sides, and had complete possession of the fort. In the mean time nearly all the officers had been killed, especially of the colored troops, and there was no one hardly to guide the men. They fought bravely, indeed, until that time. I do not think the men who broke had a commissioned officer over them. They fought with the most determined bravery, until the enemy gained possession of the fort. They kept shooting all the time. The negroes ran down the hill towards the river, but the rebels kept shooting them as they were running; shot seme again after they had fallen; robbed and plundered them. After everything was all gone, after we had given up the fort entirely, the guns thrown away and the firing on our part stopped, they still kept up their murderous fire, more especially on the colored troops, I thought, although the white troops suffered a great deal. I know the colored troops had a great deal the worst of it. I saw several shot after they were wounded; as they were crawling around, the secesh would step out and blow their brains out.

About this time they shot me. It must have been four or half-past four o'clock. I saw there was no chance at all, and threw down my sabre. A man took deliberate aim at me, but a short distance from me, certainly not more than 15 paces, and shot me.

Question. With a musket or pistol?

Answer. I think it was a carbine; it may have been a musket, but my impression is that it was a carbine. Soon after I was shot I was robbed. A secesh soldier came along, and wanted to know if I had any greenbacks. I gave him my pocket-book. I had about a hundred dollars, I think, more or less, and a gold watch and gold chain. They took everything in the way of valuables that I had. I saw them robbing others. That seemed to be the general way they served the wounded, so far as regards those who fell in my vicinity. Some of the colored troops jumped into the river, but were shot as fast as they were seen. One poor fellow was shot as he reached the bank of the river. They ran down and hauled him out. He got on his hands and knees, and was crawling along, when a secesh soldier put his revolver to his head, and blew his brains out. It was about the same thing all along, until dark that night.

I was very weak, but I finally found a rebel who belonged to a society that I am a member of, (the Masons,) and he got two of our colored soldiers to assist me up the hill, and he brought me some water. At that time it was about dusk. He carried me up just to the edge of the fort, and laid me down. There seemed to be quite a number of dead collected there. They were throwing them into the outside trench, and I heard them talking about burying them there. I heard one of them say, "There is a man who is not quite dead yet." They buried a number there; I do not know how many.

I was carried that night to a sort of little shanty that the rebels had occupied during the day with their sharpshooters. I received no medical attention that night at all. The next morning early I heard the report of cannon down the river. It was the gunboat 28 coming up from Memphis; she was shelling the rebels along the shore as she came up. The rebels immediately ordered the burning of all the buildings, and ordered the two buildings where the wounded were to be fired. Some one called to the officer who gave the order and said there were wounded in them. The building I was in began to catch fire. I prevailed upon one of our soldiers who had not been hurt much to draw me out, and I think others got the rest out. They drew us down a little way, in a sort of gulley, and we lay there in the hot sun without water or anything.

About this time a squad of rebels came around, it would seem for the purpose of murdering what negroes they could find. They began to shoot the wounded negroes all around there, interspersed with the whites. I was lying a little way from a wounded negro, when a secesh soldier came up to him and said: "What in hell are you doing here?" The colored soldier said he wanted to get on the gunboat. The secesh soldier said: "You want to fight us again, do you? Damn you, I'll teach you," and drew up his gun and shot him dead. Another negro was standing up erect a little way from me; he did not seem to be hurt much. The rebel loaded his gun again immediately. The negro begged of him not to shoot him, but he drew up his gun and took deliberate aim at his head. The gun snapped, but he fixed it again, and then killed him. I saw this. I heard them shooting all around there—I suppose killing them.

By the chairman:

Question. Do you know of any rebel officers going on board our gunboat after she came up?

Answer. I don't know about the gunboat, but I saw some of them on board the Platte Valley, after I had been carried on her. They came on board, and I think went in to drink with some of our officers. I think one of the rebel officers was General Chalmers.

Question. Do you know what officers of ours drank with them?

Answer. I do not.

Question. You know that they did go on board the Platte Valley and drink with some of our officers?

Answer. I did not see them drinking at the time, but I have no doubt they did; that was my impression from all I saw, and I thought our officers might have been in better business.

Question. Were our officers treating these rebel officers with attention?

Answer. They seemed to be; I did not see much of it, as they passed along by me.

Question. Do you know whether or not the conduct of the privates, in murdering our soldiers after they had surrendered, seemed to have the approval of their officers?

Answer. I did not see much of their officers, especially during the worst of those outrages; they seemed to be back.

Question. Did you observe any effort on the part of their officers to suppress the murders?

Answer. No, sir; I did not see any where I was first carried; just about dusk, all at once several shots were fired just outside. The cry was: "They are shooting the darkey soldiers" I heard an officer ride up and say: "Stop that firing; arrest that man." I suppose it was a rebel officer, but I do not know. It was reported to me, at the time, that several darkeys were shot then. An officer who stood by me, a prisoner, said that they had been shooting them, but that the general had had it stopped.

Question. Do you know of any of our men in the hospital being murdered?

Answer. I do not.

Question. Do you know anything of the fate of your quartermaster, Lieutenant Akerstrom?

Answer. He was one of the officers who went with me to meet the flag of truce the last time. I do not know what became of him; that was about the last I saw of him. I heard that he was nailed to a board and burned, and I have very good reason for believing that was the case, although I did not see it. The first lieutenant of company D of my regiment says that he has an affidavit to that effect of a man who saw it.

Question. Have you any knowledge in relation to any of our men being buried alive?

Answer. I have not, other than I have stated.

By Mr. Gooch:

Question. How long had your regiment been in Fort Pillow?

Answer. We reached there the 8th of February. There were no other troops there then, and we held the place alone for some time.

By the chairman:

Question. By whom were you ordered there?

Answer. By General W. S. Smith, chief of cavalry, and also by General Hurlbut.

Question. What other troops were there at the time of the fight?

Answer. Four companies of the 6th United States heavy artillery, colored, and a battery called now, I think, the 2d United States light artillery. It was before the 1st Tennessee light artillery, colored.

Question. What was about the number of our force there?

Answer. Not far from 500 men.

Question. Do you know what became of Major Bradford?

Answer. He escaped unhurt, as far as the battle was concerned. I was told the next morning on the boat that he had been paroled. I did not see him after that night.

Question. Do you know why you were left unsupported, as you were, when it was known that Forrest was in your vicinity?

Answer. I do not know why, unless it was thought that he would not attack us. I think it was supposed that he was going to make an attack on Memphis.

By Mr. Gooch:

Question. What do you estimate Forrest's force to have been?

Answer. From all I could see and learn, I should suppose he had from 7,000 to 10,000 men.

Question. Is there anything further you desire to state?

Answer. I heard some of the rebels talking during the night after the fight. They said we ought to have surrendered when we had the opportunity, but that they supposed the Yankees were afraid the colored troops would not be treated as prisoners of war; and they intimated that they would not be; and said it was bad enough to give to the "home-made Yankees"—meaning the Tennessee soldiers—treatment as soldiers, without treating the negroes so, too.

On the morning of the fight there was so much hurry and confusion that our flag was not raised for a time; we had been firing away an hour before I happened to notice that our flag was not up. I ordered it to be raised immediately, and our troops set up vociferous cheers, especially the colored troops, who entered into the fight with great energy and spirit.

Question. How many officers of your regiment were left alive?

Answer. Only two, immediately after the surrender, that I know of. We had ten officers in our regiment, and eight were in the battle, only two of whom remained alive.

Question. Were those who were killed killed before or after the fort was captured?

Answer. I don't know of but one who was killed before we were driven from the fort.

Question. Was Captain Potter, who is now lying here unable to speak, shot before or after the surrender?

Answer. He was shot in the early part of the engagement. I have been told that Major Bradford was afterwards taken out by the rebels and shot; that seems to be the general impression, and I presume it was so.

MOUND CITY, *April* 23, 1864.

Nathan G. Fulks, sworn and examined.

By Mr. Gooch:

Question. To what company and regiment do you belong?
Answer. Company D, 13th Tennessee cavalry.
Question. Where are you from?
Answer. About twenty miles from Columbus, Tennessee.
Question. How long have you been in the service?
Answer. Five months, the 1st of May.
Question. Were you at Fort Pillow at the time of the fight there?
Answer. Yes, sir.
Question. Will you state what happened to you there?
Answer. I was at the corner of the fort when they fetched in a flag for a surrender. Some of them said the major stood a while, and then said he would not surrender. They continued to fight a while; and after a time the major started and told us to take care of ourselves, and I and twenty more men broke for the hollow. They ordered us to halt, and some of them said, "God damn 'em, kill 'em! kill 'em!" I said, "I have surrendered." I had thrown my gun away then. I took off my cartridge-box and gave it to one of them, and said, "Don't shoot me;" but they did shoot me, and hit just about where the shoe comes up on my leg. I begged them not to shoot me, and he said, "God damn you, you fight with the niggers, and we will kill the last one of you!" Then they shot me in the thick of the thigh, and I fell; and one set out to shoot me again, when another one said, "Don't shoot the white fellows any more."
Question. Did you see any person shot besides yourself?
Answer. I didn't see them shot. I saw one of our fellows dead by me.
Question. Did you see any buildings burned?
Answer. Yes, sir. While I was in the major's headquarters they commenced burning the buildings, and I begged one of them to take me out and not let us burn there; and he said, "I am hunting up a piece of yellow flag for you." I think we would have whipped them if the flag of truce had not come in. We would have whipped them if we had not let them get the dead-wood on us. I was told that they made their movement while the flag of truce was in. I did not see it myself, because I had sat down, as I had been working so hard.
Question. How do you know they made their movement while the flag of truce was in?
Answer. The men that were above said so. The rebs are bound to take every advantage of us. I saw two more white men close to where I was lying. That makes three dead ones, and myself wounded.

Francis A. Alexander, sworn and examined.

By the chairman:

Question. To what company and regiment do you belong?
Answer. Company C, 13th Tennessee cavalry.
Question. Were you at Fort Pillow at the fight there?
Answer. Yes, sir.
Question. Who commanded your regiment?
Answer. Major Bradford commanded the regiment, and Lieutenant Logan commanded our company.
Qnestion. By what troops was the fort attacked?

Answer. Forrest was in command. I saw him.

Question. Did you know Forrest?

Answer. I saw him there, and they all said it was Forrest. Their own men said so.

Question. By what troops was the charge made?

Answer. They were Alabamians and Texans.

Question. Did you see anything of a flag of truce?

Answer. Yes, sir.

Question. State what was done while the flag of truce was in.

Answer. When the flag of truce came up our officers went out and held a consultation, and it went back. They came in again with a flag of truce; and while they were consulting the second time their troops were coming up a gap or hollow, where we could have cut them to pieces. They tried it before, but could not do it. I saw them come up there while the flag of truce was in the second time.

Question. That gave them an advantage?

Answer. Yes, sir.

Question. Were you wounded there?

Answer. Not in the fort. I was wounded after I left the fort, and was going down the hill.

Question. Was that before or after the fort was taken?

Answer. It was afterwards.

Question. Did you have any arms in your hand at the time they shot you?

Answer. No, sir. I threw my gun away, and started down the hill, and got about twenty yards, when I was shot through the calf of the leg.

Question. Did they shoot you more than once?

Answer. No, sir; they shot at me, but did not hit me more than once.

Question. Did they say why they shot you after you had surrendered?

Answer. They said afterwards they intended to kill us all for being there with their niggers.

Question. Were any rebel officers there at the time this shooting was going on?

Answer. Yes, sir.

Question. Did they try to stop it?

Answer. One or two of them did.

Question. What did the rest of them do?

Answer. They kept shouting and hallooing at the men to give no quarter. I heard that cry very frequent.

Question. Was it the officers that said that?

Answer. I think it was. I think it was them, the way they were going on. When our boys were taken prisoners, if anybody came up who knew them, they shot them down. As soon as ever they recognized them, wherever it was, they shot them.

Question. After they had taken them prisoners?

Answer. Yes, sir.

Question. Did you know anything about their shooting men in the hospitals?

Answer. I know of their shooting negroes in there. I don't know about white men.

Question. Wounded negro men?

Answer. Yes, sir.

Question. Who did that?

Answer. Some of their troops. I don't know which of them. The next morning I saw several black people shot that were wounded, and some that were not wounded. One was going down the hill before me, and the officer made him come back up the hill; and after I got in the boat I heard them shooting them.

Question. You say you saw them shoot negroes in the hospital the next morning?

Answer. Yes, sir; wounded negroes who could not get along; one with his leg broke. They came there the next day and shot him.

Question. Do you know anything about their burning buildings and the hospital?

Answer. I expect they burned the hospital after we got out. They said they would not while we wounded ones were in there. The hospital we were in was standing when I went down the hill on the boat.

Question. You don't know what happened to it afterwards?

Answer. I don't.

Question. Something has been said about men being nailed to the buildings, and then burned. Do you know anything about that?

Answer. No, sir; I did not see that, but I heard some of them say they drove the negroes into the houses and then burned them.

Question. Did you see anything about their burying them?

Answer. No, sir.

Wiley Robinson, sworn and examined.

By Mr. Gooch:

Question. What State are you from?

Answer. Tennessee.

Question. When did you enlist?

Answer. I think about eight months ago.

Question. How old are you?

Answer. Eighteen years old the 19th of next May.

Question. What regiment and company were you in?

Answer. Company A, 13th Tennessee cavalry.

Question. Were you at Fort Pillow at the time of the attack there?

Answer. Yes, sir.

Question. Were you wounded there?

Answer. Yes, sir.

Question. State all about that; when it was, &c.

Answer. I was wounded once in the hand before I surrendered.

Question. Were you shot afterwards?

Answer. Yes, sir; six times. I was shot twice in the foot, twice in the legs, and twice in the hands.

Question. Had you arms in your hands when they shot you?

Answer. We had retreated to the river bank and thrown down our arms.

Question. What did they say when they shot you?

Answer. They swore at us, and then shot us.

Question. Did you see any of the rebel officers there?

Answer. Yes, sir; I saw some, who came round and told them to kill us all.

Question. Did you see them shoot anybody else besides yourself?

Answer. Yes, sir; I saw them shoot one white man close beside me.

Question. Did they shoot you after you were down?

Answer. Yes, sir; through the leg with a musket.

Question. Did you see any negroes shot?

Answer. No, sir; I did not see any. I fell after they shot me, and did not see much.

Question. Were you there the next day after the fight?

Answer. Yes, sir; they took me on board the boat the next day about ten o'clock.

Question. Do you know whether they killed any persons in the hospital?

Answer. I know they killed one of our company in the hospital. They said they fired into the hospital.

Question. Do you know anything about their burying anybody alive?

Answer. No, sir.

Daniel Stamps, sworn and examined.

By the chairman:

Question. To what company and regiment do you belong?

Answer. Company E, 13th Tennessee cavalry.

Question. What was your position?

Answer. I was the company commissary sergeant.

Question. Where do you reside?

Answer. In Lauderdale county, Tennessee.

Question. What was your occupation?

Answer. I was a farmer.

Question. Were you at Fort Pillow when the fight was there?

Answer. Yes, sir.

Question. State what happened there.

Answer. The first thing, I went out sharpshooting, and was out about two hours, and then was ordered in the fort. I staid there, I reckon, about an hour. Then I was called out by Lieutenant Akerstrom to go down alongside the bluff sharpshooting again, because the rebels were coming down Cold creek. We staid there all the time until they charged into the fort. Then they all ran down under the hill, and we went down under the hill too. I reckon we staid there close on to an hour. They were shooting continually. I saw them shooting the white men there who were on their knees, holding up their hands to them. I saw them make another man get down on his knees and beg of them, and they did not shoot him. I started out to go up the hill, and just as I started I was shot in the thigh. Pretty well towards the last of it, before I got shot, while I was down under the hill, a rebel officer came down right on top of the bluff, and hallooed out to them to shoot and kill the last damned one of us.

Question. Do you know the rank of that officer?

Answer. I do not. I can't tell them as I can our officers. Their uniform is different. I went round on the hill then. I heard several of them say it was General Forrest's orders to them to shoot us and give us no quarter at all. I don't know whether they were officers who said so or not. I don't recollect anything else particularly that I saw that night. The next morning they came round there again, shooting the negroes that were wounded. I saw them shoot some 20 or 25 negroes the next morning who had been wounded, and had been able to get up on the hill during the night. They did not attempt to hurt us white men the next morning.

Question. Were any of their officers with the men who were round shooting the negroes the next morning?

Answer. One passed along on horseback, the only one I saw. He rode along while they were shooting the negroes, and said nothing to them. I said, "Captain, what are you going to do with us wounded fellows?" He said they were going to put us on the gunboats, or leave us with the gunboats. He had a feather in his cap, and looked like he might have been a captain. I don't know what he was. He was the only man I saw pass that looked like an officer while they were shooting the negroes.

Question. Where were you when the flags of truce were sent in?

Answer. I was down under the bluff sharpshooting.

Question. Is there anything else that you think of important to state?

Answer. I don't know that there is.

James P. Meador, sworn and examined.

By Mr. Gooch:

Question. To what company and regiment do you belong?

Answer. Company A, 13th Tennessee cavalry.

Question. Do you live in Tennessee?

Answer. Yes, sir; I am a native of the State.

Question. Were you in Fort Pillow at the time of the attack there?

Answer. Yes, sir.

Question. Were you wounded there?

Answer. Yes, sir; twice.

Question. When?

Answer. Once before I surrendered and once afterwards.

Question. Did you see anybody shot besides yourself after he surrendered?

Answer. Yes, sir; I saw lots of negroes shot, and some few white men, and I heard them shoot a great many. I was lying down under the bank.

Question. What were our men doing when they were shot?

Answer. They were begging for quarter when they shot them.

Question. Did you see any of them shot while begging for quarter?

Answer. Yes, sir; I heard an officer say, "Don't show the white men any more quarter than the negroes, because they are no better, and not so good, or they would not fight with the negroes." I saw them make one of our company sergeants kneel down and ask for quarter, and another secesh soldier came up and snapped his pistol at him twice; but they told him not to shoot him. I saw them shoot others when they were kneeling down.

W. J. Mays, sworn and examined.

By the chairman:

Question. To what company and regiment do you belong?

Answer. Company B, 13th Tennessee cavalry.

Question. Were you in Fort Pillow when it was attacked?

Answer. Yes, sir.

Question. State what happened there.

Answer. They attacked us about six o'clock in the morning. Sharpshooting commenced early afterwards, and kept coming closer and closer until the skirmishers were drawn in about ten o'clock. After that they made several efforts to gain the fort, and could not get the position. Under this last flag of truce they gained the position they had been trying to get all day.

Question. Did you see them moving their troops when the flag of truce was in?

Answer. Yes, sir; I showed it to the boys.

Question. What was the movement?

Answer. The place was pretty well surrounded, but they were not on the ground they had been trying to get all day. Under that flag of truce they gained the place, some 75 yards from the fort, and placed themselves under logs, with a better position.

Question. Are you sure this movement was made while the flag of truce was in?

Answer. I know it.

Question. Did others see it?

Answer. Yes, sir; two boys near me, who were both taken prisoners.

Question. Was anything said about it at the time?

Answer. We spoke of it among ourselves at the time. We remarked that under the flag of truce they were only gaining the position they had been trying for all day. I was shot in the charge on the fort. The place was then taken. I would not have fallen then, but our men after surrendering found no quarter shown them, and they flew down the bluff and ran over me and kept me down for some time, until I bled so that I could not get up. I saw them shoot a great many after they surrendered. I saw them shoot four white men and at least 25 blacks, some of them within 20 feet of me, while they were begging for quarter. They pulled one out of a hollow log by the foot and held him, when another shot him close by me. There were two negro women, and three little boys, some 8, 9 or 12 years old, about 25 steps from me. The secesh ran upon them and cursed them, and said, "Damn them;" they thought they were free to shoot them. All fell but one, a little fellow, and they took the breech of a gun and knocked him down. Then they followed up the men that were trying to get away down the bluff, and some hours afterwards they came back searching their pockets. They came on back then, looking over them, and I saw one man with a canteen and asked him for a drink of water. His reply was to turn on me with his pistol presented and shoot at me three times, saying, "God damn you; I will give you water." But he didn't hit me, though he threw the dirt over my face. I concluded it was best to lie still, and didn't move any more until after dark, and then I crawled in with some of the dead and laid there until about 9 o'clock the next morning, when the gunboat came up, and I crawled down on the gunboat with a piece of white paper in my left hand, and made signs, and the boat came ashore and I got on the boat. The general cry from the time they charged the fort until an hour afterwards was, "Kill 'em, kill 'em; God damn 'em; that's Forrest's orders, not to leave one alive." They were burning the buildings. They came with a chunk of fire to burn the building where I was in with the dead. They looked in and said, "These damned sons of bitches are all dead," and went off. I heard guns the next morning, but I was in there with the dead, and didn't see them shoot anybody.

Question. Did you see any of the men in the fort shot after they had surrendered?

Answer. Yes, sir; I saw four white men and 25 negroes that I spoke of that were shot in the fort. The white men didn't commence flying from the fort, though they threw their guns down, until they saw there was no quarter shown them.

James McCoy sworn and examined.

By the chairman:

Question. Where do you reside?

Answer. When I am suffered to live at home I live in Tennessee.

Question. You don't belong to the army?

Answer. No, sir; but I have been with the regiment six months. The head officers were old acquaintances of mine. I once lived with Major Bradford.

Question. Were you at Fort Pillow at the time the attack was made?

Answer. Yes, sir; I was in Fort Pillow at headquarters.

Question. Will you tell us what you observed there?

Answer. About daylight in the morning part of the pickets came in and said the rebels had captured some of the pickets and were coming. I had not got out of bed then. Major Bradford was up immediately the alarm was given. I had had my hands mashed a few days before. Major Bradford told me I had better go on the gunboat, as I would be in the way because I could not hold a gun. I went on board the gunboat, and about sunrise the firing commenced. The gunboat immediately played up and down the river, where I could see everything going on at the fort. I could not see over the bluff. Major Bradford had a flag and stood on the edge of the bluff and motioned to the gunboat where to throw their shells. We had a great many guns on the boat, and about 20 used their guns all the time. The rebel sharpshooters would come over the hill and shoot at the boat and everybody that passed.

Question. Where were you when the flag of truce came in?

Answer. I was on the boat.

Question. What did you see?

Answer. As soon as the flag of truce came in the gunboat stopped firing. It was about 3 o'clock when it came in, and while it was in the enemy were creeping up constantly, sharpshooters and all, nearer and nearer. I saw a great many creeping on their hands and feet, getting up to the hill close to the fort. I don't know what was back of that. Some men in the fort told me that they had advanced and got close to the fort before the flag of truce was taken out. I saw them gathering around there all the time, and all that time they were stealing from the commissary's stores blankets and everything else they could get at. I reckon I saw 200 men climbing the hill with as much as they could carry on their backs, shoes, &c.

Question. Why did our officers permit that without firing on them?

Answer. The gunboat, I think, was almost out of ammunition and had nothing to shoot; and none of them supposed the gunboat would stop shooting, but she ran out of ammunition.

Question. Were you there until the place was taken?

Answer. Yes, sir.

Question. What happened after that?

Answer. About the time the rebels got over the fort there was just a cloud of them, our men in the fort running out. About 500 secesh cavalry, as well as I could see, came up and turned in to shooting them down just as fast as they could. I heard a great deal of screaming and praying for mercy. The negroes took a scare from that and ran down the hill and into the river, but they kept shooting them. I was not more than 400 yards off, on the gunboat. I don't suppose one of them got more than 30 yards into the river before they were shot. The bullets rained as thick in the water as you ever saw a hail-storm.

Question. Were those men armed who were shot?

Answer. No, sir; they threw down their arms.

Question. How many were shot?

Answer. I don't know how many. They lay thick there the next morning, beside those they had buried.

Question. You came back there the next morning?

Answer. Yes, sir.

Question. What do you know about their burying men who were not dead?

Answer. I don't know anything myself, only what I heard.

Question. Did you go up there where they had buried them?

Answer. No, sir.

Question. What did you hear about it?

Answer. I heard one of them say that he saw where a negro was buried, and saw a large mass of foam and dirt where somebody had been breathing through the earth. He brushed it off and saw a negro there still breathing. I saw one or two who looked as if they had been buried when they came on board. I heard one ask them if they had been buried, and they said "Very near it." I don't think they were wounded. One of them had been in the dirt. I don't know whether he played dead and was buried or not.

Question. Do you know anything of their killing the men in the hospital?

Answer. Not of my own seeing. Mr. Akerstrom was in his office down under the hill after the flag of truce was in, and made some signs for us to come to him. Since that time I have been told that they wounded him and then nailed him to a door and burned him up, but I didn't see that myself.

Question. When did you hear about this nailing to a building and burning him up?

Answer. Since we came up here.

Question. Were you on board the gunboat the next day when some of the rebel officers came on board?

Answer. I was on board the Platte Valley.

Question. Did they come with a flag of truce?

Answer. A flag of truce was hoisted, and when we got in to the shore some of the rebel officers came on board the Platte Valley.

Question. How were they received by our officers?

Answer. Just as though there had been no fight. Some of the officers on the Platte Valley took one of the rebel officers up to the bar and treated him, and some would ask the rebel officers what made them treat our men as they did. He said they intended to treat all home-made Yankees just as they did the negroes. I went to Captain Marshall and asked him to let me shoot him. He said that the flag of truce was up, and it would be against the rules of war to shoot him.

Question. Do you know what officers treated him?

Answer. I don't know; they were all strangers to me. The gunboat first landed, and then the transport Platte Valley came up and took the prisoners, and then another boat came up and laid alongside of her. The three lay there together.

Question. Do you know of anything further on the subject that is important?

Answer. I don't think of anything now.

William E. Johnson, sworn and examined.

By Mr. Gooch:

Question. To what regiment do you belong?

Answer. I am a sergeant of company B, of the 13th Tennessee cavalry.

Question. Were you at Fort Pillow at the time of the attack there?

Answer. No, sir; I was at Memphis. I came up to Fort Pillow the morning after the fight, on the Platte Valley, within some six or eight miles below Fort Pillow, and then got on the gunboat 28.

Question. Did you go on shore at Fort Pillow?

Answer. No, sir; I saw some of the rebel officers come down and go on board the Platte Valley; and some of our officers were drinking with them, and making very free with them. I did not particularly notice what rank, but I took them to be captains and lieutenants.

Question. Did you hear the conversation between them?

Answer. They were making very free with one another, joking, talking, and running on. I did not feel right to see such going on, and did not go about them.

John W. Shelton, sworn and examined.

By the chairman:

Question. Where were you raised?

Answer. I was born in Arkansas, but raised principally in Tennessee.

Question. To what company and regiment do you belong?

Answer. Company E, 13th Tennessee cavalry.

Question. Were you at Fort Pillow when the attack was made there

Answer. Yes, sir.

Question. Were you wounded there?

Answer. Yes, sir.

Question. Before or after the surrender?

Answer. It was after I surrendered.

Question. Where were you when you were shot?

Answer. I was under the hill, going up the hill.

Question. What did they say when they shot you?

Answer. I asked them if they did not respect prisoners of war; they said "no, they did not," and kept on shooting; and they popped three or four caps in my face with a revolver after they had wounded me.

Question. Did you see them shoot any others after they had surrendered?

Answer. Yes, sir, lots of them; negroes and white men both. They shot them down wherever they came to them.

Question. Were you there the next day after the battle?

Answer. Yes, sir.

Question. Did you see them shoot anybody the next day?

Answer. I saw them shoot negroes, not white men.

Question. How many did you see them shoot that day?

Answer. I saw them shoot five or six on the hill where I was; they said they shot all they could find.

Question. Were you in the hospital there?

Answer. I was in a house there with the wounded.

Question. Did you see them kill anybody there that was wounded?

Answer. They took two negroes out and shot them.

Question. Did you see them burn any buildings the wounded were in?

Answer. Not the one we were in. I was told they fired some buildings that wounded negroes were in.

Question. Were you where they buried any of the killed?

Answer. I saw them bury some in a ditch in the evening.

Question. Did they separate the whites from the blacks?

Answer. I cannot tell; I was not close enough. I saw them carry them there and throw them in the ditch.

Question. Did you hear anything about their nailing a man to a building and then setting it on fire?

Answer. I heard of it, but did not see it.

Question. When did you hear of it?

Answer. After I came up here.

John F. Ray, sworn and examined.

By Mr. Gooch:

Question. To what company and regiment do you belong?

Answer. Company B, 13th Tennessee cavalry.

Question. Were you at Fort Pillow when it was attacked?

Answer. Yes, sir.

Question. At what time were you wounded?

Answer. I was wounded about 2 o'clock, after the rebels got in the breastworks?

Question. Was it before or after you had surrendered?

Answer. It was after I threw down my gun, as they all started to run.

Question. Will you state what you saw there?

Answer. After I surrendered they shot down a great many white fellows right close to me—ten or twelve, I suppose—and a great many negroes, too.

Question. How long did they keep shooting our men after they surrendered?

Answer. I heard guns away after dark shooting all that evening, somewhere; they kept up a regular fire for a long time, and then I heard the guns once in a while.

Question. Did you see any one shot the next day?

Answer. I did not; I was in a house, and could not get up at all.

Question. Do you know what became of the quartermaster of your regiment, Lieutenant Akerstrom?

Answer. He was shot by the side of me.

Question. Was he killed?

Answer. I thought so at the time; he fell on his face. He was shot in the forehead, and I thought he was killed. I heard afterwards he was not.

Question. Did you notice anything that took place while the flag of truce was in?

Answer. I saw the rebels slipping up and getting in the ditch along our breastworks.

Question. How near did they come up?

Answer. They were right at us; right across from the breastworks. I asked them what they were slipping up there for. They made answer that they knew their business.

Question. Are you sure this was done while the flag of truce was in?

Answer. Yes, sir. There was no firing; we could see all around; we could see them moving up all around in large force.

Question. Was anything said about it except what you said to the rebels?

Answer. I heard all our boys talking about it. I heard some of our officers remark, as they saw it coming, that the white flag was a bad thing; that they were slipping on us. I believe it was Lieutenant Akerstrom that I heard say it was against the rules of war for them to come up in that way.

Question. To whom did he say that?

Answer. To those fellows coming up; they had officers with them.

Question. Was Lieutenant Akerstrom shot before or after he had surrendered?

Answer. About two minutes after the flag of truce went back, during the action.

Question. Do you think of anything else to state? If so, go on and state it.

Answer. I saw a rebel lieutenant take a little negro boy up on the horse behind him; and then I heard General Chalmers—I think it must have been—tell him to "take that negro down and shoot him," or "take him and shoot him," and he passed him down and shot him.

Question. How large was the boy?

Answer. He was not more than eight years old. I heard the lieutenant tell the other that the negro was not in the service; that he was nothing but a child; that he was pressed and brought in there. The other one said: "Damn the difference; take him down and shoot him, or he would shoot him." I think it must have been General Chalmers. He was a smallish man; he had on a long gray coat, with a star on his coat.

Daniel H. Rankin, sworn and examined.

By Mr. Gooch:

Question. To what company and regiment do you belong?

Answer. Company C, 13th Tennessee cavalry.

Question. Were you at Fort Pillow at the late attack there?

Answer. Yes, sir.

Question. Will you state what happened there?

Answer. The worst thing I saw was the rebels moving up on us while the flag of truce was up at the fort. One part of their army moved right up on the brink of the ditch, and when the firing began, they rushed right into the fort. Before that the rebels were off two or three hundred yards. They tried twice to make a charge, but they did not succeed; they did not get within twenty or thirty steps of the fort then. I saw a great many men shot after they surrendered, white and black both.

Question. Are you sure you saw the rebels moving up towards the fort while the flag of truce was in?

Answer. Yes, sir; I saw them.

Question. When were you shot?

Answer. After I surrendered.

Question. Where were you when you were shot?

Answer. About half way down the bluff.

Question. Had you your gun when you were shot?

Answer. No, sir; if I had had my gun I would have shot the fellow who shot me. He was not more than ten steps from me. He was loading his gun, and I saw him shoot a man near me. As he fired at him I threw myself over the bluff, catching hold of a little locust. He aimed at my body and hit me in the leg. I then dropped down and got into the river, and afterwards got out and crawled behind a stump with two of my company. Some darkeys came there, and we told them to go away; we saw the rebels were shooting them, and we allowed if they were not with us we might get clear. I went back to where I was shot, and some fellow fired at us, but did not hit us. We begged him not to shoot; that the place was surrendered to them. One of our fellows threw up his hands, but they fired at him and hit his arm. We were carried out about two miles from the fort and then paroled.

Question. How long did you stay where you had been carried out from the fort?

Answer. I staid there some eighteen or twenty hours; from about 8 o'clock at night to about 4 o'clock the next evening. In that time my wound was dressed, and I was paroled somewhere between 3 and 5 o'clock. I got three of the rebels to help me up about a half a mile to a citizen's house, for I was not able to walk. I found out that the gunboat had a flag of truce, and I got an old man then in the house to saddle up a horse and carry me to the fort. Two rebel doctors went along with me. When we got there a rebel lieutenant colonel took my parole from me, said it was forged, and that he was going to take me back. The doctors told him my parole was right, and that I was not able to travel. They took me down to the gunboat No. 28, and then I went from that boat to gunboat No. 7, and then I went on the flag-ship.

Lieutenant William Clary, sworn and examined.

By Mr. Gooch:

Question. What is your rank and position in the service?

Answer. I am second lieutenant of company B, 13th Tennessee cavalry.

Question. Were you at Fort Pillow when it was attacked?

Answer. No, sir; I was sent to Memphis the day before, and returned to Fort Pillow the morning after the fight. I came up on gunboat No. 28. The rebels were at Fulton, about two miles and a half below Fort Pillow. We fired at them, and the rebels at Fort Pillow heard it, and thought we were bringing up re-enforcements, and then they set the town on fire.

Question. When did you get up there?

Answer. Early in the morning, or little after daylight.

Question. When did you land at Fort Pillow?

Answer. We got there about 8 o'clock in the morning, and shelled there an hour or so. The rebels were occupying the fort in large numbers. By and by the rebels came down with a flag of truce, and I went on shore to see what was wanting. One of the officers of the 6th United States heavy artillery said he did not like to go on shore for fear the rebels would kill him. I went on shore with one of the naval officers and saw General Forrest's adjutant general, Major Anderson. He said if we would recognize the parole of Forrest we might take our wounded on the gunboat; and that was agreed upon. I rode all around the battle-ground, and saw some of our dead half buried, and I saw five negroes burning. I asked Colonel Chalmers, the general's brother, if that was the way he allowed his men to do. He concluded that he could not control his men very well, and thought it was justifiable in regard to negroes; that they did not recognize negroes as soldiers, and he could not control his men. I did not see any white men burning there; if there were any, I did not recognize them as such. Their faces were burned, and some of them were sticking out of the tents and houses with their clothes partly burned. The negroes were lying upon the boards and straw in the tents which had been set on fire. It seemed to me as if the fire could not have been set more than half an hour before. Their flesh was frying off them, and their clothes were burning.

Question. How many did you see in that condition?

Answer. I saw five.

Question. Did they burn the hospital?

Answer. I saw the hospital burning, but I do not know whether they moved the sick out or not before they burned it. I understood the rebels went in where there were some 20 or 30 negroes sick, and hacked them over their heads with sabres and shot them. The negroes had been moved from the heights up on the hill into two large tents by us; but I do not think our men had been moved up there. I went through the hospital tents up there the morning before I started down to Memphis, and saw them full of colored troops. Dr. Fitch told me that he had his hospital flag on every bush around the bottom of the hill. At the commencement of the fight the major had told him to take his instruments and his medicines down under the bluff and stick up flags there, and have the wounded taken down to him. But the doctor said they did not notice his flags at all; that some of his patients were wounded there. He was wounded himself and taken prisoner and paroled.

Question. Did you see them shoot any colored men that morning?

Answer. I saw them shoot one man just before we landed with the flag of truce. An escort of about 20 men rode up to a livery stable and set it on fire. The gunboat fired at them but did not hit them, and they got on their horses and rode off at a trot. There were some paths down the hill, and a man came along down one of them; I saw them halt; the foremost one, an officer I think, pulled out a revolver and shot very deliberately at this man, and then they galloped off in quick time. He did not kill the man, however, for I saw him walking along afterwards. I do not know whether the man was white or black.

Question. Did you hear anything of their nailing men to a building and then burning it?

Answer. Yes, sir; I heard of it. And I heard a lady say that a man was nailed to a building that was burned. She said she was well acquainted with Lieutenant Akerstrom before the fight took place. Some one asked why he was not buried. Some of the rebels said he was a damned conscript that had run away from Forrest. But I never heard Lieutenant Akerstrom say any such thing.

Question. Who was that lady?

Answer. Mrs. Ruffin, the wife of Thomas Ruffin.

Question. Where is she now?

Answer. I think she is at Cairo now. Her husband did not get wounded, but he was sick. I heard an ensign on gunboat 28 invite General Chalmers and some of his aides-de-camp to come on board the gunboat, and I saw Major Anderson and several other confederate officers on the Platte Valley drinking at the bar, and I saw a couple of army officers drinking there with them, and there might have been some naval officers with them too, but I am not certain of that. The clerk of the Platte Valley, General Forrest's adjutant general, Major Anderson, and an ensign of gunboat 28, took the names of the paroles. I did not take the names myself, because I was busily engaged going over the battle-field to find out if any of our men were left alive. I heard a great many rebel soldiers say they did not intend to recognize those black devils as soldiers. They said this to me as I was speaking about the slaughter there. They also expressed the opinion that if we had not been fighting with black troops they would not have hurt us at all; but they did not intend to give any quarter to negroes.

Dr. Stewart Gordon, sworn and examined.

By the chairman:

Question. What is your position?

Answer. Acting assistant surgeon, United States army.

Question. Where are you now stationed?

Answer. I have charge of ward N, Mound City general hospital.

Question. Is that the ward in which are the colored men we first examined yesterday?

Answer. Yes, sir.

Question. Have you prepared a statement of the condition of the men in that ward whose testimony we have taken?

Answer. I have it here; it is a brief history of their cases, where they were wounded, how they were wounded, and the condition they are in.—(Appendix to this deposition.)

Question. Were you here in the hospital when those men were brought in?

Answer. I was.

Question. Had you any conversation with them then?

Answer. Yes, sir; with the greater part of them.

Question. Did you hear their testimony yesterday?

Answer. I did.

Question. Did the statements they made to us correspond with the statements they made to you when they were first brought here?

Answer. They did.

Question. So far as you can judge, from your experience as a medical man, are their statements in relation to their injuries corroborated by the appearance of the injuries themselves?

Answer. Yes, sir.

Question. How many of those men have died since they have been received here?

Answer. Only one in my ward.

Question. How many are there now who you think will not recover?

Answer. I think there are three who will not recover; perhaps more.

Ward N.—Private Elias Falls, company A, 1st Alabama artillery, shot in arm while fighting, shot in thigh after being prisoner, flesh wound, condition favorable; Private Duncan Harden, company A, 1st Alabama artillery, shot in arm while fighting, arm broke, shot in thigh after being prisoner, flesh wound, favorable; Private Nathan Hunter, company D, 1st Alabama artillery, shot in side and hip after surrender, flesh wound, condition favorable; Sergeant Benjamin Robinson, company D, 1st Alabama artillery, shot in thigh and right leg after surrender, flesh wound, favorable; Private Daniel Tylor, company B, 1st Tennessee artillery, shot in right shoulder, shot in right eye after surrender, destroying sight, unfavorable; Private John Haskins, company B, 1st Tennessee artillery, shot in left arm after surrender, flesh wound, slight, favorable; Private Thomas Adison, company C, 1st Alabama artillery, shot in nose and right eye after surrender, destroying sight, unfavorable; Private Alfred Flake, company A, 1st Alabama artillery, shot in left hand while lying sick in hospital, flesh wound, unfavorable; Private Manuel Nichols, company B, 1st Alabama artillery, shot in left side before, and right arm after surrender, flesh wound, serious, unfavorable; Private Arthur Edmonds, company C, 1st Alabama artillery, shot in head and right arm after surrender, causing fracture of arm, condition favorable; Private Henry Hanks, company A, 1st Alabama artillery, shot in left side after surrender, wound serious, condition unfavorable; Private Charles Key, company D, 1st Alabama artillery, shot in right arm after surrender, fracture of arm, condition favorable; Private Henry Christon, company B, 1st Alabama artillery, shot in back before surrender, wound serious, rather favorable; Private

Aaron Fintis, company D, 1st Alabama artillery, shot in both legs after surrender. flesh wound, slight, condition favorable; Private George Shaw, company B, 1st Tennessee artillery, shot in left side of head, shot in right wrist after surrender, not serious, favorable; Private Major William, company B, 1st Tennessee artillery, shot through nose after surrender, not serious, condition favorable; officer's servant William Jerdon, 13th Tennessee cavalry, shot in left ankle, amputation, shot in left arm, fracture of arm after surrender, very unfavorable; Corporal Alexander Naison, company C, 1st Alabama artillery, shot in right side of head after surrender, not serious, favorable; Private Thomas Gadis, company C, 1st Alabama artillery, shot in right hip after surrender, serious, condition unfavorable; Corporal Eli Cothel, company B, 1st Alabama artillery, shot in right leg while fighting, shot in left arm after surrender, flesh wound, favorable; Private Sandy Cole, company D, 1st Alabama artillery, shot in right thigh and arm after surrender, flesh wound, condition favorable; Private Nathan Modley, company D, 1st Alabama artillery, shot in right knee after surrender, injury of joint, condition unfavorable; Private John Holland, company B, 1st Tennessee artillery, shot in right thigh after surrender, flesh wound, condition favorable; Private Robert Hall, company C, 1st Alabama artillery, sabre cut of head and left hand while lying sick in hospital, died.

STEWART GORDON,
Charge of Ward N.

Dr. William N. McCoy, sworn and examined.

By Mr. Gooch:

Question. What is your position in the service?

Answer. I am an acting assistant surgeon, now stationed at Mound City general hospital, in charge of wards L, K, I, and H. Wards L, K, and H have wounded in from Fort Pillow.

Question. Have you prepared a statement of the cases of those of your patients whom we examined here?

Answer. Yes, sir; here is the statement.—(See appendix to this deposition.)

Question. Did you have any conversation with those wounded men in relation to their injuries when they first came to the hospital?

Answer. I did to some extent.

Question. Have any of the wounded from Fort Pillow died in your wards?

Answer. One in ward H.

Question. Are there others who you think will not recover?

Answer. There are two whose recovery I think is doubtful.

Wounded in wards L, K, and H, United States General Hospital, Mound City, Illinois.—W. P. Walker, sergeant, company D, 13th Tennessee cavalry, received four wounds at Fort Pillow April 12, 1864. One ball passed through left arm near middle third, fracturing humerus. Second ball struck right side of neck, 1½ inch below mastoid process, and remaining in. Third ball made flesh wound in right shoulder. Fourth ball struck left eye, supposed by himself to be a glancing shot; eye totally destroyed. Done after the surrender.

Milas M. M. Woodside, a discharged soldier from the 7th Tennessee cavalry, also from the 13th Tennessee cavalry, wounded by two balls, first (pistol) ball striking just below insertion of deltoid muscle of right arm, and remaining in; second (musket) ball striking centre of right breast over third rib, and passing to the right and downward, emerged at inner border of the scapula, about 6 inches from point of entrance. Done after surrender.

Jason London, private, company B, 13th Tennessee cavalry, received a ball, which struck the dorsal side of right hand about the junction of carpal and metacarpal bones of index finger; emerged at carpal bone of thumb; then struck thigh in front, about 6 inches above knee-joint; passing over the bone, emerged on inner side. After being wounded, he was knocked down by one of the fiends with a musket. Done after the surrender.

David H. Taylor, private, company E, 13th Tennessee cavalry, received five wounds. First (musket) ball passed in under the angle of right jaw, fracturing the symphysis, where it emerged. Second ball struck front of right shoulder-joint; emerged immediately behind caracoid process. Third ball entered 3 inches below, and a little to the right of entiform cartilage; passing downward, is lost. Fourth ball in left knee, fracturing inner condyle of femur, and passed into poplitacl space. Fifth ball, upper part of middle third thigh; lost. Done after the surrender.

David W. Harrison, private, company D, 13th Tennessee cavalry, received three wounds. First (musket) ball passed from behind head of humerus, left side; emerged between clavicle and axilla, producing compound comminuted fracture of head and upper end of shaft of bone. Second ball struck left side 2½ inches above ilium; ball not found. Third ball entered at upper edge of scapula behind, passing under the bone, is lost. Wounds received after surrender.

James Calvin Goeforth, private, company E, 13th Tennessee cavalry, received wound. Ball passed from right to left across the back, entering at upper part of scapula; emerged at a point a little below and at the opposite side, (flesh wound.) Done after the surrender.

William A. Dickey, company B, 13th Tennessee cavalry, wounded after the surrender. Ball entered abdomen 4 inches to the right of umbilicus; ball lost.

Thomas J. Cartwright, company A, 13th Tennessee cavalry, received wound in left shoulder, striking pectoral muscle near axilla, fracturing clavicle; was extracted near the vertebral column at upper and outer border of scapula. Done before the surrender.

William L. McMichael, private, company C, 13th Tennessee cavalry, received five wounds. First ball glanced along the upper portion of right parietal bone, making wound (flesh) 2½ inches long. Second ball glanced ulnar side of left forearm at wrist joint. Third ball struck left side of abdomen on a line from anterior superior process of ilium to symphysis pubis; ball not found. Fourth ball struck near the insertion of tensu of right side; passed downwards 4 inches; was extracted. Wounds received after the surrender of the fort.

Isaac J. Leadbetter, private, company E, 13th Tennessee cavalry, received wound in left side. Musket ball struck over eighth rib and plunged downward; is lost. Done after surrender.

James Walls, private, company E, 13th Tennessee cavalry, was wounded by musket ball striking over origin of gluteus minemus of left side, and passed upwards and across, emerging 11 inches from point of entrance almost over the last rib of right side, and about 2½ inches from vertebral column. Done after the surrender.

In charge of WILLIAM N. McCOY,
Acting Assistant Surgeon, United States Army.

Dr. A. H. Kellogg, sworn and examined.

By the chairman:

Question. What is your rank and position in the service?

Answer. I am an acting assistant surgeon, in charge of wards E and F, Mound City general hospital.

Question. Were you present yesterday when the testimony of the wounded men in your wards was taken?

Answer. I have but one under my charge who was wounded at Fort Pillow. I heard his testimony.

Question. Had you previously had any conversation with him in relation to the circumstances attending his being wounded?

Answer. Yes, sir.

Question. Did his statements to us yesterday correspond with the statements he made to you?

Answer. Yes, sir; except he gave a few more details yesterday as to what was said to him. He told me that he was wounded after he had surrendered.

Question. Have you prepared a statement of his case?

Answer. Yes, sir here it is.

Woodford Cooksey, private, company A, 13th regiment Tennessee cavalry, gunshot wound, with comminuted fracture of middle third of left femur, received at Fort Pillow, April 12, 1864, *after surrender.*

A. H. KELLOGG, M. D.,
Acting Assistant Surgeon, U. S. A

Doctor Charles H. Vail, sworn and examined.

By Mr. Gooch:

Question. What is your rank and position in the service?

Answer. Acting assistant surgeon in charge of wards A, B, C, and D, Mound City general hospital. The adjutant of the 13th Tennessee cavalry is in ward B.

Question. Have you prepared a statement of his case?

Answer. Yes, sir; and also of Captain Porter, who is in the same ward, and who was too weak to be examined this morning.

First Lieutenant Mack J. Seaming, adjutant 13th Tennessee cavalry, gunshot wound of right side, received at Fort Pillow, April 12, 1864. Ball entered right side below inferior angle of scapula, between sixth and seventh rib, ranged downward and was lost in muscles near hip. Wounded after he had surrendered; shot by a man standing thirty feet above him on the bank. Present condition of patient good, with fair prospect of recovery.

Captain John H. Potter, company B, 13th Tennessee cavalry, wounded at Fort Pillow, April 12, 1864. Ball fractured skull, carrying away a portion of left parietal and frontal bones, leaving brain exposed for a distance of an inch and a half; was wounded early in the fight by a sharpshooter before the surrender. Present condition almost hopeless, has remained insensible ever since he was wounded.

CHARLES H. VAIL, M. D.,
Acting Assistant Surgeon, U. S. A., in charge of officers' ward.

Doctor J. A. C. McCoy, sworn and examined.

By Mr. Gooch:

Question. What is your rank and position?

Answer. Acting assistant surgeon in charge of wards O, P, Q, and R, in Mound City general hospital.

Question. Have you any of the wounded soldiers from Fort Pillow in your wards?

Answer. I have.

Question. Have you prepared a statement of their cases?

Answer. Yes, sir; I have two statements here prepared at different times; I will hand you both of them, as each one contains some particulars not in the other.

Ward Q.—John F. Ray, private, company B, 13th Tennessee, shot in popliteal space, ball lodged, done after surrender; John W. Shelton, private, company E, 13th Tennessee, shot through left leg, middle third, flesh wound, done after surrender; Joseph M. Green, private, company A, 13th Tennessee, shot in right shoulder, behind, ball escaping at middle of right arm, flesh wound, done after surrender; James H. Stout, private, company B, 13th Tennessee, shot in right leg, producing compound fracture of tibia, done after surrender; Thomas J. Thompson, private, company D, 13th Tennessee, shot between sixth and seventh ribs, ball passing downward is lost, done after surrender; Daniel H. Rankin, private, company C, 13th Tennessee, shot through left leg, flesh wound, done after surrender; Wiley Robinson, private, company A, 13th Tennessee, shot in right arm and right index finger, flesh wounds, shot through left index finger and through inferior lobe left lung, ball lodged, shot through left thigh and through left ankle, flesh wounds, all but one shot done after surrender; Daniel Stamps, private, company E, 13th Tennessee, shot through right thigh, flesh wound, done after surrender; James P. Meador, private, company A, 13th Tennessee, shot through inferior lobe of right lung and superior lobe of left lung, one shot after surrender; William J. Mays, company B, 13th Tennessee, shot through right axilla and side, flesh wounds, done just before surrender; James N. Taylor, private, company E, 13th Tennessee, shot in right hip, ball lodged, done after surrender; Francis A. Alexander, private, company C, 13th Tennessee, shot through right leg, flesh wound, done after surrender; Nathan G. Fowlkes, private, company D, 13th Tennessee, shot in left leg, compound fracture of both bones, done after surrender.

J. A. C. McCOY,
Acting Assistant Surgeon, U. S. A.

Francis A. Alexander, company C, 13th Tennessee, shot once after surrender, dangerous; Nathan G. Fowlkes, company D, 13th Tennessee, shot once after surrender, dangerous; Wiley Robinson, company A, 13th Tennessee, shot seven times, six times after surrender, dangerous; Daniel Stamps, company E, 13th Tennessee, shot once after surrender, severe; James P. Meador, company A, 13th Tennessee, shot twice, once after surrender, dangerous; James N. Taylor, company E, 13th Tennessee, shot once after surrender, dangerous; William J. Mays, company B, 13th Tennessee, shot once just before surrender, dangerous; John F. Ray, company B, 13th Tennessee, shot once after surrender, dangerous; John W. Shelton, company E, 13th Tennessee, shot once after surrender, dangerous; Thomas J. Thompson, company D, 13th Tennessee, shot once after surrender, dangerous; Joseph M. Green, company A, 13th Tennessee, shot once after surrender, dangerous; James H. Stout, company B, 13th Tennessee, shot once after surrender, dangerous; Daniel H. Rankin, company C, 13th Tennessee, shot once after surrender, dangerous.

J. A. C. McCOY, M. D.,
Acting Assistant Surgeon, U. S. A.

The following is a statement prepared by Dr. M. Black of the cases under his charge:

Horton Casen, private, company A, 1st Alabama infantry, wounded at Fort Pillow after surrender, gunshot wounds in hip and thigh; Jacob Thompson; waiter, company B, 11th Illinois cavalry, wounded at Fort Pillow after surrender, pistol shots through thumb and head and several blows with blunt instrument (says with a gun) on head and neck, dividing skin in several places; Henry Parker, company D, 1st Alabama, wounded at Fort Pillow after surrender, gunshot wound in hip; Ransom Anderson, company B, 1st Alabama artillery, wounded at Fort Pillow after surrender, sabre cuts on head and hand and gunshot wounds in shoulder and chest; Mary Jane Robinson, wife of a soldier at Fort Pillow, wounded by a rebel after the surrender of the fort, at a distance of ten yards, gunshot wound through both knees.

M. BLACK,
Acting Assistant Surgeon, U. S. A.

Surgeon Horace Wardner, recalled and examined.

By the chairman:

Question. Have you heard our examination of the wounded in this hospital from Fort Pillow?

Answer. I have.

Question. Did you have any conversation with them when they were first brought to the hospital?

Answer. Yes, sir.

Question. Did the statements they made to you then correspond with their statements to us?

Answer. They did.

Question. Do the nature and character of their injuries sustain their statements in regard to their injuries?

Answer. The character of the injuries of these men corroborates their statements in regard to the treatment they received from the rebels.

MOUND CITY, ILLINOIS, *April* 23, 1864.

Captain Alexander M. Pennock, United States navy, sworn and examined.

By Mr. Gooch:

Question. What is your rank and position in the navy?

Answer. I am a captain in the United States navy; fleet captain of the Mississippi squadron, and commandant of the station of Cairo and Mound City.

Question. How long have you been in the naval service?

Answer. Since the first of April, 1828.

Question. Will you please state what services have been rendered by the naval forces here in checking and preventing the recent movements of the rebel Forrest and his command in this vicinity?

Answer. Two gunboats were at Paducah at the time the attack was made upon that place; they rendered efficient service there. On receiving information that Paducah had been attacked, or that there was a probability of its being attacked, I immediately went to Cairo from Mound City, with Captain Shirk, of the navy, and conferred with General Brayman and General Veatch. A regiment was sent by General Veatch up to Paducah. An armed despatch boat was also sent up, with Captain Shirk on board, and Captain Odlin, assistant adjutant general on General Brayman's staff, to ascertain the facts, and render such assistance as might be needed. I was informed by both Captain Shirk and Captain Odlin that the gunboats there, and the fort, had expended a great deal of ammunition and were getting short of it. Ammunition both for the army and navy was immediately sent up; a division of gunboats from the Cumberland river, Captain Fitch commanding, came down after the fight and re-enforced Captain Shirk at Paducah.

Information having reached me that the rebels were crossing over into Illinois in small squads, four gunboats were stationed by the two above-named naval officers between Paducah and Mound City, to prevent their crossing, and orders were given them to destroy all ferries and skiffs, in fact all means of communication across the Ohio river.

A gunboat had been stationed at Columbus, Kentucky. Hearing that the surrender of that place had been demanded, I despatched Captain Fitch with two of the Cumberland river boats, and another gunboat which was here for repairs, to Columbus, with orders if all was quiet there to go down the river a far as Hickman. I instructed him that the Mississippi river must be kept clear at all hazards. After having given this order, which was in writing, the captain of a steamboat came to me and informed me that Fort Pillow had been attacked, and that the captain of the gunboat stationed there sent word that he had expended nearly all his ammunition. I directed Captain Fitch, if he could be spared from Columbus, to go down to Fort Pillow with his three boats, and I immediately had placed on board a despatch boat the ammunition required for the gunboat then at Fort Pillow. And boats have since been cruising up and down the Ohio river, and the Mississippi river as far as Fort Pillow, for the purpose of giving convoy and keeping the river open. On the arrival of Captain Fitch near Fort Pillow, he found the enemy in force on this side of the fort, behind wood piles on the bank of the river; they were burning wood and barges there. They were shelled and driven off. Captain Fitch also prevented a detachment of rebels from crossing over to an island, where a number of transports and other boats had been detained, which the rebels desired to capture or destroy. He convoyed that fleet as far as Fort Pillow, clear of danger. Afterwards three boats were sent down to Hickman, for the purpose of giving protection to such Union men as desired to leave and bring away their goods, and if possible to capture any rebels that might be in the place. A detachment of marines accompanied this expedition. The town was surrounded twice, once by day and once by night; the guerillas had been in there and escaped. The people of Hickman were warned that if even a musket shot was again fired at a transport or other boat the place would be at once destroyed. These boats have been moving constantly day and night, and despatch boats have been furnished by the navy to convey despatches for General Sherman and General Brayman, up the Tennessee river, or wherever they might require. I would add that when Captain Fitch returned from Fort Pillow he brought away with him refugees, women and children, who had been left there, and ten wounded soldiers who had been there for two days.

Question. What, in your opinion, would be the competent military and naval force to protect the public property at Cairo and Mound City?

Answer. Two gunboats and 2,000 men.

Question. State briefly your reason for believing so large a force is required for that purpose.

Answer. For the reason that we have public property extending along the river for seven miles, and we should be ready for any emergency.

Question. What amount of property would be destroyed here, should the enemy get possession long enough to destroy it?

Answer. It is difficult to estimate its value accurately. We have here a a large number of guns, and all the ammunition and other supplies for the Mississippi fleet, consisting of at least 100 vessels.

Question. What effect would the destruction or capture of this property have upon operations here in the west?

Answer. It would paralyze the fleet.

Question. For how long a time?

Answer. For the entire season, besides giving the enemy means to act more on the offensive—means enough to last them for a campaign.

Question. Is it also true that all the army supplies for the western department pass through here?

Answer. To the best of my knowledge it is.

Question. What force have you here at Mound City now?

Answer. I have two gunboats, 85 marines, 100 mechanics, who have been armed and drilled, one company of the invalid corps, and a detachment of convalescents from the hospital. Any other forces that may be here are merely temporary.

Question. What force have you at Cairo?

Answer. Seventy-odd marines. But those we have only to protect the wharf boat and the inspection boat, which have on board provisions, ship chandlery, &c. Admiral Porter has ordered me to move them up to this point whenever I can do so without detriment to the public service. I understand that there is a permanent garrison at Cairo of between 300 and 400 men. When General Brayman was compelled to re-enforce Columbus, he was compelled to take away from there all except about 150 men.

Captain James W. Shirk, United States navy, sworn and examined.

By the chairman:

Question. What is your rank and position in the navy, and where are you stationed at this time?

Answer. I am a lieutenant commander, and commandant of the United States gunboat Tuscumbia, and the 7th district of the Mississippi squadron, which extends from the headwaters of the Tennessee river to Cairo.

Question. How long have you been in service in the west?

Answer. I have been attached to this squadron since the 6th of September, 1862.

Question. You are acquainted with the immense amount of public property at Mound City and Cairo?

Answer. Yes, sir.

Question. Do you consider that there is a permanent force here, both naval and military, large enough for its protection?

Answer. I do not consider that there has been force enough here heretofore.

Question. What, in your judgment, would be a force sufficient to render that protection and security which the place ought to have?

Answer. I should think it would take a couple of gunboats, and at least two full regiments. The great danger to be apprehended here is from fire.

Question. Will you now state what services the navy has rendered in the late raids in this region of country?

Answer. I will state in regard to my own division. I returned to Paducah, from a trip up the Tennessee river, on the 25th of March, at noon. I immediately called upon Colonel Hicks, the commandant of that post, as was my custom, to hear what news he had. He informed me that the rebels had taken Union City the day before, and that he expected an attack there that night. As I had just come down from the southern part of Tennessee, and had heard nothing of Forrest there, and as I had been told so many times before without cause that the rebels were threatening to attack Paducah, I did not put much confidence in the report; at the same time, I did not wish to leave the place unprotected by gunboats, and I accordingly left the Peosta and the Pawpaw at that place, while I came down to Cairo to communicate with Captain Pennock and the authorities here, in order to find out whether or not there was any truth in the report. I left Paducah about one o'clock and arrived here about dark. Shortly after I arrived here the telegraphic operator at Metropolis telegraphed down that Paducah was in flames. Captain Pennock and I went down to Cairo to see Generals Brayman and Veatch. General Veatch ordered a regiment of his troops up to Paducah to re-enforce Colonel Hicks, and I immediately started up in the despatch boat Volunteer with Captain Odlin, General Brayman's assistant adjutant general. On our way up we destroyed several ferry-boats and skiffs, in order to prevent the rebels crossing the river. We arrived at Paducah about daylight on the 26th of March. The enemy was in force about two miles and a half from town. It was reported to me by my subordinate officers that the enemy had attacked the place about three o'clock in the evening of the day before; that the fort had been bravely defended and preserved by the gallantry of Colonel Hicks and his small garrison, assisted very materially by the two gunboats which I had left there; that Forrest had occupied the town; that about ten o'clock that night he had been driven out by the fire of the Peosta, she having gone up and shelled the town for that purpose. I placed myself in communication with Colonel Hicks on the morning of the 26th, and found that he was short of ammunition, as were also the gunboats. I immediately telegraphed to Captain Pennock to send up a full supply of ammunition for the two gunboats, and 30,000 rounds of Enfield cartridges for Colonel Hicks. The supplies were sent up by him immediately, and reached us that evening. In the afternoon, about three o'clock, Colonel Hicks sent me a message that the enemy were forming in line of battle at the head of Jersey street, and requested me to open upon them with shell. I fired shell in that direction, and about four o'clock the enemy left in the direction of Mayfield. The captains of the Peosta and the Pawpaw both informed me that the day before the rebels took advantage of the presence of women there, behind whom they covered themselves, and fired at the officers and men on the gunboats. The women came running down towards the fort, and the rebels got behind them and fired at our people on the boats.

Question. And the boats could not fire upon the rebels without killing the women?

Answer. No, sir. And the rebels also took advantage of a flag of truce, while it was flying, to enter the town and plant their batteries there, and to get into brick houses on the levee, from which to fire on the gunboats, while the flag of truce was flying at the fort. I returned that night at midnight to Cairo, and assisted Captain Pennock as much as I could in making preparations to take care of the public property, as I knew that some few stragglers had crossed the Ohio above, and we were fearful they would come down and burn the public property here. Again, on the 12th of this month, I was at Paducah. The rebels were reported in force all around the town. I telegraphed to Captain Pennock, giving him that information, and also that in my opinion Colonel Hicks ought to be re-enforced. Another regiment was immediately sent up by General Brayman, and Lieutenant Commander Fitch, commanding the 8th district of the Mississippi squadron, by direction of Captain Pennock, sent four of his gunboats to report to me for duty. I made disposition of four gunboats, each with ten marines on board, to patrol between Paducah and Mound City. The enemy hovered around us until about noon of the 14th, when they made a dash upon the town, sending in a flag of truce to Colonel Hicks, giving him one hour to remove the women and children from the town. I immediately ordered all the transports to the Illinois shore, and took the women and children over there. When the hour was up I was informed that the rebels were in Jersey, a suburb of the town, and Colonel Hicks wished me to go up there and shell them. I did so, with two gunboats, carrying long-range rifled guns, firing about 120 rounds of shell, which fell in among them. The rebels retired, and encamped from three to six miles out of town that night. When the flag of truce was sent in to the fort, squads of rebel cavalry came into town and stole all the government horses there, and also a great many belonging to private citizens.

Question. Under the flag of truce?

Answer. Yes, sir; as the flag of truce came in and went to the fort they came into the town.

Question. Is not that a direct and utter violation of the rules of warfare?

Answer. It is a direct violation of the flag of truce. I have had three or four boats up the Tennessee river all the time. There are three up there now, one having come out the day before yesterday. There were two to have started this morning at daylight, and I received a despatch this forenoon, saying that the enemy were reported to be crossing the Tennessee river at Birmingham and above, in force, from the west to the east side. I immediately telegraphed to Paducah and had two heavy gunboats go up to ascertain the truth of the report.

I do not credit the story, but I have done all I possibly could do, with the limited number of boats at my command.

Question. How long have you been in the navy?

Answer. Fifteen years.

Question. You are acquainted with the administration of Captain Pennock, of the navy, here?

Answer. Yes, sir.

Question. What do you say of it?

Answer. I do not think any one could have done more than Captain Pennock has done, with the means at his command.

Question. Why is it that we do not hear more of the transactions of the gunboats out here, while we hear so much of what the army does?

Answer. One reason is that there is a general order by Admiral Porter, prohibiting any newspaper reporter from going on board any vessel in the Mississippi squadron.

Question. Is there a cordial understanding and co-operation between the navy here and the military forces under General Brayman?

Answer. I think there is to a very great degree. I never saw more cordiality existing between officers of the different services. I would like to say further, that during this late raid I convoyed General Veatch's division up the Tennessee river. It was ordered up there by General Sherman to land at or near Savannah, and go out to Purdy and the Hatchie, in that way intending to catch Forrest. I afterwards sent up another despatch of the same purport, from General Sherman to General Veatch, which reached him at the landing near Purdy. I sent up a third despatch to him, which was brought here by General Corse from General Sherman. That despatch never reached General Veatch for the reason that he had come back from Purdy, gone on up the Tennessee and disembarked his troops at Waterloo, Alabama, and was out of reach of my gunboats.

Captain Smith, commanding the Peosta, broke up a rebel recruiting office at Brooklyn, Illinois, a week ago last Sunday. The recruiting office was on board a trading vessel. He destroyed the boat, but saved seven new rebel uniforms that were on it. He could not discover the recruiting agent there, there being so many secesh sympathizers around there.

Question. In your opinion, has General Brayman acted with vigilance and activity, and done all he could with the forces intrusted to him, during these raids?

Answer. So far as I know, he has done all he could do.

CAIRO, ILLINOIS, *April* 24, 1864.

Major General Steven A. Hurlbut, sworn and examined.

By the chairman:

Question. What is your rank and position in the army?

Answer. I am a major general of volunteers, commanding the 16th army corps.

Question. Where have you been stationed?

Answer. I have been stationed at Memphis for the last sixteen months.

Question. How long have you been stationed along the river?

Answer. Ever since the battle of Shiloh. I have commanded at Bolivar and Jackson, Tennessee, until about the 20th of November, 1862, when I was ordered to Memphis.

Question. Now, with regard to this raid of Forrest, was that raid made in your department?

Answer. Yes, sir.

Question. Please give us, in your own way, a brief account of that raid.

Answer. Forrest first crossed the Memphis and Charleston railroad last December. I organized a force in Columbus, and moved it down and drove him out. General Sherman then ordered all the available troops in my command to be got together—leaving very small garrisons at the important points—for the Meridian expedition. I marched and crossed there, and marched back again. Two divisions of my command were then detailed to go up Red river, under General Banks. As an auxiliary to the infantry movement to Meridian, General W. S. Smith came to Memphis and took command of all my cavalry and another brigade which he brought over, all amounting to about seven thousand effective men, to move across the country, drive the enemy's force out, cut his way across to Columbus and Aberdeen, and to go down to the Mobile and Ohio railroad, and join us at Meridian. He failed to make that junction; was met by Forrest about West Point, and for some reason or other (I do not know what) retreated and fell back to Memphis. The effect of a retreat, at the rate at which they retreated, and the loss they met with, and the retreating before an inferior force, demoralized the cavalry very seriously. I returned to Memphis about the Three Points, marched, and found that Forrest was organizing a very considerable force, so far as I could find out, with the intention of moving up to West Tennessee. I had orders from the War Department to send home all the veteran regiments (cavalry especially) as rapidly as possible. I took an inventory of my force, and found that I had about six thousand cavalry to two thousand two hundred horses, which limited the efficiency of the cavalry. I furloughed and sent home the 3d Michigan, 2d Iowa, 3d, 6th, 7th, and 9th Illinois, and distributed their horses among the men that were left, so as to keep men enough always, and more, to mount with horses. Forrest moved up, and crossed the line of the Charleston and Memphis railroad, towards Jackson, Tennessee, and occupied it. General Grierson was directed by me to go out with his cavalry, feel him, attack him, and cripple him as much as possible. He went out, and reported that he was "a little too strong for him, and he could not touch him." My effective force at Memphis consisted of 2,200 cavalry, 2,100 white infantry, and 2,400 colored infantry. I had the choice to move out a force sufficiently strong to attack Forrest and leave Memphis open, with its immense amount of government stores, ordnance, hospitals, and everything of that nature. I became satisfied that if I moved out 4,000 men, (which was the lowest I considered safe to send out,) and they should move out 50 or 60 miles into the country, the enemy, being all mounted, would turn that force and come in and occupy Memphis, which I considered would be a greater disaster than to allow Forrest to range in West Tennessee. I therefore did not send them out, but I kept the cavalry out as far as we could go, or dared go. It was not possible to divine precisely what Forrest's intentions were. My own opinion was, that it was his intention to organize a force, cross the Tennessee river, and operate upon General Sherman's line of communication. I was at Cairo at the time Union City was attacked. Four regiments and a battery of one of my divisions, which were ordered up the Tennessee river, were here also. I directed General Brayman to take them and throw them up to Columbus in rear of Forrest when he was at Paducah, but they were peremptorily ordered up the Tennessee river.

Question. Ordered up by General Sherman?

Answer. Yes, sir. The result was, that there was not force enough, in my opinion, in the command on the Mississippi river, from Paducah to Memphis, to operate upon Forrest with any prospect of success.

Question. What was the estimated strength of Forrest's forces?

Answer. Forrest's entire force, according to the best of my information, was between 8,000 and 9,000 men altogether. That includes this division of Buford's that operated up here. I have somewhere among my papers a list of all his brigades. I know nearly all of them. I have run against nearly all of them. He had five of the oldest regiments in the confederate service detailed expressly for this purpose as a nucleus of his organization. These were troops that had seen a great deal of service along the line below Memphis—Chalmers's brigade, Ely's brigade, Bell's brigade, and McCullough's. I cannot estimate Forrest's force at less than between 8,000 and 9,000 men. The cause of his raid, unquestionably, was the fact that so large an amount of troops which had been holding this region of country had been removed—a portion of them up the Tennessee river to Decatur, and a portion up the Red river—also the fact that he knew perfectly well, from his spies at Memphis, the condition of our cavalry. Memphis, from the nature of the ground there, is a place that requires not less than five thousand men to garrison the outer line. It is the worst place to cover that I ever saw. We have a fort there that was built that would take seven thousand men as a reasonable amount to line the parapets. We have immense stores there, for from Memphis not only the 16th and 17th army corps are supplied, but General Steele's army at Little Rock are supplied from there also. We have large hospitals there, scattered all over the city. We have an unsteady and unreliable population; and the daily interior guard duty, for the city proper, requires over 300 men. I considered then, and I consider now, that the removal of any force competent to make any serious impression upon Forrest would have imperilled Memphis; and I believe that was what General Forrest wanted done.

Question. How large a force did you retain there for the safety of that place?

Answer. I retained the infantry—four thousand men. I kept the cavalry out all the time as far as they could go.

Question. How came you to reoccupy Fort Pillow? Had it been abandoned?

Answer. No, sir. When I moved to Meridian, the 52d Indiana regiment which had been there was withdrawn, and made a part of the expedition, and the 13th Tennessee cavalry, which was recruiting, was moved down there as a recruiting point. I afterwards re-enforced it by sending up Major Booth with four companies of colored heavy artillery and six guns, and a section of light artillery, making in all about 600 men.

Question. Do I understand you to say that the post had never been entirely abandoned?

Answer. No, sir. When the 52d Indiana was taken away it was temporarily abandoned until the 13th Tennessee came down to hold it as a recruiting point. I considered Fort Pillow as a place which ought to be held with a small garrison, and I think so yet, and any navy officer or river man will tell you that the situation of the channel there requires it.

Question. I am not questioning that at all. I merely inquired as to the fact.

Answer. I sent Major Booth there because I had great confidence in him as a soldier. He was an old soldier who had served in the regular army, and I considered him the best man I had for that purpose. I received a report from him "that he could hold that post against any force for forty-eight hours," which was all I expected him to do, and if he had not been killed I think he would have held it. I have no doubt that his death was the immediate cause of the capture of the place.

Question. Just in this connexion, please to state why you deemed it important to keep up a garrison at that place.

Answer. The steamboat channel at Fort Pillow runs right under the bluff, and brings every boat as it passes within musket-shot of the shore, and a couple of guns mounted up above there would stop most effectually the navigation of the river, and drive away any of the tin-clad gunboats we have, for a plunging fire would go right through them, and they could not get elevation enough to strike. The whole life of the army below, especially while these large movements were going on, depended upon an uninterrupted communication by the river, and the stopping that communication for two or three days might deprive us of necessary supplies just at the moment that they were required. These were my reasons for holding the place.

Question. What information have you in regard to the attack upon Fort Pillow; its capture, and the barbarities practiced there?

Answer. I am not positive about dates, but my recollection is that Fort Pillow was attacked on the 12th of April. Just about dusk of the 12th a boat came down to Memphis from Fort Pillow, bringing information that the place was attacked, but that Major Booth was perfectly confident of being able to hold out until he could be re-enforced. I immediately ordered a regiment to be got ready, with four days' rations and an extra supply of ammunition; took the steamer "Glendale," dropped her down to Fort Pickering, and the regiment was in the very act of going on board when another boat came down with the information that the fort was captured. The order to move up the regiment was countermanded, for there was no use in sending it then. There were at Fort Pillow two 10-pound Parrotts, two 6-pounder field guns, and two 12-pounder howitzers, and about 600 men. I cannot tell precisely the number of the 13th Tennessee cavalry, for it was a recruiting regiment, and filling off and on. If the men had been left in the position in which they had been placed by Major Booth, and from which position he had already repelled an assault of the enemy, I think they would have been able to have held the fort until re-enforced. I believe that the ground there is so strong that 600 men with that artillery ought to have held it; but the command devolved upon a very good gentleman, but a very young officer, entirely inexperienced in these matters. The enemy rushed on the fort from two or three directions, and confused him, I think, and broke him and carried it. The information which I have from all sources, official and otherwise, is that—whether by permission of their officers, or contrary to their permission, I cannot say—a butchery took place there that is unexampled in the record of civilized warfare. We always expect, in case of a place carried by assault, that some extravagance of passion will occur; but this seems to have been continued after resistance had ceased, when there was nothing to keep up the hot blood, and to have been of a nature brutal to an extent that is scarcely credible, and I have embodied in my official report to General McPherson (my present superior officer) my opinion that the black troops will hereafter be uncontrolable, unless the government take some prompt and energetic action upon the subject. I know very well that my colored regiments at Memphis, officers and men, will never give quarter.

Question. They never ought to.

Answer. They never will. They have sworn it; and I have some very good colored regiments there.

Question. What do you say of the fighting qualities of the colored troops?

Answer. That depends altogether upon their officers. If they are properly officered, they are just as good troops as anybody has. I have two or three regiments at Memphis that I am willing to put anywhere that I would put any soldiers which I have ever seen, with the same amount of experience.

Question. Did you learn anything of the particulars of those atrocities that were committed there at Fort Pillow?

Answer. I learned the particulars from the reports of the officers.

Question. Did you learn anything about any flags of truce being taken advantage of?

Answer. They always do that; that is a matter of habit with them.

Question. And they took advantage of them in this case, as you learn?

Answer. Yes, sir; and they did it at Paducah, and they tried it at Columbus.

Question. Did you hear anything about their setting fire to hospitals, while the wounded were in there?

Answer. I learn, from what I consider unquestionable authority, that bodies were found which had been wounded by musket shots, and then their eyes bayoneted out; men wounded in a similar way, with their bowels cut open; and I have heard many other instances of equal barbarity.

Question. Did you hear, recently after that capture, of anybody being nailed to a building and burned?

Answer. I heard that Lieutenant Akerstrom was so treated.

Question. Did you learn that from a source that you could give credit to?

Answer. I had no reason to doubt it, with the exception of the identification of the body. The fact that somebody was so treated, I consider to be sufficiently proven; the identification I think is doubtful.

Question. Is there anything more you wish to state? If so, will you state it without further questioning?

Answer. I do not know that I can state anything more than my opinion in regard to certain things that might have been done. I do not know that it is worth while to do that. As I am under censure myself, at present I prefer not to.

Question. Will you give us a description of the situation of Fort Pillow?

Answer. It is a very difficult thing to describe. The original fortifications, as made by the rebels, were very much too large to be held by any force that we could spare. It was intended for a very large force; but there are two crowning heights—bold knobs—that stand up there, which command the entire region of approach, and which Major Booth was directed to occupy. He went up and examined the ground, and reported to me. A light work was thrown up upon one of them, and there was a portion of a work upon the other. The one to the south was not occupied during the fight; the one to the north of the ravine, which leads down to the landing, was occupied. That was the point which I considered should have been held; and I think yet it could have been, and would have been, if Major Booth had lived.

Question. Can you describe the position in which the men were placed by Major Booth?

Answer. Major Booth had his artillery upon this knoll, and held the slope of the hill with some rifle pits. From these rifle pits, as I am informed, he repulsed the enemy. The troops were afterwards drawn in by Major Bradford, into the fortification proper, and that was attacked on all sides. My opinion is that Major Bradford lost his head—got confused. The rush was too strong for him. The amount of the enemy's force that actually attacked there I do not know, but from all the testimony I could get, I should judge it to have been not less than 2,500 men.

Question. Who do you understand led the enemy's forces?

Answer. Forrest was there personally. I understand, however, that the main body of the force was Chalmers's command, who was also there. There was also a portion of Forrest's force there. Forrest will carry his men further than any other man I know of; he is desperate.

Question. Have we any force at Fort Pillow now?

Answer. No, sir.

Question. Do you consider that a point which should be occupied by a force, in order to make the navigation of the river safe?

Answer. I do.

Question. What force do you deem should be placed there to hold it?

Answer. I think 500 steady troops, properly supplied with artillery, and properly covered with works, could hold the place until re-enforced—hold it, all that is necessary.

Question. Did you ever have any instructions or orders to evacuate Fort Pillow? or did you, at any time, ever propose to evacuate it?

Answer. I never had any orders to evacuate it. My orders from General Sherman were to hold certain fortified points on the river. I never had any instructions with regard to Fort Pillow one way or the other that I recollect. I considered it necessary to hold it, and never intended to abandon it.

Question. Had it been held by us for some considerable time?

Answer. It had been held since we first occupied the river.

Question. Do not the same reasons exist for holding it now, that had existed during all that period?

Answer. The same. The reasons are geographical, and do not change.

By Mr. Gooch:

Question. Then I understand you to state that your instructions, in spirit, required you to hold it, and that it was necessary that it should be held?

Answer. My opinion is distinct that it should be held always, and there is nothing in my instructions that requires it to be abandoned. Some discretion, I suppose, belongs to an officer in charge of as much range as I have had to hold; and I certainly should not abandon that place, if I had troops to hold it.

By the chairman:

Question. Will you tell us what you know about the attack on Union City?

Answer. Colonel Hawkins, of the 7th Tennessee regiment, was at Union City as an advanced post. He had in round numbers about six hundred men. He was threatened by about fifteen hundred, I should think. They attacked him, and were repulsed. General Brayman moved from here with two thousand troops, and got down as far as the bridge, six miles from Union City, before Hawkins surrendered. They commenced the flag-of-truce operation on him, when they found they could do nothing else, threatening to open upon him with artillery, and to give no quarter. Contrary to the entreaties, prayers, and advice of all his officers and all his men, he did surrender his post, with a relieving force within six miles of him; and surrendered it, as I have no doubt, from pure cowardice.

Question. Was he aware of the re-enforcements approaching?

Answer. I think so, but I will not be positive. General Brayman can tell more about that than I can. I was at Columbus when General Brayman returned.

Question. Where is Colonel Hawkins now?

Answer. He is a prisoner. This is the second time he has surrendered to Forrest.

Captain Thomas P. Gray, sworn and examined.

By Mr. Gooch:

Question. What is your rank and position in the army?

Answer. For the last four months I have been holding the place of captain in the 7th Tennessee cavalry, but I have not been mustered in yet.

Question. Had you been in service before?

Answer. Yes, sir.

Question. For how long?

Answer. I enlisted in Illinois on the 24th of July, and was mustered into the United States service August 1, 1861.

Question. Were you at Union City when the late attack was made there?

Answer. I was.

Question. Will you give us an account of what occurred there?

Answer. On the 23d of March last it was generally understood by the troops there that the rebels were advancing upon us; we supposed under General Forrest. That night two companies, I think, were ordered to keep their horses saddled. The first orders I received were about half-past four, the morning of the 24th. The adjutant of our regiment came to me and told me to have my horses saddled. In perhaps half an hour after that we were ordered into line, and I held my company in line for some time waiting for orders. As Colonel

Hawkins came by I asked him if he wanted me to take my position at the breastworks, and he said he did. I then took my position at a place where I thought I was most needed, at some breastworks that my company had thrown up on the east side. At this time the rebels were firing on our pickets. I think there was no general charge until about half-past 5 or 6 o'clock. That charge was made by cavalry, on the south side. They did not charge a great way, and were easily repulsed. The same men then reassembled, dismounted, and charged on the fort. This time they came very close to the breastworks, but were again repulsed. After that our troops were very exultant, and ready to meet the rebels anywhere. The next charge was made on the northwest; that was easily repulsed. The last charge was made on the northeast, fronting my position; that was repulsed tolerably easily, but with more loss to the rebels than previously. Then there was sharpshooting for about an hour and a half, and we were all in good spirits. At the expiration of that hour and a half a flag of truce came in in my front. I sent word to Colonel Hawkins that there was a flag of truce coming. I went in person to meet the flag, and halted it about two hundred yards from the breastworks, and asked them what they desired. They said they wished to see the commander of the forces there. I told them I had notified him, and he would be there in a moment. At that time they ordered me under arrest, because I made myself easy looking around upon their position. I demanded their right to order me under arrest under a flag of truce, and told them I had as much right to look around as they had. They then ordered me to sit down. I told them that was played out; that I was not only there under the right of a flag of truce, but that I was there to give them their orders if they made any mismoves. They gave up then, as Colonel Hawkins was in sight. When the colonel came a document was handed him. I do not know anything about it; for, as soon as the colonel came near, I went back to the breastworks. The flag of truce then retired. As soon as I got back I made it my business to go around inside the breastworks to get a view of the rebel troops. They were there upon stumps and logs, and every place where they could see.

In about twenty minutes, I think it was, they came again with another flag of truce. I met them as before. This time a demand for surrender was handed to Colonel Hawkins. I remained there this time, and saw the communication. I could once give almost the exact language of it. At any rate, it was a demand for unconditional surrender, promising us the rights of prisoners of war if the surrender was made; if not, then we must take the consequences. After consulting with them for a little time Colonel Hawkins was allowed fifteen minutes to go to camp and back again. I remained there about fifteen minutes with the rebel truce bearers. During this time I could observe in every move and remark they made that they were beaten. Perhaps I should have said before, that when Colonel Hawkins was talking about the matter, I gave my opinion in regard to it. This was before the flag of truce came in at all. Colonel Hawkins came down to my corner of the breastworks. I told him that the rebels were beaten on their first programme, at any rate; that it was my opinion that they would either consolidate and make a charge on one side, or else they would leave the field, or else lie there and sharpshoot until they could get re-enforcements. I state this merely to show what our feelings were—that we were satisfied they were whipped, were beaten.

When the colonel came back from his second flag of truce I left them and went inside the breastworks. I was satisfied from appearances that the surrender would be made, and I hid a couple of revolvers and some other things I had; I did not know whether I should ever find them again or not. The troops considered that the surrender was made as soon as they saw a rebel officer coming back with the colonel, and every man tried to hide his stuff. Some broke their guns, and all were denouncing Colonel Hawkins as a coward, in surrendering them without cause. That is all I know of the matter up to the time of the surrender.

Question. Do you say it was the opinion of all the officers and men, so far as you know, that the surrender was wholly unnecessary?

Answer. Yes, sir; every man I ever heard say anything about it.

Question. To what cause do you attribute the surrender?

Answer. Some said that the colonel was half rebel, anyway; others said that he was a little cowardly, and surrendered to an imaginary foe—to a force that was not there. Those were the reasons that I have heard.

Question. What was your force there?

Answer. About 500 men.

Question. Did you have any colored troops?

Answer. None.

Question. What was the force of the enemy?

Answer. As near as I could judge—and I tried to estimate their number—they had about 800 after the surrender; I think they must have had a thousand at first.

Question. Could you have held that position against them?

Answer. I am satisfied we could have held it all day, unless our ammunition had given out.

Question. Had you any information in regard to any re-enforcements approaching to your relief?

Answer. For the last two hours we had expected to see them at any time.

Question. What reason had you to expect re-enforcements?

Answer. We had a communication that they knew our situation at Columbus, that they knew the rebels were advancing on us, and, of course, I thought they would send us re-enforcements.

Question. From what point did you expect re-enforcements?

Answer. From Columbus. I remarked to the men, as soon as the surrender was made, that I would be ten times more mad if I should hear afterwards that our re-enforcements were right close to us, which I expected was the case.

Question. What occurred after the surrender?

Answer. The men were marched on foot; the officers were allowed to ride their horses. They were marched two days—it was rainy and muddy weather—nearly east, towards Dresden. They had nothing to eat for two days, until eight o'clock the second night, and then we got some corn-bread and meat. The second day they turned from the Dresden road, towards Trenton, through the country, not in the regular road. On the evening of the third day we arrived at Trenton, Tennessee. There all our money, and I think all our watches, were taken—I know some of them were—and the pocket-knives were taken from the men: all done officially, one company at a time.

We laid over the fourth day at Trenton. On the fifth day at noon we marched toward Humboldt, and arrived there in the evening, just before dark. At seven o'clock, or nearly seven o'clock, I left them. My intention was to go to the commander at Memphis and get him to send a force out to make the rebels release our troops. Before I left the rebels, after I had concluded to leave them, I commenced getting up a plot to break the guards, and see if we could not redeem our name a little in that way and get off. It was working finely, but I met the opposition of the officers, because it was the general opinion that if we were caught, one in every ten would be killed. I abandoned that and escaped. I travelled on foot twenty-five hours without stopping, through the brush, dodging the rebels and guerillas. I was then directed by a negro to a farm where there were no whites, and where, he said, I could get a horse. When I got there I found I was so tired and sleepy that I dared not risk myself on a horse, and I secreted myself and rested there until early the next morning; I got a little refreshment there, too. I then got an old horse, with no saddle, and rode into Fort Pillow, just forty miles, in a little more than five hours. I reached there a little before noon, on the 30th of March.

The morning after I escaped from the rebels I wrote myself a parole, which screened me from a great many rebels whom I could not avoid. I was chased by two guerillas for some distance at this place, where I stopped over night, and got a horse. I knew two guerillas had been chasing me over ten miles. I told the negroes, as I laid down, that if any strangers came on the place, or any one inquiring for Yankees, to tell them that one had been there and pressed a horse and gone on. They did so; and more than that, they told the guerillas that I had been gone but a few minutes, and if they hurried they would catch me. They dashed on five miles further, and then gave up the chase and turned back. That is the way I avoided them.

After I got to Fort Pillow I got on a boat and went to Memphis, reaching there before daybreak on the morning of the 31st of March, and waked General Hurlbut up just about daybreak, and reported to him.

Question. Did you have much conversation with these rebels, or hear them express opinions of any kind, while you were with them?

Answer. I was talking almost continually with them. Somehow or other I got a little noted in the command, and a great many came to me to discuss matters about the war. They seemed to be confident that they were all right, and would succeed. I did not hear the command I was with say they intended to attack Fort Pillow; but while I was on my way from there to Fort Pillow, the report was current along the road that the rebels were going to attack it. But I reported to Major Booth, when I got to Fort Pillow, that I did not think there was any danger of an attack, because I thought I should have seen or heard something more to indicate it. I told him, however, that I thought it would be well to be on the lookout, though I did not think they would attack him. I heard the rebels say repeatedly that they intended to kill negro troops wherever they could find them; that they had heard that there were negro troops at Union City, and that they had intended to kill them if they had found any there. They also said they had understood there were negro troops at Paducah and Mayfield, and that they intended to kill them if they got them. And they said that they did not consider officers who commanded negro troops to be any better than the negroes themselves.

Question. With whom did you have this conversation?

Answer. With officers. I did not have any extensive conversation with any officer higher than captain. I talked with three or four captains, and perhaps twice that number of lieutenants.

Question. Did you see Colonel Hawkins, or have any conversation with him, after the surrender?

Answer. I did not. I felt so disgusted with him that I never spoke a word to him after the surrender.

Captain John W. Beattie, sworn and examined.

By Mr. Gooch:

Question. To what regiment do you belong?

Answer. I am a captain in the 7th Tennessee cavalry.

Question. Were you at Union City when it was surrendered?

Answer. Yes, sir.

Question. What was our force there?

Answer. Something near five hundred, altogether. There were some there that did not belong to our regiment.

Question. What was the force that attacked you?

Answer. From 1,500 to 1,800, as near as we could learn from the rebel officers while we were with them.

Question. What rebel officers were in command there

Answer. The surrender was made to Colonel Duckworth; but I am not certain whether it was Duckworth or Faulkner who had the command.

Question. Will you state briefly the circumstances attending the attack and surrender of Union City?

Answer. Our pickets were driven in about 4 o'clock in the morning. We sent some men out to see what force it was. As soon as it was light enough to see we found the rebels were all around our camp. Skirmishing commenced all around. Those of our men who were out, and could get in, came in; but some of the pickets did not get in at all. My company were almost all out on picket. The enemy, mounted men, made a charge on our camp; they came up on all sides, but we drove them back. They then dismounted and made three other charges, and we drove them back each time. I did not see but one of our men killed; and I did not see any that were wounded at all. One of my sergeants was killed. About 9 o'clock, I should think, the enemy got behind logs and stumps, and all such places, and commenced sharpshooting. If a man raised his head up, there would be a shot fired at him. We put out the best of our men as sharpshooters. A great many of our men lay down inside of our works and went to sleep, as they felt altogether easy about the matter. I think it was about half past ten o'clock when the bugle was sounded to cease firing; and fifteen minutes before eleven they sent in a flag of truce demanding an unconditional surrender. Colonel Hawkins called the officers together and asked them what they thought best to be done. All were in favor of fighting. When he asked me about it I told him that if they had artillery they could whip us; but if they had no artillery we could fight them till hell froze over; those were my very words. Then the telegraph operator said that he had seen two pieces of artillery. He had my glass, and had been up in a little log shanty, where he could see all over the ground. Colonel Hawkins said if they had artillery, and we renewed the fight, like enough they would kill every man of us they got. So we agreed then he should make the surrender on condition that we should be paroled there, without being taken away from the place, and each one allowed to keep his private property, and the officers allowed to keep their fire-arms. He went out to make the surrender on those conditions; and if they did not accept them, then we were to fight them as long as a man was left. He went out, and the next thing I knew there was an order came there for us to march our men out and lay down their arms. We marched them out in front of his headquarters and laid down our arms. The rebels then piled into our camp and cleaned out everything; what they could not carry off they burned. We were then marched off. The colonel had not then told us on what conditions the surrender was made; he only said he supposed we would be paroled.

Question. The enemy had used no artillery?

Answer. No, sir.

Question. Did you find out subsequently whether or not they had any artillery?

Answer. They had two pieces of artillery, but they did not have them at Union City.

Question. Where was it?

Answer. On the way from Dresden to Paducah. They told me it was in supporting distance; that they could have had it at Union City in a short time; but I heard so many stories I did not know what to believe.

Question. Did you suppose at the time you made the surrender that re-enforcements were approaching you?

Answer. The colonel could not tell us whether any re-enforcements were coming or not.

Question. How far was Union City from Columbus?

Answer. I think it was twenty-six miles; but I am not certain.

Question. You supposed re-enforcements would come from there, if at all?
Answer. From Cairo.
Question. How far were you from Cairo?
Answer. It is about forty-six miles from here to Union City. You would have to go from here to Columbus, and from Columbus out to Union City.
Question. How long did you remain with the enemy?
Answer. From Thursday until Monday night.
Question. How did you effect your escape?
Answer. We were not guarded very closely. When I was ready to leave I went into the kitchen, just after supper, and asked for some bread and meat for a man who was sick. The cook gave it to me, and I then went out the door and called Captain Parsons, and asked him if he did not want to go down and see the boys; that I had got a piece of meat to take down. He said yes; but instead of going down to see the boys we turned off into the woods.
Question. At what point did you come into our lines?
Answer. We came in at Waverly landing.

By the chairman:

Question. Have you heard since that re-enforcements under General Brayman were approaching to your relief?
Answer. Yes, sir.
Question. Did you hear how near they had got to you?
Answer. Within six miles of the place at four o'clock that morning.

By Mr. Gooch:

Question. Had you any conversation with the rebel officers while you were with them?
Answer. Yes, sir.
Question. Did you hear them say anything about negro troops, &c.?
Answer. Not much. I was talking with them about our regiment. They said when they first started to come there that they were going to get us, and seemed to be surprised to think we had fought them as well as we did, for they said they expected to get us without any trouble.
Question. Did they say why they expected to get you without any trouble?
Answer. No, sir. They said they would parole Hawkins again, and let him get some more horses, and knives, and things, and then they would come when they wanted him again.
Question. How did they treat our men?
Answer. They gave them nothing to eat until the second night, when they gave them about an ounce of fat bacon each. Some got a little bread, but a a few of them, however. On Sunday morning they marched the men up in front of the court-house, passed them in one at a time and searched them, taking boots, hats, coats, blankets, and money from them.
Question. Did they leave you without boots, coats, or blankets?
Answer. There were a great many of our men who had new boots, and the rebels would take the new boots and give them their old ones, and so they exchanged hats and blankets.
Question. How many days were you in reaching our lines after you escaped from the rebels?
Answer. I reached Waverly landing on Thursday, the 7th of April, and Cairo in two weeks from the time that I got away from them.

Captain P. K. Parsons, sworn and examined.

By Mr. Gooch:

Question. Were you at Union City when that place was surrendered?
Answer. Yes, sir.

Question. State briefly the circumstances attending the attack there and the surrender.

Answer. I think it was a few minutes after 4 o'clock in the morning that our pickets were driven in by the enemy. I was then sent out to look after them, and commenced skirmishing with them just at daylight. Before sun-up they had surrounded the fort. They then made three or four charges, two on horseback, I believe, but they were repulsed very easily. They then did not do anything but use their sharpshooters until about ten minutes before 11 o'clock, when they sent in a flag of truce demanding an unconditional surrender. The colonel went out and received the demand and brought it in. He then called the officers together and asked what we thought of the matter. He turned to Captain Harris, as the oldest officer, and asked him what we should do. The captain said he was for fighting, and I believe other officers there said "fight." The colonel then asked me to ride out with him, and I did so. On our way out I told the colonel that I thought we had the rebels whipped unless they had re-enforcements, which I did not think they had. They gave us fifteen minutes more to consider. Then some officers said they thought they saw artillery out there. Captain Beattie said if they had artillery they could whip us, but not without. The colonel then went out and made an unconditional surrender of the fort, about sixteen officers and about 500 men. I guess there were 300 men and officers out of the 500 who wanted to fight.

Question. Did you see any artillery?

Answer. No, sir.

Question. They had none there?

Answer. No, sir; I rode out as far as I dared go to see, and I did not see anything with the glass I had but an ambulance; there was no artillery there at all.

Question. To what do you attribute the surrender by Colonel Hawkins?

Answer. It is hard for me to make up my mind about that. Colonel Hawkins was a first lieutenant of a company in the Mexican war and I fought under him there, and I have fought under him in this war, and I never saw any cowardice about him before. I think this was one of the most cowardly surrenders there ever was. Still, I cannot think Colonel Hawkins is a coward; at least I never saw any show of cowardice in him before. I could see no reason for surrendering when we had but one man killed or hurt in the fort.

Question. You escaped from the enemy?

Answer. Yes, sir.

Question. How did you effect your escape?

Answer. I escaped with Captain Beattie.

Question. How long were you with the enemy?

Answer. Four days and a half.

Question. Who did you understand was in command of the rebels?

Answer. Colonel Duckworth.

Question. How many men did he have?

Answer. From the best information I could get there were about 1,500 of them. Several of their officers said they had 1,250 men, regular troops, and four independent companies. That was their statement to me.

Question. Had you a good position at Union City?

Answer. It was a very good position against small arms; it was not strong against artillery.

Question. Did you know anything about re-enforcements coming to you?

Answer. We were looking for re-enforcements. We had a despatch to hold the place, that re-enforcements would be sent.

Question. From whom was that despatch?

Answer. From General Brayman.

Question. Did Colonel Hawkins receive that despatch before he surrendered?

Answer. Yes, sir; the day before the fight, before the wire was cut. He was getting a despatch when the wire was cut; we did not know what that despatch was. But the one he got before was an order to hold the place, that re-enforcements would be sent to him. We were looking for them to come that morning or that night. I heard some rebel officers and men say they had come 450 miles for our regiment, and that they had known they would get it. I asked them how they knew they would get it, but they would not tell me. A rebel cursed Colonel Hawkins; said he was a God damned coward, but he had good men.

Question. Were our men in good spirits before the surrender?

Answer. They were just as cool and quiet as you ever saw men; not a bit excited, but talking and laughing.

Mrs. Rosa Johnson, sworn and examined.

By Mr. Gooch:

Question. Where have you been living?

Answer. I have a home at Hickman, Kentucky, but have been at Fort Pillow.

Question. Did you live there?

Answer. No, sir; my son was there, and I went down to stay with him.

Question. Where were you during the fight?

Answer. I was on a big island, where the gunboat men took us. I staid there a part of two days and one night.

Question. Did you go back to Fort Pillow after the fight?

Answer. Yes, sir; the gunboat took us over there.

Question. When did you go back there?

Answer. The battle was on Tuesday, and I went back Wednesday evening.

Question. Had our wounded men been taken away when you went back?

Answer. Yes, sir, I believe so.

Question. How long did you stay there?

Answer. I went about 2 o'clock in the evening, and staid till night.

Question. Did you go about the fort after you went back?

Answer. Yes, sir; I went up in it, expecting to find my son lying there, and I went around, where I saw some half buried, some with feet out, or hands out, or heads out; but I could not find him. I was so distressed that I could not tell much about it.

Question. Did you see anybody nailed to any boards there?

Answer. We saw a man lying there, burned they said; but I did not go close to him. I was looking all around the fort for my child, and did not pay attention to anything else.

Question. You came away that night?

Answer. I think we did.

Question. Is that all you know about it?

Answer, That is about all I know about it. There was a pile of dirt there, and there was a crack in it, which looked like a wounded man had been buried there, and had tried to get out, and had jammed the dirt, for they buried the wounded and the dead altogether there. There were others knew about that.

Mrs. Rebecca Williams, sworn and examined.

By Mr. Gooch:

Question. Where do you reside?

Answer. In Obion county, Tennessee.

Question. Was your husband in that fight at Fort Pillow?

Answer. Yes, sir.

Question. Were you there during the fight?

Answer. I was over on the island with Mrs. Johnson.

Question. Did you go back to Fort Pillow after the battle?

Answer, Yes, sir.

Question. What did you see there?

Answer. I did not see anything more than what Mrs. Johnson saw. I saw a burned man. He was lying right where a house was burned. He was a white man, but as I was alone by myself, I felt frightened, and did not look at it. I saw many buried there, some half buried, and negroes lying around there unburied. I heard that there was a man nailed up to a building and burned, but I did not see it.

Question. What time of day was it that you were there?

Answer. About 2 o'clock, the day after the fight. I saw that the man who was burned was a white man. Mrs. Ruffin was there and examined it, and can tell you all about it.

Captain James H. Odlin, sworn and examined.

By the chairman:

Question. What is your rank and position in the service?

Answer. I am a captain, and assistant adjutant general and chief of staff for General Brayman, for the district of Cairo, where I have been stationed since the 23d of January, 1864.

Question. Do you know anything about the capture of Fort Pillow?

Answer. Only from hearsay.

Question. You are acquainted somewhat with the circumstances attending the surrender of Union City?

Answer. Yes, sir.

Question. Will you tell us about that?

Answer. About 4 o'clock on the evening of the 23d of March we received a telegram that it was likely Union City would be attacked within two days. Shortly afterwards we received a telegram from Colonel Hawkins that he would be attacked within 24 hours. He said his men had not seen the enemy, but that his information was reliable. General Brayman instructed me to proceed by special boat to Columbus, and from thence, by special train, to Union City, to inquire into the matter, find out the truth of the case, and let him know; also, to find out whether re-enforcements were necessary. I left Cairo about 5 p. m. on the 23d, arrived at Columbus about half past seven o'clock, and immediately proceeded to the telegraph office and telegraphed to Colonel Hawkins, asking him if he had any further information. He answered that he had none. I then asked him if his information and his despatches could be relied upon, and whether he had seen the enemy. He answered that none of his men had seen the enemy; that he had not seen any one who had seen the enemy, but that his information was entirely reliable, and that he would be attacked, there was no doubt of it.

I then proceeded, by special train, to Union City, and had a consultation with Colonel Hawkins. He told me that the ferries on the Obion had been destroyed, and that scouts whom he had expected in the day before had not returned; that he supposed that they were captured, or that it was impossible for them to get across the Obion. He said that his men had not seen the enemy; that he could not get any of them across the Obion in consequence of the rebel forces having destroyed the private ferries, and guarding the other places.

About half past 3 o'clock on the morning of the 24th a messenger came in and stated that the pickets at the bridge on the Dresden and Hickman road had been attacked and driven in, and that they were probably cut off, which afterwards proved to be the fact. The messenger also reported that, when shots were exchanged, he thought the rebels had brought artillery to the front, but he could not be certain of that; that it sounded on the bridge like artillery. I immediately directed Colonel Hawkins to have his men saddle their horses ready for a fight. I instructed him, if he saw fit, and thought he could not hold the place, to abandon it and fall back on Columbus. He asked me how soon I would re-enforce him if he remained there. I told him I would re-enforce him just as quick as I could get the troops up there. He said he thought he could hold the place with his regiment if he had some artillery; but that he could not contend against artillery without he had some himself. I told him I did not want him to retreat without having seen the enemy; that he must have a skirmish with them, and feel their strength, before falling back to Columbus; that I did not want the command disgraced by retreating without seeing the enemy, which it would be if the reports should prove false, or he found that he had fallen back before a small number of men.

I then told Colonel Hawkins I must leave, for my orders were not to endanger the train, but to save it. The train consisted of nine cars and a locomotive, and was loaded with stores from Union City belonging to the government and to the railroad company, and 150 contrabands, (railroad hands.) The last words I said to Colonel Hawkins were, that if he found he could not whip the enemy, he should immediately retreat to Columbus. He said that, if he did not fall back, he would hold the place until re-enforcements reached him. I told him I would immediately push forward re-enforcements; that the garrison at Columbus consisted of only 1,100 men in all, and that 900 and odd of them were negroes, who had never been in a fight, and that re-enforcements would have to come from Cairo. I wrote a telegraphic despatch at the time to General Brayman, giving all the facts. But while it was being sent, the wires were cut, and we did not get the half of it through.

I then started to return to Columbus with the train, with the distinct understanding with Colonel Hawkins that he should either hold Union City until re-enforcements should arrive, or fall back to Columbus. The State line bridge was burning as I crossed it with the train, the evident intention of the rebels being to capture the train. I succeeded, however, in getting it through to Columbus safe.

Colonel Lawrence, commanding at Columbus, had telegraphed General Brayman that communications with Union City were cut off; that I was on the opposite side of the bridge, and that Colonel Hawkins was probably attacked. General Brayman immediately forwarded re-enforcements to Columbus, taking 2,000 men belonging to General Veatch's command, then on their way up the Tennessee river. He had received telegraphic orders from General Sherman not to take any of those troops out of their proper course, but forward them as soon as possible up the Tennessee. As transports were not ready for them, and as General Brayman could go to Union City and back again before transportation would be ready, he concluded to use some of the troops for the purpose of re-enforcing Union City. The movement was made with as little delay as possible. He arrived at Columbus about ten or half past ten o'clock on the morning of the 24th, and immediately proceeded on a railroad train towards Union City. Upon arriving within about seven miles of Union City, we were informed, by citizens and some scouts, that Colonel Hawkins had surrendered at 11 o'clock of that day; that the rebels had destroyed all the works and the government property, and had retreated. General Brayman being fully convinced that Union City had been surrendered, everything there destroyed, and that the enemy had fled, returned to Columbus, and from thence to Cairo, with the troops ready to be forwarded up the Tennessee in obedience to the orders of General Sherman.

Question. Will you now state what you know in relation to the attack on Paducah?

Answer. About 8 o'clock on the night of the 25th of March we received a telegraphic despatch from the operator at Metropolis, stating that a big light was seen in the direction of Paducah; that it looked as if the town or some boats were burning. The despatch also stated that the telegraph repairer had come in and reported that he had been within two miles of Paducah, and had heard firing there. We had received, previous to this, no intimation from Colonel Hicks, commanding at Paducah, that the place was in danger of an attack. In obedience to instructions from General Brayman, I immediately got on a despatch boat, furnished by Captain Pennock, of the navy, and with Captain Shirk, of the navy, proceeded to Paducah. We found, on our arrival there, that General Forrest, with his command of about 6,500 men, had attacked Paducah in the afternoon, about 3 o'clock, the troops under Colonel Hicks having only about fifteen minutes notice of their coming. Colonel Hicks's scouts had returned from the road over which the rebels had come in, and reported that they had heard nothing of the enemy. They were just about sending out new scouts when the rebels dashed into the town, driving our pickets in, and driving our troops into the fort. As the rear of the battalion of the 16th Kentucky cavalry were marching into the fort they were fired upon by the rebels.

After fighting a short time, the rebels sent in a demand, under flag of truce, for the unconditional surrender of all the forces under Colonel Hicks's command, and all the government property, stating that, if he should comply with the demand, his troops should be treated as prisoners of war; if not, then an overwhelming force would be thrown against him, and no quarter would be shown him. Colonel Hicks replied by stating that he had been placed there by his government to hold and defend the place and the public stores there, and that he should obey the command of his superior officer, and do so; that he was prepared for the enemy, and should not surrender.

Forrest then again attacked the fort, making three different charges. Our troops, both black and white, behaved in the most gallant and meritorious manner, fighting most bravely. After fighting until half past seven or eight o'clock in the evening our ammunition began to run short, so much so that men and officers began to count their cartridges. Colonel Hicks had only 3,000 rounds of small ammunition left when Forrest made the second demand for a surrender. But Colonel Hicks, as before, positively refused to comply with the demand. Firing then ceased until daylight the next morning.

During this cessation of firing I succeeded in getting into the fort with reenforcements and a small supply of ammunition from the gunboats. The supply of ammunition from Cairo did not arrive until the evening. As it was impossible to get any despatches through from Colonel Hicks, the line being cut, we knew nothing when I left Cairo of his being short of ammunition. The understanding we had with Colonel Hicks, before any attack was made, was that we had a large supply of ammunition on hand; that there were about 33,000 cartridges, calibre 58, on hand—that being the calibre used by the troops there—and a large supply of artillery ammunition in the fort.

The next morning, about six o'clock, the enemy again advanced in line of battle towards the fort. There was some firing on both sides, but it did not amount to much. Some of the rebel troops, while their main body was firing at the fort, were engaged in pillaging the town, stealing property from private citizens, horses, and government stores, burning houses, and committing all sorts of depredations.

While the flag of truce was at the fort the first, second, and third times, the rebel troops were taking new positions in line of battle, although they had made a distinct agreement and understanding with Colonel Hicks that while the flag of truce was in there should be no movements of troops on either side; that everything should remain as it was.

While the fight was going on, women, children, and other non-combatants came running down to the river towards the gunboats. The officers in the fort and on the gunboats called to them to run down to the river bank to the left of our fort. They did so, and under cover of the gunboats they got on a wharf boat or a little ferry-boat and were ferried across the river as fast as possible. While they were doing this the rebel sharpshooters got in among them, so that we could not fire upon them without killing the women and children, and fired on our troops in the fort and on the gunboats, wounding one officer on a gunboat and two men. They also made women stand up in front of their sharpshooters, where it was impossible for us to return the fire without killing the women. They also fired into houses where there were women, and where there were none of our soldiers. They also went into a hospital, took the surgeon of the hospital prisoner, and took a lady that was there and carried her off and took her clothing from her, leaving her nothing but an old dress to cover herself with. This woman, as well as Dr. Hart, the surgeon of the hospital, were taken away by them as prisoners. All the prisoners taken there by Forrest, with the exception of three or four men, were sick men from the hospital, unable to move or walk from the hospital to the fort without injury to their health. All the men who were able to walk were brought from the hospital to the fort. They took the rest of the men from the hospital, and under the third flag of truce offered to exchange them. This Colonel Hicks and myself refused, because we thought it treachery on their part. We also refused for the reason that we did not think they had a right to take as prisoners of war men in the hospital who were unable to walk without danger to their lives. Yet the rebels took those men and marched them ten miles, and then camped them down in a swampy piece of ground at night, with their clothes nearly all taken from them. Some of them were left bareheaded and barefooted, with nothing on but their pants and shirts, compelled to stay in that swampy ravine all night long, with nothing to eat, and not permitted to have fires. The next morning they were marched off again. I have certain knowledge that for two days and one night those sick men were compelled to march with the rebel troops without anything to eat, with hardly any clothing, and a number of them without any boots or shoes.

Question. Do you know that the rebels placed women and other non-combatants in front of their lines as they advanced towards the fort?

Answer. They had women and children between us and their lines, and they stood behind them, the women and children forming a sort of breastwork for the rebels, as we were unable to return their fire for fear of killing the women and children. Colonel Hicks reported to me that they took several women and compelled them to stand in front of their lines during the fight; that there were women and children between our fire and theirs; that as the women moved the rebels moved along with them, keeping behind them.

Question. Have you any idea of the number of women and children they had thus placed in front of them?

Answer. It varied at different times. Colonel Hicks informed me that at one time the rebels held six women in front of them, refused to let them escape, but compelled them to stand there under the hottest of the fire.

Question. Were those women so placed that we could not fire upon the enemy with advantage without endangering the lives of the women?

Answer. We could not fire upon them at that particular point without endangering the lives of the women and children.

Question. Do you know whether the flag of truce was violated by the rebels at any time?

Answer. Yes, sir, it was. While the flag of truce was in they moved their troops into new positions; they marched their troops around to the back of the fort, and brought them up through the timber, dashed up towards the fort at full speed, then turned off towards the right of the fort, taking up their position between the fort and the town. During the first flag of truce they marched the majority of their forces, if not the whole of them, down into an open common between the fort, the river, and the town, along the river bank, then obliqued off to the left, and took position in line of battle off to the right of the fort as you faced the town; and at one time, while their troops were taking position between the town and the fort during a flag of truce, they had women placed in front of their lines.

Question. While they were making the movement?

Answer. Yes, sir. The rebel General Thompson with his forces took position on the right of the fort between the hospital and the fort while the flag of truce was at the fort. The fact of the rebel movements was reported to Colonel Hicks, and he requested of the flag of truce that they should be stopped, as they had violated their word, it being distinctly understood that there should be no movements during that time, and the officer sent an orderly to stop it, but it was not done; the troops continued to move. After they had placed their troops in position the flag of truce left the fort. As the flag of truce passed from the fort down through the town, the rebel troops escorting the flag shot down in the streets some citizens and some men straggling from the hospital. A charge was then immediately made on the fort, at which time the rebel General Thompson was killed. The rebels also, while the flag of truce was at the fort, pillaged the town, and robbed citizens on the streets who were on their way down to the river for the purpose of going across. They pillaged the town right in view of our gunboats; and as soon as the flag of truce left the fort our gunboats opened upon the rebels, and drove them out of that part of the town.

The morning after I arrived there, when the rebel forces advanced on the fort, they sent in a flag of truce asking for an exchange of prisoners, which was refused. It was a written communication from General Forrest, asking, if his request was granted, that Colonel Hicks, with one or two staff officers, would meet him at a point designated, when they would agree between themselves upon the exchange. Colonel Hicks replied that he had no authority to exchange prisoners; otherwise he would be happy to do so. When this written reply was handed to the rebel officer in charge of the flag of truce, he asked three or four questions for the purpose of gaining time. Colonel Hicks and I both noticed this, and sent him off as soon as possible. While this flag of truce was at the fort the rebels were taking position. They afterwards fell back into the timber.

The main body of the rebels, Forrest with them, retreated on the Mayfield road, while about 300 of his men remained in the town making movements and feints on the fort, to prevent our sending out and ascertaining his movements. Forrest, by that time, had found out that we had been re-enforced with troops, and that more boats were arriving; also, that the navy had re-enforced us with two or three more gunboats.

In the afternoon, about 5 o'clock, by Colonel Hicks's consent and direction, I sent word to the gunboats to move up opposite the town and shell it at the head of Jersey street, our troops having seen squads of rebels in that part of the city. This the gunboats did. After that the town was quiet, the rebels who had remained there having been driven out by the shells.

Question. Do you know what was our loss and the loss of the enemy there?

Answer. Our loss altogether was 14 killed—of which 11 were negroes—and 46 wounded; I do not know how many of them were negroes. The rebels lost about 300 killed, and from 1,000 to 1,200 wounded. That is what the citizens reported Forrest said, and we believed it to be correct from the number of graves we found, and from other circumstances. Forrest seized the Mayfield and Paducah train and carried all his wounded off to Mayfield, except a few who lay near the fort.

Our black troops were very much exposed. The fort was in bad condition, and the negro troops, with the heavy artillery, were compelled to stand up on the platforms to man the guns, their only protection there being a little bank or ridge of earth about knee high. Our loss in killed resulted from this exposure. The rebel troops got up on the tops of houses, and also in the hospital, and fired down into the fort upon our gunners. But the troops fought bravely, without flinching; as soon as a man fell at the guns, one of his comrades would drag him out of the way and take his place. The black troops, having muskets as well as serving the artillery, would load and fire their muskets while the artillery was being fired. The white troops were better covered and had more protection; but they fought as well as any men could be expected to fight.

Question. Will you state to us what you know about the operations of the rebels against Columbus?

Answer. The first news we received of any operations against Columbus was about 12 o'clock in the day—I do not remember the exact day, but it was just before the attack on Fort Pillow. I received a written communication by despatch boat from Colonel Lawrence, commanding the post at Columbus, stating that he had received a communication from General Buford demanding an unconditional surrender of the forces under his command, with all government property, with the assurance that the white troops would be treated as prisoners of war, while the black troops, I think, would either be returned to their masters, or made such disposition of as the rebels should see fit. To this Colonel Lawrence replied that he had been placed there by his government to defend the place and the government property and stores there, and that he should obey the orders of his superiors; surrender, therefore, was out of the question. The rebel general then offered to give Colonel Lawrence half an hour to remove the women and children out of the town. Colonel Lawrence replied that he should immediately notify the women and children to leave on a boat; that if he (the rebel general) attempted to attack the place, the lives of the women and children would rest on his head, but if he waited half an hour he would have them all out; that he (Colonel Lawrence) would not ask them to wait, for he felt amply prepared to receive their attack.

The flag of truce then returned. On their way out, or while the flag of truce was at the fort, the rebel cavalry occupied themselves in stealing horses that had been brought in by Union citizens, and stabled near our picket lines for protection. The rebels stole something like twenty-five or thirty horses belonging to Union men while this flag of truce was in. That was the last Colonel Lawrence heard of the enemy that day. Colonel Lawrence then gave notice that he should receive no more flags of truce from Forrest; that as Forrest did not respect them, he should not himself respect them. That was all that occurred at Columbus.

Question. You have said that you went up to Paducah on a gunboat with Captain Shirk, of the navy: did he co-operate cordially with the land forces in repelling the attack upon Paducah?

Answer. He did. Captain Shirk and all his officers did everything in their power to aid us. He was very accommodating, even furnishing us with ammunition, although he himself was getting short of it. He had but a very small amount, yet he divided with us, giving us a share of what he had. He also sent by boat to Metropolis all the despatches that were sent by Colonel Hicks and myself to General Brayman, and he sent a despatch boat to Cairo. To make sure that the information should get through, and to have supplies forwarded to us, the gunboats did everything in their power, and rendered great assistance in defending the place.

Question. Has Captain Pennock, of the navy, co-operated cordially with the military authorities in their operations in this vicinity, where it has been possible for the navy to co-operate?

Answer. Yes, sir; Captain Pennock has always been on hand, always had boats ready; has made such dispositions of his boats that he could at any moment throw from one to three boats, and at one time as many as five boats, on any one point in the district, whenever asked to do so. At the time of the attack upon Paducah he was very prompt in furnishing us with a despatch boat and supplying us with ammunition. I believe he has done everything in his power to assist us in carrying out all our movements and operations. At the same time Captain Pennock has labored under the difficulty of being compelled to send some of his boats up the Tennessee river with despatches for General Veatch. I mention that to show that he has had to send some of his boats away. Yet he has always been ready to assist us at any time, night or day. The best feeling has always existed, and still exists, between the naval officers and the military authorities at this post, and at all the posts in the district; and they co-operate cordially in carrying out all orders and measures that are deemed for the good of the service.

John Penwell, sworn and examined.

By the chairman:

Question. Where do you reside?
Answer. Detroit, Michigan.
Question. Do you belong to the army?
Answer. I do not.
Question. Were you at Fort Pillow when it was attacked?
Answer. Yes, sir; this last time.
Question. In what capacity were you there?
Answer. As a volunteer for the occasion.
Question. Will you tell us, in your own way, what you saw there?
Answer. Nothing occurred of much account—only the fighting part of it—until after they sent the last flag of truce there. They kept on fighting, but the fort was not surrendered. While the flag of truce was outside the fort, and they were conferring together, I noticed and spoke about seeing men going around behind the fort. They who were out with the flag of truce came back and said they were not going to surrender, and commenced fighting again. I had just fired my musket off, and heard a shot behind me. I saw the rebels come running right up to us. I was just feeling for a cartridge. They were as close as from here to the window, (about 10 feet.) I threw my musket down. A fellow who was ahead asked "if I surrendered." I said, "Yes." He said, "Die, then, you damned Yankee son of a bitch," and shot me, and I fell. More passed by me, and commenced hallooing "Shoot him down," and three or four stopped where I was and jumped on me and stripped me, taking my boots and coat and hat, and $45 or $50 in greenbacks.
Question. Where did they shoot you?
Answer. In the breast, and the ball passed right through.
Question. Did you see other men shot after they had surrendered?
Answer. I did not see any after I laid down, but I heard the hallooing around me, and begging them "Not to shoot," and then I heard them say "Shoot them down, shoot them down!" In fact, when they stripped me, one of them said "He ain't dead," and they jerked me up and took off my coat. It hurt me pretty bad, and I cried out to them "Kill me, out and out." One of them said "Hit him a crack on the head," but another said "Let the poor fellow be, and get well, if he can. He has nothing more left now." I fainted then. After I revived I crawled into a tent near where I was. A captain of artillery was in there very badly wounded. Some one had thrown an overcoat over us after I got in there. In the night they roused us up, and wanted to know "If we wanted to be burned up." I said "No." They said "They were going to fire the tent, and we had better get out," and wanted to know if we could walk. I said "I could not." They helped me out and made me walk some, but

carried the officer out. They took us to a house and left us there. They would not give us any water, but told us to get it for ourselves. There were other wounded men there. Some petty officer came in there and looked at us, and wanted to know how badly we were hurt. I said, "Pretty bad," and asked him for water, and he made some of the men fetch us some. We lay there until the gunboat came up and commenced shelling, when they made us get out of that—help ourselves out the best way we could. Three of our own men were helping the wounded out of the houses, when they commenced burning them. As soon as they saw I could walk a little, they started me up to headquarters with a party. When we got to the gully the gunboat threw a shell, which kind of flurried them, and we got out of sight of them. I got alongside of a log, and laid there until a party from the boat came along picking up the wounded.

Question. Did they have a hospital there that the wounded were put in?

Answer. There were four or five huts there together which they put them in. That was all the hospital I saw.

Question. Do you know whether they burned anybody in there?

Answer. I do not know, but they hallooed to us to "Get out, if we did not want to get burned to death." I told an officer there, who was ordering the houses to be burned, to let some of the men go in there, as there were some eight or nine wounded men in there, and a negro who had his hip broken. He said "The white men can help themselves out, the damned nigger shan't come out of that." I do not know whether they got the wounded out or not. I got out, because I could manage to walk a little. It was very painful for me to walk, but I could bear the pain better than run the risk of being burned up.

Question. Do you know anything about rebel officers being on the boat, and our officers asking them to drink?

Answer. Yes, sir. There were several rebel officers on board the Platte Valley. I went on board the boat, and took my seat right in front of the saloon. I knew the bar-tender, and wanted to get a chance to get some wine, as I was very weak. I was just going to step up to the bar, when one of our officers, a lieutenant or a captain, I don't know which, stepped in front of me and almost shoved me away, and called up one of the rebel officers and took a drink with him; and I saw our officers drinking with the rebel officers several times.

COLUMBUS, KENTUCKY, *April* 24, 1864.

Colonel Wm. H. Lawrence, sworn and examined.

By the chairman:

Question. What is your rank and position in the army?

Answer. I am colonel of the 34th New Jersey volunteers.

Question. Where are you stationed now, and how long have you been there stationed?

Answer. I am stationed at Columbus, and have been there since the end of January last.

Question. What do you know with regard to the attack and capture of Fort Pillow?

Answer. All I know about that is, that General Shipley arrived here on the 13th of April. He took me one side, and told me that as he passed Fort Pillow he was hailed from a gunboat, and told that there had been severe fighting there; that he saw a flag of truce at Fort Pillow, and that, after passing the fort a little distance, he saw the American flag hauled down, or the halliards shot away, he did not know which; and he afterward saw a flag, which was not raised higher than a regimental flag, and that he believed Fort Pillow had surrendered. He then offered me two batteries of light artillery, which he said were fully manned and equipped. He repeated this same conversation to General Brayman, as I understand, after arriving at Cairo.

Question. Did he give any reason why he did not undertake to assist the garrison at Fort Pillow?

Answer. No, sir.

Question. From his conversation, did you gather that he was in a condition to render assistance?

Answer. [After a pause.] It struck me as the most remarkable thing in the world that he had not found out positively; had not landed his batteries, and gone to the assistance of Fort Pillow.

Question. Under what circumstances did you understand he was there?

Answer. The steamer on which he was passed by there. I am under the impression that he had also two or three hundred infantry on the steamer.

Dr. Chapman Underwood, sworn and examined.

By Mr. Gooch:

Question. Where do you reside?

Answer. I reside in Tennessee.

Question. Were you at Fort Pillow, or on board a gunboat, during the attack there?

Answer. Yes, sir; I was there.

Question. What was your position?

Answer. I was sent from there, about ten days before that, on detached service, looking after convalescents, and returned on the Saturday evening before the fight on Tuesday morning. I was acting assistant surgeon. The regiment was not full enough to have a surgeon with the regular rank.

Question. Will you state what came within your own observation in connexion with the attack and capture?

Answer. I roomed with Lieutenant Logan, first lieutenant of company C, 13th Tennessee cavalry. About sun-up, I got up as usual. About the time I got up and washed, the pickets ran in and said Forrest was coming to attack the fort. I started up to the fort. Lieutenant Logan knew the feeling the rebels had towards me, and told me to go on the gunboat.

Question. What do you mean by that?

Answer. Well, they had been hunting me—had shot at me frequently. Faulkner's regiment, and a part of another, was raised in the country where I knew all of them. I was a notorious character with them, and always had to leave whenever they came around. The lieutenant advised me to go on board the gunboat for safety, and I did so. The attack came on then, and we fired from the gunboat, I think, some 260 or 270 rounds, and the sharpshooters on the boat were firing, I among the rest. We fought on, I think, until about one or half past one. The rebels had not made much progress by that time. They then came in with a flag of truce, and firing ceased from the fort and gunboat, and all around. They had a conference, I think, of about three-quarters of an hour. They returned with the flag of truce; but in a very short time came back again with it to the fort, and had another interview. During the time the flag of truce was in there, there was no firing done from either side, but we could see from the gunboat up the creek that the rebels were moving up towards the fort. The boat lay about 200 yards from the shore, right opposite the quartermaster's department. By the time the first flag of truce got to the fort, they commenced stealing the quartermaster's stores, and began packing them off up the hill. For an hour and a half, I reckon, there seemed to be above one or two hundred men engaged in it.

Question. This was before the capture of the fort?

Answer. Yes, sir; while under the protection of the flag of truce. When the last flag of truce started back from the fort, in three minutes, or less, the firing opened again, and then they just rushed in all around, from every direction, like a swarm of bees, and overwhelmed everything. The men—white and black—all rushed out of the fort together, threw down their arms, and ran down the hill; but they shot them down like beeves, in every direction. I think I saw about 200 run down next to the water, and some of them into the water, and they shot them until I did not see a man standing.

Question. How many do you think were shot after the capture of the fort, and after they threw down their arms?

Answer. Well, I think, from all the information I could gather, there were about 400 men killed after the capture, or 450. I think there were about 500 and odd men killed there. A very great majority of them were killed after the surrender. I do not suppose there were more than 20 men killed before the fort was captured and the men threw down their arms and begged for quarter.

Question. Was there any resistance on the part of our soldiers after the capture of the fort?

Answer. None in the world. They had no chance to make any resistance.

Question. And they did not attempt to make any?

Answer. None that I could discover. There were about 500 black soldiers in all there, and about 200 whites able for duty. There were a great many of them sick and in the hospital.

Question. What happened after that?

Answer. They then got our cannon in the fort, and turned them on us, and we had to steam off up the river a little, knowing that they had got a couple of 10 or 12-pounder Parrott guns. They threw three shells towards us. We steamed off up the river, anchored, and lay there all night. We returned the next morning. We got down near there, and discovered plenty of rebels on the hill, and a gunboat and another boat lying at the shore. We acted pretty cautiously, and held out a signal, and the gunboat answered it, and then we went in. When we got in there, the rebel General Chalmers was on board, and several other officers—majors, captains, orderlies, &c.—and bragged a great deal about their victory, and said it was a matter of no consequence. They hated to have such a fight as that, when they could take no more men than they had there. One of the gunboat officers got into a squabble with them, and said they did not treat the flag of truce right. An officer—a captain, I think—who was going home, came up and said that, "Damn them, he had 18 fights with them, but he would not treat them as prisoners of war after that," and that he intended to go home, and would enlist again. Chalmers said that he would treat him as a prisoner of war, but that they would not treat as prisoners of war the "home-made Yankees," meaning the loyal Tennesseeans. There were some sick men in the hospital, but I was afraid to go on shore after the rebels got there. I merely went on shore, but did not pretend to leave the boat.

Question. Did you see any person shot there the next morning after you returned?

Answer. I heard a gun or a pistol fired up the bank, and soon afterwards a negro woman came in, who was shot through the knee, and said it was done about that time. I heard frequent shooting up where the fort was, but I did not go up to see what was done.

FORT PILLOW, TENNESSEE, *April* 25, 1864.

Captain James Marshall, sworn and examined.

By the chairman:

Question. What is your rank and position in the naval service?

Answer. I am an acting master, commanding the United States steamer New Era, gunboat No. 7.

Question. Where is your boat?

Answer. My boat has been twenty-four hours' run from Fort Pillow. Since the attack here, that has been changed. At the time the fort was attacked, I was to make my principal headquarters here.

Question. Were you present with your gunboat at the time Fort Pillow was attacked and captured?

Answer. I was.

Question. Please describe that affair.

Answer. At six o'clock, on the morning of the 12th of April, Major Booth sent me word that the rebels were advancing on us. I immediately got the ship cleared for action. I gave the men their breakfasts. I had no idea that there would be a fight. I thought it would merely be a little skirmish. I went out into the stream. Major Booth and myself had previously established signals, by which he could indicate certain points where he would want me to use my guns. He first signalled me to commence firing up what we call No. 1 ravine, just below the quartermaster's department, and I commenced firing there. Then he signalled me to fire up Coal Creek ravine No. 3, and I then moved up there. Before I left down here at ravine No. 1 the rebel sharpshooters were firing at me rapidly. I came along up, and the women and children, some sick negroes, and boys, were standing around a great barge. I told them to get into the barge if they wanted to save themselves, and when I came down again I would take them out of danger. They went in, and I towed them up and landed them above Coal Creek, where the rebel sharpshooters commenced firing at them. The next time I moved up Coal Creek ravine I told them to go on up to a house, as the rebels were firing upon them. The trees and bushes around them there probably prevented them from being hit. On knowing that they were fired at much, I kept a steady fire up to about one o'clock. At that time the fire had ceased or slackened, and everything seemed to be quieting down, and I thought, perhaps, they were waiting to get a little rest. My men were very tired, not having had anything to eat since morning, and the officers nothing at all. I ran over on the bar to clean out my guns and refresh my men. We had fired 282 rounds of shell, shrapnell, and canister, and my guns were getting foul. While we were lying on the bar a flag of truce came in—the first one. It was, I should judge, about half past six o'clock. While the flag of truce was in, some of the officers came to me and told me the rebels were robbing the quartermaster's department. I went out on the deck and saw them doing so. Some of the officers said that we should go in and fire upon them; that we could slay them very nicely. I remarked to them that that was not civilized warfare; that two wrongs did not make a right; and that if the rebels should take the fort afterwards they would say that they would be justified in doing anything they pleased, because I had fired on them while the flag of truce was in, although they were thus violating that flag of truce themselves. They were also moving their forces down this hill, and were going up the ravine. When I saw that, I got under way, and stood off for the fort again, intending to stop it. I had only seventy-five rounds of ammunition left, but I told the boys that we would use that at any rate. The flag of truce started and went out, and I do not think it had been out more than five minutes when the assault was made. Major Bradford signalled to me that we were whipped. We had agreed on a signal that, if they had to leave the fort, they would drop down under the bank, and I was to give the rebels canister. I was lying up above here, but the rebels turned the guns in the fort on us—I think all of them—and a Parrott shot was fired but went over us. I had to leave, because, if I came down here, the channel would force me to go around the point, and then, with the guns in the fort, they would sink me. Had I been below here at the time, I think I could have routed them out; but part of our own men were in the fort at the same time, and I should have killed them as well as the rebels. The rebels kept firing on our men for at least twenty minutes after our flag was down. We said to one another that they could be giving no quarter. We could see the men fall, as they were shot, under the bank. I could not see whether they had arms or not. I was fearful that they might hail in a steamboat from below, capture her, put on 400 or 500 men, and come after me. I wanted to get down so as to give warning, and I did send word to Memphis to have all steamboats stopped for the present. The next morning the gunboat 28 and the transport Platte Valley came up.

Question. When did you go ashore after the fort had been captured?

Answer. I went ashore the next morning, about ten o'clock, under a flag of truce, with a party of men and an officer, to gather up the wounded and bury the dead. I found men lying in the tents and in the fort, whose bodies were burning. There were two there that I saw that day that had been burned.

Question. What was the appearance of the remains? What do you infer from what you saw?

Answer. I supposed that they had been just set on fire there. There was no necessity for burning the bodies there with the buildings, because, if they had chosen, they could have dragged the bodies out. There was so little wood about any of those tents that I can hardly understand how the bodies could have been burned as they were.

Question. Were the tents burned around the bodies?

Answer. Yes, sir. On the 14th of April (the second day after the capture) I came up again. I had a lot of refugees on board, and as I came around I hoisted a white flag, intending to come in and see if there were any wounded or unburied bodies here. When I landed here, I saw, I should judge, at least fifty cavalry over on Flower island, and while I was lying here with a white flag they set fire to an empty coal barge I had towed over there. I put the refugees on the shore, took down the white flag, and started after them, and commenced shelling them, and the gunboats 34 and 15 and the despatch boat Volunteer came down and opened on them. We did not see the rebels then, but saw where they were setting wood piles on fire, and we followed them clear round and drove them off. At this time I received information that the body of Lieutenant Akerstrom had been burned; that it was he who was burned in the house. Some of the refugees told me this, and also that they had taken him out and buried him. There was also one negro who had been thrown in a hole and buried alive. We took him out, but he lived only a few minutes afterwards. After we had followed these rebels around to the head of Island 30, I came back to the fort, landed, and took on board the refugees I had put on shore. The next morning the three gunboats landed here, and we sent out pickets, and then sent men around to look up the dead. We found a number there not buried, besides one man whose body was so burnt that we had to take a shovel to take up his remains.

Question. Was he burned where there was a tent or a building?

Answer. Where there was a building.

Question. Do you know whether there were any wounded men burned in those buildings?

Answer. I do not. All I know about that is what I was told by Lieutenant Leming, who said that while he was lying here wounded, he heard some of the soldiers say that there were some wounded negroes in those buildings, who said, "You are trying to get this gunboat back to shell us, are you, God damn you," and then shot them down. I went to Memphis, and then had to go to Cairo. I was then ordered to patrol the river from here (Fort Pillow) to Memphis. I started down on my first trip on Friday morning last. I arrived at Memphis on Friday afternoon. I mentioned there the manner in which our men had been buried here by the rebels, and said that I thought humanity dictated that they should be taken up and buried as they ought to be. The general ordered some men to be detailed, with rations, to come up here and rebury them properly. They have come here, and have been engaged in that work since they came up.

Question. How many have you already found?

Answer. We have found already fifty-two white men and four officers, besides a great many colored men.

Question. Had the blacks and whites been buried together indiscriminately?

Answer. We have not found it so exactly; we have found them in the same trench, but the white men mostly at one end, and the black men at the other; but they were all pitched in in any way—some on their faces, some on their sides, some on their backs.

Question. Did you hear anything said about giving quarter or not giving quarter on that occasion?

Answer. No, sir; but our paymaster here could tell you what he heard some of their officers say.

Question. Do you know anything about the transport Platte Valley being here?

Answer. She was lying alongside the gunboat 28 here when I came down the day after the fight, and came alongside of her.

Question. Do you know anything about any of our officers showing civilities to the rebel officers after all these atrocities?

Answer. I saw nothing of that kind but one lieutenant, who went up around with them on the hill. Who he was I do not know, but I recollect noticing his stripe.

Question. Did he belong to the navy or army?

Answer. He belonged to the army. I saw the rebel General Chalmers but once. When I came down here that morning I was the ranking officer; but the captain of gunboat 28 had commenced negotiations with the flag of truce, and I told him to go on with it. I met those men in the cabin of the 28 on business. I was not on board the Platte Valley but once, except that I crossed over her bow once or twice. I was not on her where I could see anything of this kind going on.

Question. How many of our men do you suppose were killed after they had surrendered?

Answer. I could not say. I have been told that there were not over 25 killed and wounded before the fort was captured.

Question. Do you know how many have been killed in all?

Answer. My own crew buried, of those who were left unburied, some 70 or 80. The Platte Valley buried a great many, and the gunboat 28 buried some.

Question. What number do you suppose escaped out of the garrison?

Answer. I have no means of knowing. I have understood that the rebels had 160 prisoners—white men—but I think it is doubtful if they had that many, judging from the number of men we have found.

By Mr. Gooch:

Question. Where did those men come from whose bodies we have just seen unburied?

Answer. I should judge they came from the hospital. One of them had a cane, showing that he was not a well man, and they had on white shirts—hospital clothing—and, as you saw, one looked thin, very thin, as if he had been sick.

Question. How far are these bodies lying from the hospital?

Answer. I should think about 150 yards.

Question. Would men, escaping from the fort, run in that direction?

Answer. They would be very apt to run in almost any direction; and they would be more likely to run away from the stores that these rebels were robbing.

By the chairman:

Question. From the hospital clothing they had on; from their appearance, showing that they had been wounded or sick persons; and from the bruised appearance of their heads, as if they had been killed by having their brains knocked out, do you infer that they were hospital patients that had been murdered there?

Answer. I should. I should be just as positive of that as I should be of anything I had not actually seen.

Question. You take it that they were sick or wounded men endeavoring to escape from the hospital, who were knocked in the head?

Answer. I should say so.

Paymaster William B. Purdy, sworn and examined.

By the chairman:

Question. What is your rank, and where have you been stationed, and in what service?

Answer. Acting assistant paymaster of the navy. I have no regular station or quarters at present; but on the day of the attack on Fort Pillow I was acting as signal officer on the gunboat No. 7.

Question. Will you state what you observed that day, and afterwards, in relation to that affair?

Answer. After our flag was down, I saw the rebels firing on our own men from the fort, and I should say that while the flag of truce was in, before the fort was captured, I could see the rebels concentrating their forces so as to be better able to take the fort.

Question. Do you mean that they took advantage of the flag of truce to place their men in position so as to better attack the fort?

Answer. Yes, sir; I could see them moving down to their new positions, and, as soon as the flag of truce was out, firing commenced from these new positions.

Question. Do you understand such movements to be in accordance with the rules of warfare?

Answer. No, sir; I do not.

Question. Had you any coversation with one of General Chalmers's aids about their conduct here?

Answer. Yes, sir; with one who said he was an aide-de-camp to General Chalmers, and a captain in the 2d Missouri cavalry. He told me that they did not recognize negroes as United States soldiers, but would shoot them, and show them no quarter—neither the negroes nor their officers.

Question. When was this?

Answer. That was the day after the capture of the fort, while the flag of truce was in. He then spoke in relation to the Tennessee loyal troops. He said they did not think much of them; that they were refugees and deserters; and they would not show them much mercy either.

Question. Was this said in defence of their conduct here?

Answer. No, sir; there was not much said about that. He opened the conversation himself.

Question. How many of our men do you suppose were killed here after our flag was down and they had surrendered?

Answer. I have no idea, only from what citizens have told me. They said there were not more than 25 or 30 killed before the place was captured; that all the rest were killed after the capture, and after the flag was down.

Question. Were you on the ground the day after the fight?

Answer. Yes, sir.

Question. Did you discover upon the field, or learn, from any information derived there, of any act of peculiar barbarity?

Answer. I saw men who had been shot in the face, and I have since seen a body that was burned outside of the fort. The day after the fight I did not go inside the fort at all.

Question. Did you see the remnants of one who had been nailed to a board or plank?

Answer. I did not see that.
Question. Then it was another body that had been burned which you saw?
Answer. Yes, sir.
Question. It has been said that men were buried alive. Did any such information come to your notice?
Answer. I heard of it, but did not see it.
Question. What was said about it?
Answer. A young man said he saw one in the morning up there who was alive, and he went back a short time afterwards to attend to him, but he was then dead; and I have heard of others who crawled out of their graves, and were taken up on the Platte Valley, but I do not know about them.
Question. Where was this man you found burned?
Answer. He was inside of a tent.
Question. Do you suppose him to have been burned with the tent?
Answer. Yes, sir. I took him to be a white man, because he was in the quarters where the white men were.
Question. So far as you could observe, was any discrimination made between white and black men, as to giving no quarter?
Answer. I should think not, from all I could see, because they were firing from the top of a hill down the bluff on all who had gone down there to escape.
Question. Did you notice how these men had been buried by the rebels?
Answer. I saw officers and white men and black men thrown into the trenches—pitched in in any way, some across, some lengthways, some on their faces, &c. When I first saw them, I noticed a great many with their hands or feet sticking out.
Question. Have you lately discovered any that are still unburied?
Answer. Yes, sir.
Question. Did you see the three there to-day that were lying unburied?
Answer. No, sir; I heard about them, but did not go to see them.

Eli A. Bangs, sworn and examined.

By the chairman:

Question. Do you belong to the navy or the army?
Answer. To the navy.
Question. In what capacity?
Answer. Acting master's mate for the New Era gunboat.
Question. Were you here on the day of the fight at Fort Pillow?
Answer. I was.
Question. Tell us what you observed in regard to the battle, and what followed.
Answer. I did not observe much of the first part of the engagement, because I was stationed below, in a division, with the guns; but after we hauled out into the stream I saw the flag of truce come in, and then I saw our colors come down at the fort, and saw our men running down the bank, the rebels following them and shooting them after they had surrendered.
Question. What number do you suppose the rebels killed after they had surrendered?
Answer. I could not say, only from what I saw the next day when I went ashore.
Question. You were there the next day?
Answer. Yes, sir; we came in under a flag of truce.
Question. What did you see?
Answer. Captain Marshall sent me out with a detail of men to collect the wounded and bury the dead. We buried some 70 or 80 bodies, 11 white men and one white woman.
Question. Did you bury any officers?

Answer. No, sir; I buried none of them. They were buried by the rebels.

Question. Did you observe how the dead had been buried by the rebels?

Answer. Yes, sir; I saw those in the trench. Some had just been thrown in the trench at the end of the fort—white and black together—and a little dirt thrown over them; some had their hands or feet or face out. I should judge there were probably 100 bodies there. They had apparently thrown them in miscellaneously, and thrown a little dirt over them, not covering them up completely.

Question. Did you see or hear anything there that led you to believe that any had been buried before they were dead?

Answer. I did not see any myself, but I understand from a number of others that they had seen it, and had dug one out of the trench who was still alive.

Question. Did you see any peculiar marks of barbarity, as inflicted upon the dead?

Answer. I saw none that I noticed, except in the case of one black man that I took up off a tent floor. He lay on his back, with his arms stretched out. Part of his arms were burned off, and his legs were burned nearly to a crisp. His stomach was bare. The clothes had either been torn off, or burned off. In order to take away the remains, I slipped some pieces of board under him, and when we took him up the boards of the tent came up with him; and we then observed that nails had been driven through his clothes and his cartridge-box, so as to fasten him down to the floor. His face was not burned, but was very much distorted, as if he had died in great pain. Several others noticed the nails through his clothes which fastened him down.

Question. Do you think there can be any doubt about his having been nailed to the boards?

Answer. I think not, from the fact that the boards came up with the remains as we raised them up; and we then saw the nails sticking through his clothes, and into the boards.

Question. Did you notice any other bodies that had been burned?

Answer. Yes, sir; I buried four that had been burned.

Question. What was the appearance of them?

Answer. I did not notice any particular appearance about them, except that they had been burned.

Question. How came they to be burned?

Answer. They were in the tents, inside of the fort, which had been burned. I am certain that there were four that lay where the tent had been burned, for there were the remains of the boards under them, which had not been fully burned. Those that were burned in the fort were black men.

Charles Hicks, sworn and examined.

By the chairman:

Question. Were you on the ground after the battle of Fort Pillow?

Answer. Yes, sir; the day after the battle.

Question. What did you see there?

Answer. A great many dead men.

Question. Did you see any man there that had been nailed down to a board and burned?

Answer. Yes, sir; I saw the nails through his clothes after he was taken up.

Question. In what position did he lie?

Answer. On his back. There were nails through his clothes and through the cartridge-box.

Question. So that it fastened him to the boards in such a way that he could not get up, even if he had been alive?

Answer. Yes, sir, in just that way.

Question. When you tried to take him up you raised the boards with him?

Answer. Yes, sir.

A. H. Hook, sworn and examined.

By the chairman:

Question. Did you see the man that Charles Hicks has just spoken of?

Answer. Yes, sir; I saw him. His body was partly burned, and I saw the nails through his clothes, and into the floor of the tent.

Question. The tent had been burned?

Answer. Yes, sir; there were three or four bodies burned there, but this man in particular was nailed down.

George Mantell, sworn and examined.

By the chairman:

Question. Were you on the ground at Fort Pillow at the time that these men, who have just testified, spoke of?

Answer. Yes, sir.

Question. You have heard their testimony?

Answer. Yes, sir.

Question. Do you agree with them?

Answer. Yes, sir; I saw the same.

Sergeant Henry F. Weaver, sworn and examined

By Mr. Gooch:

Question. To what company and regiment do you belong?

Answer. To company C, 6th United States heavy artillery, colored. I am a sergeant.

Question. You were here at Fort Pillow at the time of the fight?

Answer. Yes, sir.

Question. State briefly what you saw, particularly after the capture.

Answer. The rebels charged after the flag of truce, the Tennessee cavalry broke, and was followed down the hill by the colored soldiers. They all appeared to go about the same time, as near as I could tell in the excitement of the battle. I came down the hill to the river and jumped into the water, and hid myself between the bank and the coal barge. They were shooting the negroes over my head all the time, and they were falling off into the water. The firing ceased a little, and I began to get out. I saw one of the rebels and told him I would surrender. He said, "We do not shoot white men." I went up to him and he ordered me away; he kept on shooting the negroes. There were six or eight around there, and he and another one shot them all down. I went up about a rod further and met another rebel, who robbed me of watch, money, and everything else, and then he left me. I went on to the quartermaster's building below here, and was taken by another rebel and taken up into the town. He went into a store and I went in with him. He went to pillaging. I slipped on some citizen's clothing, and it was not long before I saw that they did not know who I was. I staid with them until the sun was about an hour high, and then I went away. I walked off just as if I had a right to go.

Question. Where did you go?

Answer. I went down the river, just back of the old river batteries. I then got on board a tug-boat and came down here, and the Sunday afterwards went to Memphis.

Question. Did you have any conversation with these rebels?

Answer. Not anything of any consequence about the fight.

Question. What were they doing when you were with them?

Answer. Just pillaging the store. They commenced going down to the river, and I came down with them. They went into the quartermaster's department and went a carrying off things.

Question. Did they give any quarter to the negroes?

Answer. No, sir.

Question. Did the negroes throw away their arms?

Answer. Yes, sir; and some of them went down on their knees begging for their lives. I saw one shot three times before he was killed.

By the chairman:

Question. What number of our troops do you suppose were killed before the fort was captured?

Answer. I could not tell exactly, but I do not think over a dozen of the cavalry were killed, and probably not more than fifteen or twenty of the negroes. There were a great many of the negroes wounded, because they would keep getting up to shoot, and were where they could be hit.

Question. The rebels must have killed a great many of the white men after they had surrendered?

Answer. Yes, sir. I saw yesterday afternoon a great number of cavalry taken up, and almost every one was shot in the head. A great many of them looked as if their heads had been beaten in.

Question. That must have been done after the fort had been captured?

Answer. Yes, sir; two-thirds of them must have been killed after the fort was taken.

Question. Do you know why the gunboat did not fire upon the rebels after the fort was captured, while they were shooting down our men?

Answer. They could not do that without killing our own men, too, as they were all mixed up together.

Charles A. Schetky, sworn and examined.

By the chairman:

Question. What is your position?

Answer. I am acting ensign of the gunboat New Era.

Question. Were you here at the time of the attack on Fort Pillow?

Answer. Yes, sir.

Question. State what you saw after the fort was captured.

Answer. After the flag was down I saw the rebels pouring down their bullets on our troops under the hill, although they were unarmed, and held up their hands in token of surrender.

Question. Were they shooting the black men only, or the black and white together?

Answer. The black and white were both together under the hill, and the sick and wounded were there, too.

Question. How many do you think you saw shot in that way?

Answer. I should think I saw not less than fifty shot.

Question. How many white men among those?

Answer. I could not tell. I judge that the number of whites and blacks were nearly equal.

Question. You were here the day after the fight?

Answer. Yes, sir, but I was not ashore at all that day. My duty kept me on board the boat all the time.

Frank Hogan, (colored,) sworn and examined.

By the chairman:

Question. Were you at Fort Pillow on the day of the fight?

Answer. Yes, sir.

Question. In what company and regiment?

Answer. Company A, 6th United States heavy artillery.

Question. What did you see there that day, especially after the fort was taken?

Answer. I saw them shoot a great many men after the fort was taken, officers and private soldiers, white and black.

Question. After they had given up?

Answer. Yes, sir. I saw them shoot a captain in our battalion, about a quarter of an hour after he had surrendered. One of the secesh called him up to him, and asked him if he was an officer of a nigger regiment. He said, "Yes," and then they shot him with a revolver.

Question. Did they say anything more at the time they shot him?

Answer. Yes, sir; one of them said, "God damn you, I will give you a nigger officer." They talked with him a little time before they shot him. They asked him how he came to be there, and several other questions, and then asked if he belonged to a nigger regiment, and then they shot him. It was a secesh officer who shot him. I was standing a little behind.

Question. What was the rank of the secesh officer?

Answer. He was a first lieutenant. I do not know his name.

Question. Do you know the name of the officer he shot?

Answer. Yes, sir; Captain Carson, company D.

Question. Why did they not shoot you?

Answer. I do not know why they didn't.

Question. How long did you stay with them?

Answer. I staid with them two nights and one day. They took me on Tuesday evening, and I got away from them Thursday morning, about two hours before daylight. They were going to make an early move that morning, and they sent me back for some water, and I left with another boy in the same company with myself.

Question. Where did you go then?

Answer. Right straight through the woods for about three or four miles, and then we turned to the right and came to a road. We crossed the road, went down about three miles, and crossed it again, and I kept on, backwards and forwards, until I got to a creek about five or six miles from here.

Question. Do you know anything of the rebels burning any of the tents that had wounded men in them?

Answer. I know they set some on fire that had wounded men in them, but I did not see them burn, because they would not let us go around to see.

Question. About what time of the day was that?

Answer. It was when the sun was about an hour or three-quarters on from the day of the battle.

Question. Did you hear the men in there after they set the building on fire?

Answer. Yes, sir; I heard them in there. I knew they were in there. I knew that they were there sick. I saw them shoot one or two men who came out of the hospital, and then they went into the tents, and then shot them right in the tents. I saw them shoot two of them right in the head. When they charged the fort they did not look into the tents, but when they came back afterwards they shot those sick men in the head. I knew the men, because they belonged to the company I did. One of them was named Dennis Gibbs, and the other was named Alfred Flag.

Question. How long had they been sick?

Answer. They had been sick at the hospital in Memphis, and had got better a little, and been brought up here, but they never did any duty here, and went to the hospital. They came out of the hospital and went into these tents, and were killed there. They were in the hospital the morning of the fight. When the fight commenced, they left the hospital and came into the tents inside the fort.

Question. Did you see them bury any of our men?

Answer. I saw them put them in a ditch. I did not see them cover them up.

Question. Were they all really dead or not?

Answer. I saw them bury one man alive, and heard the secesh speak about it as much as twenty times. He was shot in the side, but he was not dead, and was breathing along right good.

Question. Did you see the man?

Answer. Yes, sir.

Question. How came they to bury him when he was alive?

Answer. They said he would die any how, and they would let him stay. Every once in a while, if they put dirt on him, he would move his hands. I was standing right there, and saw him when they put him in, and saw he was not dead.

Question. Have you seen the three bodies that are now lying over beyond the old hospital?

Answer. Yes, sir.

Question. Did you know them?

Answer. I knew one of them. I helped to take him to the hospital on the Sunday before the fight. There was another man there. I knew the company he belonged to, (company B,) but I do not know his name. He was a colored man, but he had hair nearly straight, like a white man or an Indian. He had been sick a great while.

Captain James Marshall, recalled.

By the chairman:

Question. Does this witness (Hogan) speak of the same men that you supposed were fleeing from the hospital when they were killed?

Answer. Yes, sir, the same men.

Frank Hogan, resumed.

By the chairman:

Question. What did they do with the prisoners they took away with them?

Answer. I saw several officers of our regiment, and some of the men.

Question. Did you hear anything said about Major Bradford?

Answer. The first night after they had taken the fort, Major Bradford was there without any guard. Colonel McCullough waked us up to make a fire, and Major Bradford walked up and asked the liberty to go out a while. He came back, and I went to sleep, leaving Major Bradford sitting at the fire. When they waked up the next morning, they asked where Major Bradford was, and I told them he was lying there by the fire. They uncovered the head of the man who was lying there, but they said it was not Major Bradford. That was only a short distance from here. I did not see him afterwards.

Alfred Coleman, (colored,) sworn and examined.

By Mr. Gooch:

Question. To what company and regiment do you belong?

Answer. Company B, 6th United States heavy artillery.

Question. Were you at Fort Pillow at the time of the fight?

Answer. Yes, sir.

Question. Were you captured here?

Answer. Yes, sir.

Question. About what time?

Answer. About six o'clock, I should think.

Question. Where did they take you to?

Answer. Out towards Brownsville, between twelve and eighteen miles.

Question. What did you do after you were captured?

Answer. I helped to bury some of the dead; then I came to the commissary store, and helped to carry out some forage.

Question. Did you hear the rebels say anything about a fight?

Answer. Nothing more than it was the hardest fight they had been in, with the force we had here. I was then with the 2d Missouri cavalry.

Question. What did they say about giving quarter?

Answer. They said they would show no quarter to colored troops, nor to any of the officers with them, but would kill them all.

Question. Who said that?

Answer. One of the captains of the 2d Missouri. He shot six himself, but, towards evening, General Forrest issued an order not to kill any more negroes, because they wanted them to help to haul the artillery out.

Question. How do you know that?

Answer. This captain said so.

Question. Were colored men used for that purpose?

Answer. Yes, sir. I saw them pulling the artillery, and I saw the secesh whip them as they were going out, just like they were horses.

Question. How many men did you see that way?

Answer. There were some ten or twelve men hold of a piece that I saw coming out. The secesh said they had been talking about fighting under the black flag, but that they had come as nigh fulfilling that here as if they had a black flag.

Question. How long did you stay with them?

Answer. I was taken on the Tuesday evening after the fight, and remained with them until about an hour before day of Thursday morning. I then took a sack of corn to feed the horses, and got the horses between me and them, and, as it was dark and drizzling rain, I left them and escaped.

Question. Did you see any of the shooting going on?

Answer. Yes, sir. I was lying right under the side of the hill where the most of the men were killed. I saw them take one of the Tennessee cavalry, who was wounded in one leg, so that he could not stand on it. Two men took him, and made him stand up on one leg, and then shot him down. That was about four o'clock in the afternoon.

Question. How many do you think you saw them shoot?

Answer. The captain that carried me off shot six colored men himself, with a revolver. I saw him shoot them. I cannot state about the rest.

Question. Did you see more than one white man shot?

Answer. No, sir. The others that were killed were a little nearer the water than I was. I was lying down under a white-oak log near the fort, and could not see a great way.

Question. Do you know how many of their men were lost?

Answer. I heard some of them say, when they went out towards Brownsville, that they had lost about 300 killed, wounded, and missing.

Question. How many of our men were killed before the fort was taken?

Answer. I do not think there were more than ten or fifteen men killed before the fort was taken.

MEMPHIS, TENNESSEE, *April* 26, 1864.

Lieutenant Colonel Thomas H. Harris, sworn and examined.

By the chairman:

Question. What is your rank and position in the service?

Answer. I am a lieutenant colonel and assistant adjutant general of the 16th army corps.

Question. How many troops do your records show to have gone from the 6th United States heavy artillery (colored) to Fort Pillow?

Answer. There were 221 officers and men left Memphis to go to Fort Pillow.

Question. How many whites went there?

Answer. None were sent from here. I understand, unofficially, that the colored troops were recruited, to some extent, after they arrived at Fort Pillow; but I have no official knowledge of that fact. Of the 221 officers and men who went from here, there are thirty here who escaped, and some twenty or more above at Mound City and Cairo.

Question. Do you know what was the character and military experience of Major Bradford?

Answer. To the best of my knowledge and belief, Major Bradford had no military experience. I had known him for about a year. He never claimed to have had any military experience.

Question. What was the character of Major Booth as a military man?

Answer. It was good. He was originally sergeant major of the 1st Missouri light artillery, and was an officer of experience and tried courage, and of irreproachable character.

Question. Do you know whether or not any information was received here that Fort Pillow was threatened before it was actually attacked?

Answer. I know that Major Booth assured General Hurlbut that he stood in no danger, and begged him not to feel any apprehension. General Hurlbut, I believe, answered that report by sending Major Booth two additional guns, with a fresh supply of ammunition.

Question. How long have you been here in this department?

Answer. Since the 1st of August, 1862.

Question. Have you, during that time, been familiar with the condition of the garrison at Fort Pillow?

Answer. I have been familiar with it since the 1st of May, 1863.

Question. Has the garrison been entirely withdrawn from Fort Pillow at any time since then?

Answer. Yes, sir.

Question. Why?

Answer. In order to send troops for the Meridian expedition into Mississippi, under General Sherman.

Question. For how long a period was Fort Pillow without a garrison?

Answer. Fort Pillow was evacuated about the 25th of January, 1864, and remained unoccupied for a short time afterwards.

Question. Why was a garrison again placed there?

Answer. Major Bradford was with his command at and near Columbus and Paducah, Kentucky, in the early part of this year. Finding recruiting very difficult there, he applied for permission to proceed to Fort Pillow and establish his headquarters there, as he believed that he could easily fill his regiment at that point.

Question. It was then occupied rather as a recruiting station than for any other purpose at that time?

Answer. Yes, sir.

Question. Do you know whether it has been considered a military necessity to keep a garrison at Fort Pillow since the gunboats have been in the river?

Answer. It is one of the most important points on the whole river. It commands a very long stretch of the river, and a single well-manned field-piece there would stop navigation entirely.

Question. When the garrison was removed from Fort Pillow, was it in pursuance of any order from either General Grant or General Sherman?

Answer. I cannot answer that definitely without looking at the records.

Papers forwarded by Lieutenant Colonel Harris to Washington.

HEADQUARTERS 16TH ARMY CORPS,
Memphis, Tennessee, April 26, 1864.

I wish to state that one section of company D, 2d United States light artillery, colored, (1 commissioned officer and 40 men,) were sent to Fort Pillow about February 15, as part of the garrison.

The garrison of Fort Pillow, by last reports received, consisted of the 1st battalion 6th United States heavy artillery, colored, eight commissioned officers and 213 enlisted men; one section company D, 2d United States light artillery, colored, one commissioned officer and forty men; 1st batallion 13th Tennessee cavalry, Major H. F. Bradford, ten commissioned officers and 285 enlisted men.

Total white troops	295
Total colored troops	262
	557

Six field pieces: two 6-pounders, two 12-pounder howitzers, and two 10-pounder Parrotts.

T H. HARRIS,
Lieutenant Colonel and Assistant Adjutant General.

HEADQUARTERS 16TH ARMY CORPS,
Memphis, Tennessee, March 28, 1864.

SIR: You will proceed with your own battalion to Fort Pillow, and establish your force in garrison of the works there. As you will be, if I am correct in my memory, the senior officer at that post, you will take command, conferring, however, freely and fully with Major Bradford, 13th Tennessee cavalry, whom you will find a good officer, though not of much experience.

There are two points of land fortified at Fort Pillow, one of which only is now held by our troops. You will occupy both, either with your own troops alone, or holding one with yours, and giving the other in charge to Major Bradford.

The positions are commanding and can be held by a small force against almost any odds.

I shall send you at this time two 12-pound howitzers, as I hope it will not be necessary to mount heavy guns.

You will, however, immediately examine the ground and the works, and if, in your opinion, 20-pound Parrotts can be advantageously used, I will order them to you. My own opinion is, that there is not range enough. Major Bradford is well acquainted with the country, and should keep scouts well out and forward; all information received direct to me.

I think Forrest's check at Paducah will not dispose him to try the river again, but that he will fall back to Jackson and thence cross the Tennessee; as soon as this is ascertained I shall withdraw your garrison.

Nevertheless, act promptly in putting the works into perfect order, and the post into its strongest defence. Allow as little intercourse as possible with the country, and cause all supplies which go out to be examined with great strictness. No man whose loyalty is questionable should be allowed to come in or go out while the enemy is in West Tennessee.

Your obedient servant,

S. A. HURLBUT,
Major General.

Major L. F. Booth,
Com'dg 1st Batt. 1st Alabama Siege Artillery.

Headquarters 16th Army Corps,
Memphis, Tennessee, April 26, 1864.

A true copy.

T. H. HARRIS,
Assistant Adjutant General.

[Extract.]

Headquarters Fort Pillow,
Fort Pillow, Tennessee, April 3, 1864.

General: * * * * * * * *

Everything seems to be very quiet within a radius of from thirty to forty miles around, and I do not think any apprehensions need be felt or fears entertained in reference to this place being attacked, or even threatened. I think it perfectly safe.

I have the honor to be, general, very respectfully, your obedient servant,

T. F. BOOTH,
Major 6th U. S. Heavy Artillery, colored, Com'dg Fort.

Major General Hurlbut.

Headquarters 16th Army Corps,
Memphis, Tennessee, April 25, 1864.

A true extract from the last report received from Major L. F. Booth, 6th United States heavy artillery, commanding Fort Pillow.

T. H. HARRIS,
Lieutenant Colonel and Assistant Adjutant General.

Without application or requisition being made for the guns, General Hurlbut concluded to add two to the four already at the fort, and made the following order:

Special Orders, No. 88.

Headquarters 16th Army Corps,
Memphis, Tennessee, April 7, 1864.

* * * * * * * * * * *

III. Captain J. C. Heely, commanding ordnance depot, Memphis, Tennessee, will turn over to Major L. F. Booth, 6th United States heavy artillery, two 10-pounder Parrott guns, complete, except caissons, with 150 rounds of ammunition per piece, and will ship same, to-day, to Major Booth, at Fort Pillow, Tennessee. The quartermaster's department will furnish necessary transportation.

* * * * * * * * * *

By order of Major General S. A. Hurlbut.

T. H. HARRIS,
Assistant Adjutant General.

A true copy.

T. H. HARRIS,
Assistant Adjutant General.

UNITED STATES STEAMER SILVER CLOUD,
Off Memphis, Tennessee, April 14, 1864.

SIR: In compliance with your request that I would forward to you a written statement of what I witnessed and learned concerning the treatment of our troops by the rebels at the capture of Fort Pillow by their forces under General Forrest, I have the honor to submit the following report:

Our garrison at Fort Pillow, consisting of some 350 colored troops and 200 of the 13th Tennessee cavalry, refusing to surrender, the place was carried by assault about 3 p. m. of the 12th instant. I arrived off the fort at 6 a. m. on the morning of the 13th instant. Parties of rebel cavalry were picketed on the hills around the fort, and shelling those away, I made a landing and took on board some twenty of our troops, some of them badly wounded, who had concealed themselves along the bank, and came out when they saw my vessel. Whilst doing so I was fired upon by rebel sharpshooters posted on the hills, and one wounded man limping down to the vessel was shot. About 8 a. m. the enemy sent in a flag of truce, with a proposal from General Forrest that he would put me in possession of the fort and the country around until 5 p. m., for the purpose of burying our dead and removing our wounded, whom he had no means of attending to. I agreed to the terms proposed, and hailing the steamer Platte Valley, which vessel I had convoyed up from Memphis, I brought her alongside, and had the wounded brought down from the fort and battle-field and placed on board of her. Details of rebel soldiers assisted us in this duty, and some soldiers and citizens on board the Platte Valley volunteered for the same purpose.

We found about seventy wounded men in the fort and around it, and buried, I should think, 150 bodies. All the buildings around the fort, and the tents and huts in the fort, had been burned by the rebels, and among the embers the charred remains of numbers of our soldiers, who had suffered a terrible death in the flames, could be seen.

All the wounded, who had strength enough to speak, agreed that after the fort was taken an indiscriminate slaughter of our troops was carried on by the enemy, with a furious and vindictive savageness which was never equalled by the most merciless of the Indian tribes. Around on every side horrible testimony to the truth of this statement could be seen.

Bodies with gaping wounds, some bayoneted through the eyes, some with skulls beaten through, others with hideous wounds, as if their bowels had been ripped open with Bowie knives, plainly told that but little quarter was shown to our troops, strewn from the fort to the river bank, in the ravines and hollows, behind logs and under the brush, where they had crept for protection from the assassins who pursued them. We found bodies bayoneted, beaten, and shot to death, showing how cold-blooded and persistent was the slaughter of our unfortunate troops. Of course, when a work is carried by assault there wlll always be more or less blood shed, even when all resistance has ceased; but here there were unmistakable evidences of a massacre carried on long after any resistance could have been offered, with a cold-blooded barbarity and perseverance which nothing can palliate.

As near as I can learn, there were about 500 men in the fort when it was stormed. I received about 100 men, (including the wounded and those I took on board before the flag of truce was sent in.) The rebels I learned had few prisoners, so that at least 300 of our troops must have been killed in this affair. I have the honor to forward a list of the wounded officers and men received from the enemy under flag of truce.

I am, general, your obedient servant,

W. FERGUSON,

Acting Master U. S. N., Com'dg U. S. Steamer Silver Cloud.

Major General HURLBUT,

Commanding 16th Army Corps.

HEADQUARTERS 16TH ARMY CORPS,
Memphis, Tennessee, April 24, 1864.

A true copy.

T. H. HARRIS,
Assistant Adjutant General.

W. R. McLagan sworn, and examined.

By Mr. Gooch:

Question. Where were you born?

Answer. In Tennessee.

Question. Where do you now reside?

Answer. St. Paul, Minnesota.

Question. Were you at Fort Pillow on the day of its capture?

Answer. No, sir.

Question. Where were you?

Answer. About sixteen miles off, at Covington.

Question. Have you seen that statement? (showing witness statement appended to this deposition.)

Answer. Yes, sir; I made that statement myself.

Question. It is correct then?

Answer. Yes, sir.

Question. Did you yourself see Major Bradford shot?

Answer. I did.

Question. How do you know it was Major Bradford?

Answer. He represented himself to me as a Major Bradford?

Question. Did you have any conversation with him?

Answer. Yes, sir; and while we were marching from Covington to Brownsville I heard them call him Major Bradford. He told me himself that he was Major Bradford, but he did not wish it to be known, as he had enemies there; and it never would have been known but for a detective in the confederate army from Obion county, Tennessee, named Willis Wright, who recognized him as Major Bradford, and told them of it. Wright is a notorious spy and smuggler in Forrest's command. There is no doubt that the man was Major Bradford.

Question. Was there anything said at the time he was shot?

Answer. Nothing more than what I said.

Question. What did he say?

Answer. He simply said that he had fought them honorably and as a brave man, and wished to be treated as a prisoner of war. He was taken prisoner at

Fort Pillow, and was then sent to Covington, to the custody of a Colonel Duckworth, commanding the 7th Tennessee rebel cavalry, and from that place he was sent under guard, with about thirty of us conscripts. We arrived at Brownsville on the 13th; we started out on the evening of the 14th instant, about dusk. Previous to our leaving Brownsville, five of the guards were ordered back to Duckworth's headquarters. Those five guards seemed to have received special instructions about something, I don't know what. After marching about five miles from Brownsville, we halted, that is, the two companies of the rebels. These five guards then took Major Bradford out about fifty yards from the road. He seemed to understand what they were going to do with him. He asked for mercy, and said that he had fought them manfully, and wished to be treated as a prisoner of war. Three of the five guards shot him. One shot struck him about in the temple; a second in the left breast, and the third shot went through the thick part of the thigh. He was killed instantly. They left his body lying there. I escaped from the rebels at Jackson. I left on the Friday morning about 2 o'clock, and Saturday night about 12 o'clock I came back where the murder was committed, and saw his body there, yet unburied. The moon was shining brightly, and it seemed to me that the buzzards had eaten his face considerably.

Question. Did you hear them give any reason for shooting Major Bradford?

Answer. Simply that he was a Tennessee traitor, and to them they showed no quarter. They said that he was a Tennessean, and had joined the Yankee army, and they showed them no quarter. I think myself that the order for shooting Major Bradford was given by Colonel Duckworth, for the reasons I have stated.

Question. What was the officer in command at the time he was shot?

Answer. A lieutenant went out with him. He was one of the five guards.

Question. Who commanded the two companies of rebels?

Answer. I do not know who ranked in these two companies. Russell and Lawler commanded the companies. Duckworth, who, I think, gave the order for killing Major Bradford, belongs to Chalmers's command. He is a notorious scoundrel. He never had any reputation, either before the war or afterward.

Question. Did Major Bradford have on his uniform?

Answer. No, sir. He had tried to conceal his identity as much as possible, by putting on citizen's clothes, as he said that he had enemies among them, who would kill him if they knew him.

Question. Did you hear any of their officers say anything as to the manner in which they treated our soldiers whom they had captured, and the way in which they intended to treat them?

Answer. On the evening of the 12th I was in Colonel Duckworth's headquarters. I had not been conscripted then. I saw a despatch there from Forrest to Duckworth, dated that afternoon. It read something like this:

"Colonel W. L. Duckworth, Covington, Tennessee. I have killed 300 and captured 300."

Duckworth remarked to me previous to the attack that no quarter would be shown at Fort Pillow at all; that they were a set of damned Yankees and Tennessee traitors there, and they intended to show them no quarter.

Question. When did he say this?

Answer. On the evening of the 11th of April, at Covington.

Question. How long had you known Duckworth?

Answer. I never saw him before I saw him there.

Question. Did he say this to you?

Answer. I was not in conversation with him, but I heard him say this to a Captain Hill, a retired confederate captain, who formerly belonged to his command. He was within five or six feet of me when he said it.

Question. Were they talking at that time about the intended attack on Fort Pillow?

Answer. Yes, sir; and five days' rations were ordered then, and Duckworth said they were going to take Fort Pillow, and no quarter would be shown at all.

Question. Do you know how Major Bradford got to Covington, and when?

Answer. I think he arrived there on the evening of the 12th, just about dusk.

Question. Did Major Bradford state to you that he desired to disguise himself?

Answer. Yes, sir. He said that he had personal enemies in that command, among whom was this Willis Wright, who recognized him and told them who he was. Major Bradford was a native Tennesseean.

Question. Did any of the conscripts who were with you see Major Bradford shot?

Answer. Yes, sir; and I understand that one or two others, who escaped when I did, are here in the city; and I shall try to get their statements.

W. R. McLagan, a citizen of the United States, being first duly sworn, states, upon oath, that for the last two years he has been trading between St. Louis, Missouri, and Covington, Tennessee; that at the time of the attack upon Fort Pillow, April 12, 1864, he was at Covington, Tennessee, and was taken by General Forrest as a conscript on the 13th of April, with about thirty other citizens; that on the evening of the 12th of April Major Bradford, 13th Tennessee cavalry, United States forces, arrived at Covington, under guard, as a prisoner of war, and was reported as such to Colonel Duckworth, commanding 7th Tennessee cavalry, confederate forces; that on the 13th of April Major Bradford and the conscripts, including the affiant, were placed in charge of two companies of the 7th Tennessee cavalry, Captains Russell and Lawler commanding. They were taken to Brownsville, Tennessee, and started from there to Jackson, Tennessee. When they had proceeded about five miles from Brownsville a halt was made, and Major Bradford was taken about fifty yards from the command by a guard of five confederate soldiers in charge of a lieutenant, and was there deliberately shot, three of the confederate soldiers discharging their fire-arms, all of which took effect, killing him instantly. This was on the 14th day of April, 1864, near dusk; that the body of Major Bradford was left unburied in the woods about fifty yards from the road. The affiant, with the other conscripts, were taken on to Jackson, and on the 22d day of April the affiant and twenty-five others of the conscripts made their escape from the confederate forces at Jackson. On the way back he saw the body of Major Bradford lying in the same place where he was shot. This was on Saturday night, the 23d of April. Major Bradford, before he was shot, fell on his knees and said that he had fought them manfully, and wished to be treated as a prisoner of war.

W. R. McLAGAN.

HEADQUARTERS DISTRICT OF WEST TENNESSEE,
Memphis, Tennessee, April 25, 1864.

Subscribed and sworn to before me this day.

T. H. HARRIS,
Lieut. Col. and Ass't Adj't Gen'l 16*th Army Corps.*

APPENDIX.

The following papers and affidavits were furnished the committee by General Mason Brayman, at Cairo, and are herewith submitted:

CAIRO, *Illinois, April* 18, 1864.

We have the honor of reporting to you, as the only known survivors of the commissioned officers of the 13th Tennessee cavalry, that, on the morning of the 12th day of the present month, at about the hour of daylight, the rebels, numbering from five thousand to seven thousand, attacked our garrison at Fort Pillow, Tennessee, numbering as it did only about five hundred effective men. They at first sent in a flag of truce demanding a surrender, which Major Booth, then commanding the post, (Major Booth, of the 6th United States heavy artillery, colored,) refused. Shortly after this Major Booth was shot through the heart and fell dead. Major William F. Bradford, then commanding the 13th Tennessee cavalry, assumed command of the fort, and under his orders a continual fire was kept up until about one o'clock p. m., when our cannon and the rifles of the sharpshooters were mowing the rebels down in such numbers that they could not make an advance. The rebels then hoisted a second flag of truce and sent it in, demanding an unconditional surrender. They also threatened that if the place was not surrendered no quarter would be shown. Major Bradford refused to accept any such terms, would not surrender, and sent back word that if such were their intentions they could try it on. While this flag of truce was being sent in the rebel officers formed their forces in whatever advantageous positions they were able to select. They then formed a hollow square around our garrison, placed their sharpshooters within our deserted barracks, and directed a galling fire upon our men. They also had one brigade in the trenches just outside the fort, which had been cut by our men only a few days before, and which provided them with as good protection as that held by the garrison in the fort. Their demand of the flag of truce having been refused, the order was given by General Forrest in person to charge upon the works and show no quarter. Half an hour after the issuance of this order a scene of terror and massacre ensued. The rebels came pouring in solid masses right over the breastworks. Their numbers were perfectly overwhelming. The moment they reached the top of the walls, and commenced firing as they descended, the colored troops were panic-stricken, threw down their arms, and ran down the bluff, pursued sharply, begging for life. But escape was impossible. The confederates had apprehended such a result, and had placed a regiment of cavalry where it could cut off all effective retreat. This cavalry regiment employed themselves in shooting down the negro troops as fast as they made their appearance. The whites, as soon as they perceived they were also to be butchered inside the fort, also ran down. They had previously thrown down their arms and submitted. In many instances the men begged for life at the hands of the enemy, even on their knees. They were only made to stand upon their feet and then summarily shot down. Captain Theo. F. Bradford, of company A, 13th Tennessee cavalry, was signal-officer for the gunboat, and was seen by General Forrest with the signal flags. The general, in person, ordered Captain Bradford to be shot. He was instantly riddled with bullets, nearly a full regiment having fired their pieces upon him. Lieutenant Wilson, of company A, 13th Tennessee cavalry, was killed after he had surrendered, he having been previously wounded. Lieutenant J. C. Akerstrom, company E, 13th Tennessee cavalry, and acting regimental quartermaster, was severely wounded after he had surrendered, and then nailed to the side of a house and the house set on fire, burning him to death. Lieutenant Cord. Revelle, company E, 13th Tennessee cavalry, was shot and killed after surrender. Major William F. Bradford, commanding our forces, was fired upon after he had surrendered the garrison. The rebels told him he could not surrender. He ran into the river and swam out some fifty yards, they all the time firing at him, but failing to hit him. He was hailed by an officer and told to return to the shore. He did so. But as he neared the shore the riflemen discharged their pieces at him again. Again they missed. He ran up the hillside among the enemy with a white handkerchief in his hand in token of his surrender, but still they continued to fire upon him. There were several confederate officers standing near at the time. None of them ordered the firing to cease; but when they found they could not hit him, they allowed him to give himself up as a prisoner, and paroled him to the limits of the camp. They now claim that he violated his parole the same night and escaped. We have heard from prisoners who got away from the rebels that they took Major Bradford out in the Hatchie Bottom and there dispatched him. We feel confident that the story is true. We saw several negroes burning up in their quarters on Wednesday morning. We also saw the rebels come back that morning and shoot at the wounded. We also saw them at a distance running about hunting up wounded that they might shoot them. There were some whites also burning. The rebels went to the negro hospital, where about thirty sick were kept, and butchered them with their sabres, hacking their heads open in many instances, and then set fire to the buildings. They killed every negro soldier Wednesday morning upon whom they came. Those who were able they made stand up to be shot. In one case a white soldier was found wounded. He had been lying upon the ground nearly twenty-four hours without food or drink. He asked a rebel soldier to give him something to drink. The latter turned about upon his heel and fired three deliberate shots at him, saying, "Take that, you negro equality." The poor fellow is alive yet and in the hospital. He can tell the tale for himself. They ran a great many into the river, and shot or drowned them there. They immediately killed all the officers who were over the negro troops, excepting one who has since died from his wounds. They took out from Fort Pillow about one hundred and some odd prisoners, (white,) and forty negroes. They hung and shot the negroes as they passed along toward Brownsville until they were rid of them all. Out of the six hundred troops (convalescents included) which were at the fort they have only about one hundred prisoners, (all whites,) and we have about fifty wounded who are paroled.

Major Anderson, Forrest's assistant adjutant general, stated that they did not consider colored men as soldiers, but as property, and as such, being used by our people, they had destroyed them. This was concurred in by Forrest, Chalmers, and McCullough, and other officers.

We respectfully refer you to the accompanying affidavit of Hardy N. Revelle, lettered "A," and those of Mrs. Rufin, lettered "B," and Mrs. Williams, lettered "C."

Respectfully submitted.

F. A. SMITH,
First Lieut. Co. D, 13th Tenn. Vol. Cavalry.
WILLIAM CLEARY,
Second Lieut. Co. B. 13th Tenn. Vol. Cavalry.

General M. BRAYMAN.

A true copy.

C. B. SMITH,
Lieutenant and A. D. C.

Affidavit of Hardy N. Revelle.

I was in business at Fort Pillow previous to the fight on Tuesday last. Was engaged as a dry-goods clerk for Messrs. Harris & Co. Went into the fight at six o'clock on the morning of Tuesday, the 12th of April. Remained outside of the federal fortifications until about 8.30 a. m., acting as a sharpshooter. At this time we were all ordered within the fort. Lieutenant Barr was killed outside the fort, also Lieutenant Wilson, latter of the 13th Tennessee cavalry. It was not long after nine o'clock that I took my position behind the fortifications and resumed the fight. I was standing not more than ten paces from Major Booth when he fell, struck in the heart by a musket bullet. It was but a few minutes past nine. He did not die immediately, but was borne from the field. At this time there was continued firing on both sides. Rebels were not using artillery; our troops were.

The next thing I recollect is a flag of truce coming in, the bearers of which—General Forrest of the rebel army, and some parties of his staff—demanded a surrender of the garrison. Major Bradford was then in command. Forrest did not come within the breastworks, but remained some fifty yards outside, and Major Bradford went out to meet him. They conferred in a southeasterly direction from what was known as "old headquarters." Bradford is said to have replied that he would not surrender. Forrest told him that if he did not there would not be any quarter shown. They were in conference about fifteen minutes, during which time there was a cessation of firing. Bradford asked for one hour's time in which to confer with the commander of the gunboat. Forrest refused it; but I think there was a pause in actual hostilities of nearly that length of time. The rebels were busily engaged in plundering our hastily deserted encampment outside the fortifications, as well as robbing some of the stores below the hill. They were also massing their troops and placing them in eligible positions while the flag of truce was being considered. It is my opinion that they could never have gained the positions had they not done so under that flag of truce. They had already consumed seven or eight hours in attempting it with no success.

At about half-past two in the afternoon a large force of infantry came upon us from the ravine toward the east of where I stood. It seemed to come down Cold creek. They charged upon our ranks. Another large force of rebel cavalry charged from the south of east, and another force from the northward. They mounted the breastworks at the first charge where I stood. We fired upon them while upon the breastworks. I remember firing two shots while the enemy were upon the walls. The negro troops, frightened by the appearance of such numbers, and knowing they could no longer resist, made a break and ran down the hill, surrendering their arms as the rebels came down on our side of the fortifications. When we found there was no quarter to be shown, and that, white and black, we were to be butchered, we also gave up our arms and passed down the hill. It is stated that at this time Major Bradford put a white handkerchief on his sword point and waved it in token of submission; but it was not heeded if he did. We were followed closely and fiercely by the advancing rebel forces, their fire never ceasing at all. Our men had given signals themselves that they surrendered, many of them throwing up their hands to show they were unarmed and submitted to overwhelming odds.

I was about half way down the hill, partially secreted in a kind of ravine with Dr. Fitch, when I saw two men, white men, belonging to the 13th Tennessee cavalry, standing behind a stump on which they had fixed a white handkerchief, their hands thrown up. They asked for quarter. When they stood on their feet they were exposed, and I saw them shot down by rebel soldiers and killed. A captain of the rebel troops then came where we were and ordered all the federals, white and black, to move up the hill, or he would "shoot their G–d d—d brains out." I started up the hill with a number of others, in accordance with the order. I was surrendered with our men. While going up I saw white men fall on both sides of me who were shot down by rebel soldiers who were stationed upon the brow of the hill. We were at the time marching directly toward the men who fired upon us. I do not know how many fell, but I remember to have seen four killed in this way. I also saw negroes shot down with pistols in the hands of rebels. One was killed at my side. I saw another negro struck on the head with a sabre by a rebel soldier; I suppose he was also killed. One more, just in front of me, was knocked down with the but of a musket. We kept on up the hill. I expected each moment to meet my fate with the rest. At the top of the hill I met a man named Cutler, a citizen of Fort Pillow. He spoke to a rebel captain about me, and we then went, under orders from the captain, to one of the stores under the hill, where the captain got a pair of boots. This was about 4 p. m. on Tuesday. The captain and Cutler and myself then left to find General McCullough's headquarters, where we were to report and be disposed of. The captain introduced me to a lieutenant and to a surgeon of the rebel army. The surgeon made me show him where goods could be found. The lieutenant got a saddle and bridle and some bits, and then we helped them to carry them to where their horses were outside of the fortifications. I also met Mr. Wedlin, a citizen, and he accompanied us. He helped the lieutenant to mount and pack his goods, and then he gave Wedlin and myself permission to depart, and instructed us as to the best means of escape.

I am positive that up to the time of the surrender there had not been more than fifty men (black and white) killed and wounded on the Union side. Of these, but about twenty had been among the killed. The balance of all killed and wounded on our side were killed and wounded after we had given undoubted evidence of a surrender, and contrary to all rules of warfare.

H. N. REVELLE.

Sworn to before me at Cairo, Illinois, this 17th day of April, 1864.

JNO. H. MUNROE,
Captain and A. A. Gen'l.

A true copy.

C. B. SMITH,
Lieutenant and A. D. C.

Statement of Ann Jane Rufin.

I am the wife of Thomas Rufin, a member of the 13th Tennessee cavalry; was at Fort Pillow on Tuesday, the 12th day of April, A. D. 1864, and was removed to an island during the progress of the battle. Returned to Fort Pillow on Wednesday morning, the 13th of April, and saw the remains of a man lying upon the back, its arms outstretched, with some planks under it. The man had to all appearances been nailed to the side of the house, and then the building set on fire. I am satisfied that the body was that of Lieutenant John C. Akerstrom, second lieutenant company A, 13th Tennessee cavalry, who was on duty as quartermaster of the post of Fort Pillow. I was well acquainted with Lieutenant Akerstrom when living. After examining the body I walked around to a ditch where a large number of dead and wounded had been thrown and partially covered. I saw several places where the wounded had dug holes and attempted to get out, but had been unable to do so.

her
ANN JANE × RUFIN.
mark.

CAIRO, *April* 18, 1864.

Subscribed and sworn to before me this 18th day of April, 1864.

ISAAC M. TALMADGE,
Captain and District Provost Marshal.

A true copy.

C. B. SMITH,
Lieutenant and A. D. C.

Statement of Mrs. Rebecca Williams.

I am the wife of William F. Williams, a private in the 13th Tennessee cavalry, company D.

I was at Fort Pillow on the Wednesday morning after the fight of Tuesday, the 12th of April, 1864, and saw the body of a man, which had the appearance of having been burned to death. It was pointed out to me as the body of Lieutenant John C. Akerstrom, of the 13th Tennessee cavalry. I know it was the corpse of a white man.

her
REBECCA × WILLIAMS.
mark.

CAIRO, *April* 18, 1864.

Subscribed and sworn to before me this 18th day of April, 1864.

ISAAC M. TALMADGE,
Captain and District Provost Marshal.

I, the undersigned, do certify that I also witnessed the same spectacle described by Mrs. Williams.

her
NANCY M. × HOPPER.
mark.

CAIRO, *April* 18, 1864.

Subscribed and sworn to before me this 18th day of April, 1864.

ISAAC M. TALMADGE,
Captain and District Provost Marshal.

A true copy.

C. B. SMITH,
Lieutenant and A. D. C.

James R. Brigham, a resident of Fredonia, Chautauque county, New York, deposes and says:

He was and had been a clerk in a store at Fort Pillow over a year previous to the 12th April instant. On learning, early on the morning of the 12th instant, that the post was to be attacked by the confederates, he went immediately to the fort, and was engaged with a musket in defending the fort, when General Chalmers was repulsed twice. After this, I was detailed to carry wounded down the hill, on which the fort was situated, to the river bank, where, beside a large log, I raised a red flag as a sign of a hospital. The flag was made from part of a red flannel shirt. The last attack was made by General Forrest in person, who headed the column. Forrest was wounded in three (3) different places, and had his horse shot under him.

Major Booth, of the regular army, was in command. He was killed about 11 o'clock by a sharpshooter, when Major Bradford, of the 13th Tennessee regiment, took command. Major Bradford was taken prisoner, and killed near Judge Green's, some six miles from the fort, while a prisoner.

When the confederates rushed into the fort, having taken advantage of a flag of truce to get their men close to the fort in a ravine and directly under the embankments, this force numbered some fifteen hundred, with a large reserve in sight. As soon as the confederates got into the fort, the federals threw down their arms in token of surrender, and many exclaimed, "We surrender." Immediately an indiscriminate massacre commenced on both black and white soldiers. Up to the time of the surrender, I don't think more than from twenty to twenty-five had been killed, and not more than fifteen wounded. I was taken prisoner, and when marching with other prisoners, black and white, I saw the confederates shoot and kill and wound both white and black federal prisoners. Some negroes were severely beaten, but still able to go along. We were taken a few miles into the country, when myself and a few others got relieved by General McCullough, on the ground of being private citizens. I saw General Forrest, and knew he was wounded, as before stated. There were from twenty-five to thirty black soldiers carried off as prisoners, and not over thirty to thirty-five white. All the rest of that faithful and heroic garrison, some five or six hundred in number, were killed or wounded in action, or murdered or wounded after the surrender. I saw officers as well as privates kill and wound prisoners, and heard them say, while held a prisoner with them in the country, that they intended taking the prisoners still further into the country, and make an example of them.

Captain Bradford, of the 13th Tennessee, was engaged with a blue signal flag in connexion with gunboat No. 7. Captain Bradford was ordered shot by General Forrest, who said "Shoot that man with the black flag." This was after the surrender. His body was literally shot to pieces. All, both black and white, fought manfully. I saw several negroes wounded, with blood running from their bodies, still engaged loading and firing cannon and muskets cheerfully. There was no giving way till fifteen hundred confederates rushed inside the fort. Most were killed outside the fort when prisoners. The fort was defended successfully for over eight hours by from 500 to 600 men against 3,500 to 4,000 barbarians. I heard confederate officers say it was the hardest contested engagement that Forrest had ever been engaged in. I heard officers say they would never recognize negroes as prisoners of war, but would kill them when overtaken. Even if they caught a negro with blue clothes on (uniform) they would kill him. Officers of negro troops were treated and murdered the same as negroes themselves.

After lying in the woods two days and nights, I was picked up by gunboat No. 7, some 5 or 6 miles below the fort.

On my return to the fort I saw and recognized the remains of Lieutenant Akerstrom; he had been nailed to a house and supposed burned alive.

There were the remains of two negroes lying where the house burned. I was told they were nailed to the floor. I also found a negro partially buried, with his head out of the ground, alive. I went for assistance and water for him; when I returned he was so near dead that no assistance could save him. We sat by him till he died.

I can recount but a small part of the barbarities I saw on that fatal day, when hundreds of loyal soldiers were murdered in cold blood.

JAS. R. BINGHAM.

Sworn before me at Cairo, Illinois, this 18th day of April, 1864.

JNO. H. MUNROE,
Assistant Adjutant General.

A true copy.

J. H. ODLIN,
Assistant Adjutant General.

CAIRO, ILLINOIS, *April* 23, 1864.

Elvis Bevel, being duly sworn, deposeth and says:

I am a citizen of Osceola, Arkansas. I was driven from my home by guerillas. I arrived at Fort Pillow, Tennessee, on the night of the 11th of April, 1864. I was at Fort Pillow during the engagement between the rebel forces under Forrest and Chalmers, and the United States garrison at that place, on the 12th of April instant, 1864. About sun-up, the alarm of rebels being in the fort was received at Major Booth's headquarters. I took a position where I could see all that was done by the rebel and United States forces. Deponent further saith: I saw the contraband camps in flames at different points. Could see the skirmishers of the rebels. Signals were given by Captain Bradford to Captain Marshal, of the navy, commanding gunboat No. 7, to shell them from post No. 1, which is in sight of the fort, which was done by Captain Marshall. About one hour after sunrise, brisk skirmishing began. The bullets from rebel infantry caused me to move from where I was, and take position behind a large stump near the fort. About nine o'clock I moved to the rear of the fort, where I could better see the rebels who swarmed the bluff.

The rebels were here so near the gunboat that the crew under Captain Marshall had to close their ports and use their small-arms. At one o'clock p. m the firing on both sides ceased. A flag of truce was sent from the rebel lines to demand an unconditional surrender. While the flag of truce was approaching the fort, I saw a battery of artillery moved to a better position by the rebels, and saw their sharpshooters approaching the fort from another quarter. At two o'clock the fight began again; about fifteen or twenty minutes after I saw a charge made by about two thousand on the breastworks and near it on the bluff. Sharp fighting took place inside the fort of about five minutes' duration. I saw their bayonets and swords. I saw the Union soldiers, black and white, slaughtered while asking for quarter; heard their screams for quarter, to which the rebels paid no attention. About one hundred left the fort and ran down the bank of the bluff to the river, pursued by the rebels, who surrounded them; in about twenty minutes, every one of them, as far as I could see, were shot down by the rebels without mercy.

I left at this time, getting on the gunboat. On Thursday, the 14th of April, I met Captain Farris, of Forrest's command, about six miles from Fort Pillow, at Plum point: his soldiers said they were hunting for negroes. I asked him if they took any prisoners at Fort Pillow. He said they took some of the 13th Tennessee, who surrendered, but no others.

ELVIS BEVEL.

Signed and sworn to before me this 23d day of April, A. D. 1864, at Cairo, Illinois.

C. B. SMITH,
Lieut. and A. A. A. G.

A true copy

C. B. SMITH,
Lieut. and A. D. C

Statement of Wm. B. Walker, company D, 13*th Tennessee cavalry.*

I hereby certify that I was at Fort Pillow, Tennessee, on the 12th day of the present month, when it was attacked by the confederates. I saw nothing more than has probably been related by a dozen others, until about the time of the panic and the retreat down the bluff by both white and black Union troops. We were followed closely by the rebels, and shot down, after surrender, as fast as they could find us. One of the rebels, after I had given him up my money as he had ordered me, fired upon me twice, after I had surrendered, and while I begged for my life. One ball struck me in the left eye. The rebels had almost ceased firing upon us, when an officer came down and told them to "shoot the last d—d one of us," and "not to take one prisoner." He said it was the order of the general, (I could not hear the name plainly, but I think it was Chalmers.) Then the slaughter of the prisoners was resumed. I saw some six white and ten colored soldiers thus shot, long after they had surrendered, and while the negroes were on their knees begging to be spared.

his
WILLIAM B. × WALKER.
mark.

Witness: Wm. Cleary,
2d Lieut. Co. B, 13th Tennessee Cavalry.

Mound City, *Illinois, April* 23, A. D. 1864.

Sworn and subscribed to before me this 25th day of April, 1864, at Mound City, Illinois.

WM. STANLEY,
Lieutenant and Assistant Provost Marshal.

A true copy

C. B. SMITH,
Lieutenant and A. D. C.

Statement of Jason Lonan, company B, 13th Tennessee cavalry.

I do hereby certify that I was at Fort Pillow, Tennessee, on the twelfth (12th) of the present month, when it was attacked by the rebels under General A. B. Forrest. I was ordered into the fort at the commencement of the engagement. We kept up a continual fire on both sides until about 1 o'clock p. m., when a flag of truce was sent in, and firing ceased. While the flag of truce was being considered I saw the enemy plundering our evacuated quarters, and moving their forces up in large bodies, getting them in position. We had been driving them all the morning. They were at the same time placing their sharpshooters in the buildings we had occupied as barracks. The object of the flag of truce not having been agreed to, the firing again commenced. About one hour afterwards the enemy charged on our works in overwhelming numbers, and the negro soldiers, being panic-stricken, dropped their arms and ran down the bluff. The whites also, when they found there was to be no quarter shown, also ran down the bluff. The rebels ran after us, shooting all they came to, both black and white. I also certify that I was myself shot after I had surrendered, and while I had my hands up and was imploring them to show me mercy. They also shot Sergeant Gwalthney, of my company, while he was within ten feet of me, after he had given up his revolver, and while he had his hands up crying out for mercy. They took his own revolver and shot him with its contents twice through the head, killing him instantly. I also certify that I saw the rebels shoot, in all, six men who had surrendered, and who had their hands up asking quarter. I further certify that I saw the rebels come about on the ensuing morning, the 13th day of April, A. D. 1864, and despatch several of the colored soldiers of the 6th United States heavy artillery, who had survived their wounds received on the previous day.

his
JASON + LONAN.
mark.

Witness: William Cleary,
2d Lieut. Co. B, 13th Tenn. Vol. Cav.

MOUND CITY, ILLINOIS, *April* 23, 1864.

Sworn and subscribed to before me this 23d day of April, 1864, at Mound City, Illinois.

WM. STANLEY,
Lieutenant and Assistant Provost Marshal.

A true copy.

C. B. SMITH,
Lieutenant and A. D. C.

Statement of Corporal Wm. P. Dickey, company B, 13th Tennessee cavalry.

I do hereby certify that I was at Fort Pillow, Tennessee, on the 12th day of April, A. D. 1864, when that place was attacked by the rebel General Forrest. I went into the fort at the commencement of the action. We kept up a continuous fire upon both sides until about 1 o'clock p. m., when a flag of truce was sent in by the rebels, and while it was being considered the firing was ordered to cease. I also certify that while this was going on I plainly saw the enemy consolidating their forces and gaining positions they had been endeavoring to gain without success. At the same time their men were plundering our deserted camp, and stealing goods from the quartermaster's depot, and from the stores of the merchants of the post. They also at the same time put their sharpshooters into our deserted barracks, whence they had fair view, and were in fair range of our little garrison. The firing recommenced after the flag of truce had retired About one hour thereafter the rebels stormed our works. They had no sooner obtained the top of our walls when the negroes ran, and the whites, obtaining no quarter, ran after them. The rebels followed closely, shooting down all who came in the way, white and black. I also certify that I was myself shot by a rebel soldier after I had surrendered, and while I had my hands up begging for mercy. I also certify that I saw the rebels shoot down ten men, white soldiers, within ten paces of me, while they had their hands up supplicating quarter. I also certify that I saw twelve negro soldiers killed long after they had surrendered. I also certify that I saw the rebels throw several negroes into the river while they were begging for life. One rebel came to me and took my percussion caps, saying he had been killing negroes so fast that his own had been exhausted. He added that he was going to shoot some more. I also certify that I saw negroes thrown into the river by rebels, and shot afterwards, while struggling for life.

his
WM. P. + DICKEY.
mark.

Witness: WM. CLEARY,
2d Lieut. Co. B, 13th Tenn. Vol. Cav.

MOUND CITY, *April* 23, A. D. 1864.

Sworn and subscribed to before me this 23d day of April, 1864, at Mound City, Illinois.

WM. STANLEY,
Lieutenant and Assistant Provost Marshal.

A true copy.

C. B. SMITH,
Lieutenant and A. D. C.

MOUND CITY, *April* 25, 1864.

Statement of Sergeant William A. Winn, company B, 13th Tennessee cavalry volunteers.

I was in Fort Pillow on Tuesday, the 12th of April, 1864, when the attack was made by General Forrest upon that place. At the firing of the first gun I hastened on board the gunboat, as I had been wounded some time before and could not fight. The first thing I saw afterwards was the rebel sharpshooters on the top of the hill and ours at quartermaster's department, firing at each other, and the rebels were also firing at the gunboat. The next thing I saw was a flag of truce come in, which was in waiting some half an hour. This was about one o'clock p. m., and as soon as it started back, the enemy immediately started up the hill on the double-quick, not waiting for the flag of truce to return. As soon as they came close to the fort and had their sharpshooters distributed through our barracks, (which were just outside the fort,) they opened fire upon the garrison, and then charged the works. Those troops which I saw came from the direction that the flag of truce did. I saw our men run down the bluff, the rebels after them, shooting them down as fast as they came up with them. I saw twelve or fifteen men shot down after they had surrendered, with their hands up begging for mercy. Next I saw them turn their cannon on us (the boat) and throw several shells at the boat, trying to sink her, but she steamed up the river, out of range, leaving behind us a scene of cold-blooded murder too cruel and barbarous for the human mind to express.

W. A. WINN.

Sworn and subscribed to before me this 25th day of April, 1864.

WM. STANLEY,
Lieutenant and Assistant Provost Marshal.

A true copy.

C. B. SMITH, *Lieutenant and A. D. C.*

MOUND CITY, *April* 18, 1864.

Statement of William F. Mays, company B, 13th Tennessee cavalry.

I was at Fort Pillow on the 12th of April, 1864, and engaged in the fight there. The pickets were driven in about six o'clock a. m., when skirmishers were thrown out to ascertain the position and number of the enemy. The contraband camp was then discovered to be on fire, and the firing of small-arms was heard in the same direction. The skirmishing lasted about one hour, when our skirmishers were gradually drawn back towards the fort on the bluff. They then attacked the fort. Two assaults were made by them, and both repulsed. This was about eleven or twelve o'clock a. m., when a flag of truce was sent in, demanding a surrender. While the flag was being received and the firing suspended, the enemy were moving their forces into position, and occupied one position which they had been fighting to obtain all day, but had not been able to gain, except under the protection of a flag of truce. It was from this position they made their heaviest assault, it being impossible to bring our artillery to bear upon them.

Question. Do you believe they could have taken the fort or that particular position had they not done so under cover of the flag of truce?

Answer. I do not. They had been kept from it for six hours.

Question. What further took place? Go on with your statement.

Answer. In about five minutes after the disappearance of the flag of truce, a general assault was made upon our works from every direction. They were kept at bay for some time, when the negroes gave way upon the left and ran down the bluff, leaving an opening through which the rebels entered and immediately commenced an indiscriminate slaughter of both white and black. We all threw down our arms and gave tokens of surrender, asking for quarter. (I was wounded in the right shoulder and muscle of the back, and knocked down before I threw down my gun.) But no quarter was given. Voices were heard upon all sides, crying, "Give them no quarter; kill them; kill them; it is General Forrest's orders." I saw four white men and at least twenty-five negroes shot while begging for mercy; and I saw one negro dragged from a hollow log within ten feet of where I lay, and as one rebel held him by the foot another shot him. These were all soldiers. There were also two negro women and three little children standing within twenty-five steps from me, when a rebel stepped up to them and said, "Yes, God damn you, you thought you were free, did you," and shot them all. They all fell but one child, when he knocked it in the head with the breech of his gun. They then disappeared in the direction of the landing, following up the fugitives, firing at them wherever seen. They came back in about three-quarters of an hour, shooting and robbing the dead of their money and clothes. I saw a man with a canteen upon him and a pistol in his hand. I ventured to ask him for a drink of water. He turned around, saying, "Yes, God damn you, I will give you a drink of water," and shot at my head three different times, covering my face up with dust, and then turned from me, no doubt thinking he had killed me, remarking, "God damn you, it's too late to pray now," then went on with his pilfering. I lay there until dark, feigning death, when a rebel officer came along, drawing his sabre and ordered me to get up, threatening to run his sabre into me if I did not, saying I had to march ten miles that night. I succeeded in getting up and got among a small squad he had already gathered up, but stole away from them during the night, and got among the dead, feigning death for fear of being murdered. The next morning the gunboat came up and commenced shelling them out, when I crawled out from among the dead, and with a piece of paper motioning to the boat, she came up and I crawled on board.

his
WM. F. + MAYS.
mark.

Sworn and subscribed to before me this 27th day of April, 1864.

WM. STANLEY,
Lieutenant and Assistant Provost Marshal.

A true copy.

C. B. SMITH, *Lieutenant and A. D. C.*

Official statement of facts connected with the attack, defence, and surrender of the United States military post at Union City, Tennessee, on the 24th of March, 1864.

CAIRO, ILLINOIS, *April* 4, 1864.

On the 23d of March it was generally understood at the said post that at least a portion of the rebel General Forrest's command were advancing on us. At about eight o'clock p. m. of that day the advance of the enemy were seen and fired upon, near Jacksonville, six miles from Union City, by a small scouting party sent in that direction from our post. This party reported the facts immediately to Colonel Hawkins, of the 7th Tennessee cavalry, who was commander of the post.

The picket guard was then doubled, and two or three companies were ordered to keep their horses saddled during the night.

I was notified at 4.30 a. m. of the 24th of March to order my horses saddled. About five o'clock firing commenced all around the line of pickets. The main part of company B, Captain Martin, were abreast, and a part of company I, also, I think. The remaining force, about 500 strong, were distributed around at the breastworks. The pickets were driven in, with a loss of two killed and several wounded. About 5.30 a. m. a cavalry charge was made from the south side. It was repulsed with but little difficulty. The same were immediately dismounted and charged again, this time coming within twenty or thirty yards of the breastworks. They were repulsed again, and with considerable loss this time. Immediately following this another charge was made in front, from the northwest, and again repulsed. Immediately following this, the fourth charge, and last, was made from the northeast, which charge confronted my company, and were repulsed again with loss. This charge was made at about 8 a. m. About this time the colonel came to this part of the works; I remarked to him that it was my opinion the rebels were defeated in their first programme; that they would either leave the field or assemble and make a consolidated charge. Our troops were in fine spirits. Sharpshooting lasted till 9.30 a. m., when an escort, with a flag of truce, approached my position. I sent notification to Colonel Hawkins of the approaching truce flag, and then advanced in person and halted the truce escort two hundred yards from the defences. Then Colonel Hawkins came; a document was handed him, the contents of which I know not. At this time the rebel troops were in full view, in the logs and stumps. The truce escort retired, and in twenty minutes after again came. I again halted them on the same ground as before, and remained with them during this interview. This time an order was handed to Colonel Hawkins, which I read. As near as I can remember, it read as follows:

"HEADQUARTERS CONFEDERATE STATES FORCES,
"*In the Field, March* 24, 1864.

"*Commanding Officer United States Forces, at Union City, Tennessee:*

"SIR: I have your garrison completely surrounded, and demand an unconditional surrender of your forces. If you comply with the demand, you are promised the treatment due to prisoners of war, according to usages in civilized warfare. If you persist in a defence, you must take the consequences.

"By order of

"N. B. FORREST, *Major General.*"

Then followed a council of our officers, in which a large majority violently opposed any capitulation whatever with the enemy. Notwithstanding this, the colonel made a surrender at 11 a. m., which, to the best of my knowledge and belief, was unconditional. No artillery was seen or used. The surrendered troops were very indignant on hearing of the surrender. Only one man had been killed and two or three wounded inside of the works. It was generally believed to be a rebel defeat. Our troops, after grounding arms, were marched away on foot. The rebel troops were commanded by Colonel Duckworth, and as nearly as I could estimate them, there were 800.

A list of prisoners was made on the 26th, at Trenton, which numbered 481, including ten of Hardy's men and a few of the 24th Missouri infantry, who were doing provost duty.

T. P. GRAY,
Captain, Company C, 7th Tennessee Cavalry.

HEADQUARTERS POST OF PADUCAH,
Paducah, Kentucky, April 6, 1864.

SIR: I have the honor to report in relation to the late engagement with the rebel General Forrest. On the 25th instant my scouts came in at about 12 o'clock m., bringing no news of the enemy's whereabouts. I immediately ordered out others, and directed them to proceed on the Mayfield road. They had gone but three miles when they were met by Forrest's advance guard, who fired upon them. They hurriedly fell back and gave the alarm, and in less than ten minutes after they reported, the enemy were driving in my pickets, who opened a skirmish-fire and fell back to Fort Anderson, according to previous instructions. I immediately ordered the little force under my command to double-quick to the fort, which order was promptly obeyed; yet, before they could reach there, such was the impetuosity of the attack, that their rear was fired into by the enemy.

At 2 p. m. the enemy took position surrounding the fort, and a sharp fight commenced, which in a few minutes became furious, and continued for about one hour, when it was announced that a flag of truce was approaching. I immediately ordered my men to cease firing, and sent out to meet the bearer, from whom I received the following demand for a surrender:

"HEADQUARTERS FORREST'S CAVALRY CORPS,
"*Paducah, Kentucky, March 25, 1864.*

"COLONEL: Having a force amply sufficient to carry your works and reduce the place, and in order to avoid the unnecessary effusion of blood, I demand the surrender of the fort and troops, with all public property. If you surrender, you shall be treated as prisoners of war; but if I have to storm your works, you may expect no quarter.

"N. B. FORREST,
"*Major General, Commanding Confederate Troops.*

"Colonel HICKS,
"*Commanding Federal Forces at Paducah.*"

To which I replied as follows:

"HEADQUARTERS POST OF PADUCAH,
"*Paducah, Kentucky, March 25, 1864.*

"I have this moment received yours of this instant, in which you demand the unconditional surrender of the forces under my command. I can answer that I have been placed here by my government to defend this post, and in this, as well as all other orders from my superior, I feel it to be my duty as an honorable officer to obey. I must, therefore, respectfully decline surrendering as you may require.

"Very respectfully,

"S. G. HICKS,
"*Colonel, Commanding Post.*

"Major General N. B. FORREST,
"*Commanding Confederate Forces.*"

While the flag of truce was near the fort, and during its pendency, the enemy were engaged in taking position and planting a battery. As soon as the answer was returned they moved forward, and our forces opened on them, and the fight became general. They attempted to storm our works, but were repulsed. They rallied and tried it again, and met the same fate. They made a third effort, but were forced to abandon their design. It was in this last srtuggle that Brigadier General A. P. Thompson (confederate) was killed.

I now discovered, on examination, that my ammunition was growing short, and out of 30,000 rounds, (the amount we commenced the fight with,) 27,000 had been already expended. In this emergency I ordered the remainder to be equally distributed; the men to fix their bayonets; to make good use of the ammunition they had, and, when that was exhausted, to receive the enemy on the point of the bayonet, feeling fully determined never to surrender while I had a man alive. When this order was repeated by the officers to their respective commands, it was received with loud shouts and cheers.

The enemy's sharpshooters in the mean time got possession of the houses around and near the fort, from which position they picked off some of my gunners, shooting nearly all of them in the head.

Towards dark the enemy took shelter behind houses, in rooms, and hollows, and kept up a scattering fire until half past 11 o'clock, when it entirely ceased, and the rebel general withdrew his command out of the range of my guns, and went into camp for the night.

On the morning of the 26th the enemy again made a demonstration by surrounding the fort in the distance. As soon as I discovered this, I ordered Major Barnes, of the 10th Kentucky cavalry, to send out squads to burn all the houses within musket range of the fort, from which the sharpshooters had annoyed us the day previous.

While the houses were burning General Forrest sent in a second flag of truce, with the following communication:

"HEADQUARTERS FORREST'S CAVALRY CORPS,
"*Near Paducah, Kentucky, March* 26, 1864.

"SIR: I understand you hold in your possession in the guard-house at Paducah a number of confederate soldiers as prisoners of war. I have in my possession about thirty-five or forty federal soldiers who were captured here yesterday, and about five hundred who were captured at Union City. I propose to exchange man for man, according to rank, so far as you may hold confederate soldiers.

"Respectfully, N. B. FORREST,
"*Major General, Commanding Confederate Forces.*

"Colonel S. G. HICKS,
"*Commanding Federal Forces at Paducah, Ky.*"

In answer to which I sent the following:

"HEADQUARTERS POST OF PADUCAH,
"*Paducah, Kentucky, March* 26, 1864.

"SIR: I have no power to make the exchange. If I had, I would most cheerfully do it.

"Very respectfully, S. G. HICKS,
"*Colonel* 40*th Illinois Infantry, Com'dg Post.*

"Major General N. B. FORREST,
"*Commanding Confederate Forces.*"

With the above General Forrest sent a list of the names of the prisoners captured, (!) all of whom, with one exception, were convalescents in the general hospital, and too feeble to get to the fort.

The following troops composed my command during the fight:

Companies C, H, and K, 122d Illinois infantry, commanded by Major J. F. Chapman, one hundred and twenty men; 16th Kentucky cavalry, Major Barnes commanding, two hundred and seventy-one men; 1st Kentucky heavy artillery, (colored,) two hundred and seventy-four men, commanded by Lieutenant R. D. Cunningham, of the 2d Illinois artillery, making a total of six hundred and sixty-five men.

Opposed to this was the rebel force under the command of Generals Forrest, Buford, J. G. Harris, and A. P. Thompson, of six thousand five hundred men.

The casualties of my command were fourteen killed and forty-six wounded.

The enemy's loss, according to the most reliable information that I can obtain, was three hundred killed and from one thousand to twelve hundred wounded. His killed and wounded may be safely set down at fifteen hundred.

General Forrest admitted, in conversation with some of his friends in this city, that in no engagement during the war had he been so badly cut up and crippled as at this place.

Our loss in government stores was inconsiderable. The quartermaster's depot, a temporary wooden building, was burned, and in consequence thereof a small lot of quartermaster's property was lost. Our commissary stores, and most of our government horses, mules, wagons, &c., were saved.

In justice to the officers and soldiers under my command, allow me to say they acted *well* their part, proving themselves worthy of the great cause in which they are engaged, and all deserving of the highest praise.

The three companies of the 122d Illinois were the only portion of my command that had ever been under fire before.

And here permit me to remark that I have been one of those men who never had much confidence in colored troops fighting, but those doubts are now all removed, for they fought as bravely as any troops in the fort.

The gunboats Peosta, Captain Smith, and Paw Paw, Captain O'Neal, were present and rendered valuable aid in shelling the city and operating on the flank of the enemy as they surrounded the fort.

A list of the names of the killed and wounded I will furnish hereafter.

Respectfully submitted.

S. G. HICKS,
Colonel 40th Illinois Infantry, Commanding Post.

Captain J. H. ODLIN,
Assistant Adjutant General.

HEADQUARTERS CONFEDERATE STATES,
Before Columbus, Kentucky, April 13, 1864.

Fully capable of taking Columbus and its garrison by force, I desire to avoid the shedding of blood, and therefore demand the unconditional surrender of the forces under your command. Should you surrender, the negroes now in arms will be returned to their masters. Should I, however, be compelled to take the place, no quarter will be shown to the negro troops whatever; the white troops will be treated as prisoners of war.

I am, sir, yours,

A. BUFORD, *Brigadier General.*

The COMMANDING OFFICER
United States Forces, Columbus, Kentucky.

HEADQUARTERS OF THE POST,
Columbus, Kentucky, April 13, 1864.

GENERAL: Your communication of this date to hand. In reply, I would state that, being placed by my government with adequate force to hold and repel all enemies from my post, surrender is out of the question.

I am, general, very respectfully,

WILLIAM HUDSON LAWRENCE,
Colonel 34th New Jersey Volunteers, Commanding Post.

Brigadier General A. BUFORD,
Commanding Confederate Forces before Columbus, Ky.

The following affidavit was furnished, at the request of the committee, by General W. S. Rosecrans, from St. Louis:

"HEADQUARTERS DEPARTMENT OF THE MISSOURI,
"*Saint Louis, April* 26, 1864.

"Respectfully forwarded to Hon. B. F. Wade, Cairo, Illinois, chairman congressional Committee on Conduct of the War.

"W. S. ROSECRANS,
"*Major General, Commanding.*
"By O. D. GREEN, *A. A. G.*,
"*Absence of General.*"

Statement of Edward B. Benton, upon oath, relative to the massacre by the confederate troops under General Forrest, at Fort Pillow, Tennessee.

I was born in Waltham, Vermont.

Question. Where have you resided last?

Answer. I was in Missouri engaged in furnishing beef to the government troops on the North Missouri railroad until a year ago last July. I then went down to Fort Pillow, and have been there ever since.

Question. What was your business there?

Answer. I owned 215 acres of the fort, bordering on the river, and the very land we fought on. I was putting in 100 acres of cotton just outside the fortifications, which was my principal business.

Question. You lived outside the fort?

Answer. Yes, sir—slept there. I was in the fort every day; it was only about a mile from the landing—not a mile from the fortifications.

Question. Just say when you saw Forrest's men; the day and the time of day, and what you did.

Answer. On Tuesday morning, the 12th of this month, I was awakened about five o'clock, or half past five, by a little darkey boy, who came up to my room and says: "Oh, Mr. Benton, all of Forrest's men have come, and they are just going into the fort. What will I do?" I got out of bed and looked out of the window towards the fort, and saw about three or four hundred of Forrest's men drawn up in line, and some one was making a speech to them, which was answered by cheering. They cheered, and then the pickets fired. I put some things in my valise and started for the fort in a roundabout way, and got in, by running the pickets, about six o'clock, and went immediately to Major Booth and asked for a gun, and took my stand with the soldiers inside the breastworks, where I remained and shot at every person of Forrest's men that I could get a chance at, firing forty-eight shots in all, until the flag of truce was sent in.

Question. About what was the time of day it came in?

Answer. It came in about two o'clock, I should think—half past one or two o'clock in the afternoon.

Question. Had they made any attack then?

Answer. Oh, yes, sir.

Question. Had they tried to carry the fort by storm and been repulsed?

Answer. At one time the confederate troops had all disappeared.

Question. Were four hundred all there were there?

Answer. Those were all I saw there. This was when they first made their appearance when I first saw these four hundred. After getting into the fort we saw more than a thousand coming in at the different passes, and the sharpshooters were stationed on every hill on every side of us except the river side.

Question. Do you recollect how many attacks they made to carry the fort before the flag of truce came?

Answer. It is not proper to call their fighting but one attack upon the fort, although they all, or nearly all, seemed to be driven outside the outside works at one time, and soon came back fighting harder and in greater force than before.

Question. Did they use artillery?

Answer. Yes, sir. They did not hurt us with that; they shot at the gunboats.

Question. When the flag of truce came in did they make any disposition of their troops around the fort there?

Answer. Yes, sir; after the flag of truce was sent in and the firing ceased they came up on all sides to within ten yards of the very embankments that screened us.

Question. While the flag of truce was waiting?

Answer. Yes, sir; more especially on the northern side, just under the bank looking towards Coal Creek.

Question. How long was that flag inside of our lines?

Answer. One hour was the time. I suppose it was all of an hour.

Question. Do you know the nature of it?

Answer. It was for an unconditional surrender.

Question. It was refused by Major Booth?

Answer. By Major Bradford, yes, sir. Major Booth had been killed. He asked for time to consult with the gunboat, and finally returned the answer that there was none of Hawkins's men there, and he never would surrender.

Question. Did not Major Bradford make any protest against troops coming up under the flag in that way?

Answer. I don't know, sir.

Question. When the flag went back did they commence firing again?

Answer. Yes, sir.

Question. Kept it up for how long?

Answer. They commenced firing again, but the firing didn't last fifteen minutes. Up to this time there had not been twenty killed on our side.

Question. What was the strength of the garrison?

Answer. 580, I think, just.

Question. How many of these were negroes?

Answer. About 380—nearly 400—I don't know exactly to a man.

Question. How many citizens besides yourself?

Answer. William W. Cutler, of Chicago, and a young man by the name of Robinson; he was a soldier but in citizen's clothes, and got off on that plea.

Question. The second flag that came in—about how long was it after the first?

Answer. Well, there was no *second* flag of truce, except the one. There was no firing in the interim.

Question. Was there no firing while the first was in?

Answer. No, sir, not a single shot fired on either side. After the flag of truce had been rejected, or the surrender had been rejected, they were so close to the fort that about 3,000 of them just sprang right in, and the whole garrison threw down their arms at once. The bigger portion of the darkeys jumped down the bank towards the Mississippi river, without any arms at all, and were followed by Forrest's men and shot indiscriminately, black and white, with handkerchiefs held over them in a great number of instances—as many as fifty I should think.

Question. Did you see any of those prisoners formed in line and shot down?

Answer. Yes, sir.

Question. How many?

Answer. They were collected at least four different times.

Question. How long a line?

Answer. Well, it was more in a collection than it was properly in a straight line. There was a line probably as long as this room, or longer—about thirty or thirty-five feet.

Question. These lines were scattered by rebel shots several times?

Answer. They were.

Question. These men were unarmed?

Answer. Unarmed; no arms of any description, and they holding up both hands begging for quarter.

Question. Were you put in the line?

Answer. No, sir; I was not. It was attempted to put me in line, but I clung to a man who tried to shoot me, but I caught his gun and prevented him, and he took my money from me, some seventy dollars, and ordered me into line, raising his gun to strike me; and as I came to the line the captain made a feint to strike me with his sword, and told me to give him my pocket book, which I did, and as he turned to look after others, I sprang away and clung close to this man that had just taken my money. I said to him that he had taken all my money, and he must keep me from being shot like a dog, as I was a citizen, and had nothing to do with the fight. He abused me in every way by bad language, saying that we had fought them like devils, and tried to kill all of Forrest's men, until we came to the back of the stores, where he gave me a soldier's coat and told me to wait a moment until he could step in and steal his share. As soon as I was left I took some clothing, a saddle blanket, and halter that were there and started out of the fort as one of Forrest's men, but on the way I saw three persons shot—mulattoes and blacks—shot down singly in cold blood. I succeeded in getting over the fortifications and hid under fallen timber, where I remained until dark. After dark I attempted to go towards Hatchie River bottom, but the fallen timber being so bad I got lost, and wandered near the Pass No. 2, leading out of the fort, inside of it, where I could see all, where I laid until the next day about two o'clock. I heard fifty-one or fifty-two shots fired singly at different times within the fort during that time, and screams and cheers. About two o'clock the dogs were getting so close to me that I knew they were on my track.

Question. What do you mean by the dogs?

Answer. Hunting out people everywhere. They have dogs.

Question. They had bloodhounds?

Answer. Yes, sir. I left the most of my clothing and hastened down a ravine in the timber, and kept on through the ravines till I came to the Coal Creek bottom, some mile and a half, and swam across. Finally, I succeeded in getting to the island. I had to swim across the river and a bayou. That is all that I saw. Oh! I was there at the fort two days after the battle and saw the remains of burned persons; helped to bury one of the dead that I saw shot in cold blood lying right where he was left, and saw many of them, white and black, all buried together, and a number, three days afterwards, not buried.

Question. How many did you see shot in this way?

Answer. I should think probably about two hundred.

Question. It was an indiscriminate butchery, was it?

Answer. Yes, sir. There were about fifteen or twenty that lay close in one pile, huddling together, shot after they were wounded.

Question. Some white soldiers shot after they were wounded?

Answer. Yes, sir, with the hospital flag flying, and they holding white handkerchiefs over their heads. I saw at least ten soldiers shot individually with white handkerchiefs over their heads. They tore off pieces of their shirts—anything they could get—for flags of truce and to denote surrender.

Question. You say these men were shot down in hospital, with hospital flag flying?

Answer. Yes, sir, lying right down under it—not up walking at all. Every man lying near me was killed—lying close to me and on me. Two lay over me, because they kept piling themselves right up on top close under the bank. It was just down under the brow of the hill. A great many were lying in the water and were shot. Trees that were lying one end in the water and the other on shore, they would just go over on the other side of them and hide in the water, and the rebels would go over and shoot them.

Question. Your citizen's clothes saved you?

Answer. Yes, sir; I told them I had nothing to do with them. They robbed every citizen, taking off most of their clothing.

Question. How much did they take from you?

Answer. Seventy dollars.

Question. You say you were robbed twice.

Answer. Yes, once by the captain of the company and once by the private. I carry my money in my vest pocket always, and had my pocket-book in my pocket with notes in it.

Question. That was what you gave to the captain, wasn't it?

Answer. Yes, sir.

Question. And the seventy dollars in money to the soldier?

Answer. Yes, sir. He asked, "Give me your money," and the other for the pocket-book.

Question. You say they had bloodhounds; did you see any of them?

Answer. Yes, sir; and not only I but others saw them. One other, Mr. Jones, was treed by them, and staid there a long time.

Question. What Jones was that?

Answer. I don't know his given name. He lives on Island 34. I can find out his name. He is not any too good a Union man, but is rather southern in his feelings.

Question. State about Bradford's death—when he was shot. What was done? Was he wounded before the surrender?

Answer. No, sir; but it was reported by very reliable persons that Bradford was shot and hung near Covington, in Hatchie River bottom.

Question. Who told you this?

Answer. This same Jones; and there were some darkeys came in to the gunboat and said that. Darkey evidence is very correct there. You might not think it worth while to take their evidence, but it is a great deal more to be relied upon than the southern evidence there. I might state that I was inquired after by a large number of officers, and it was said they would hang me on a flag-pole.

Question. What for?

Answer. From the fact that I employed government darkeys from Colonel Phillips, at Memphis.

Question. On your plantation?

Answer. Yes, sir. And they shot all my horses unfit for cavalry.

Question. Did they shoot your darkeys?

Answer. I understand they did, and burned them all. I understand they took one yellow woman, and two or three boys escaped that I tried to take to the fort with me in the morning to help fight. The balance, a darkey whose name I don't know, said they were killed and burned in the house.

Question. You did not go back there, then?

Answer. I did not go back there. That is only what is told me. It was told me by persons who were hid right near, and I saw persons bury the bodies after they were burned.

Question. Where?

Answer. In the fort, sir—burned in the house.

Question. In connexion with the fort buildings?

Answer. Yes, sir, and out on timber. There was a large number of them burned in the buildings, but they had been buried the day before.

Question. You say there were 580 men, you think, in the fort?

Answer. Yes, sir.

Question. How many do you suppose escaped?

Answer. Well, I know there were not more than 100 as they marched out there surrounded by the other troops, and I would not think there were fifty of them. There were five darkeys in Cairo hospitals who were buried alive. Two of them have died since they got there.

Question. Did you see any of these men buried alive?

Answer. No, I did not; but they are facts that can easily be proved by the darkeys—the darkeys themselves—and those who saw it done, and saw the quartermaster burned, too.

EDWARD B. BENTON.

Subscribed and sworn to before me this 22d April, 1864.

ISAAC J. DODGE,
Lieutenant and Assist. Paymaster General, Department of Missouri.

In consequence of some portions of the evidence of General Brayman and Colonel Lawrence, which, unexplained, might impeach the good conduct of General Shepley, Mr. Gooch, of the sub-committee, telegraphed to General Shepley, giving him the substance of the testimony relating to himself, and asking him to forward to the committee any explanation he might deem necessary in writing. The following communication was received from General Shepley, and the testimony of Captain Thornton, an officer of his staff, was taken. The sub-committee deemed the explanation therein contained to be entirely satisfactory, and directed that the following communication and testimony be incorporated with the testimony in relation to Fort Pillow.

HEADQUARTERS DISTRICT OF NORFOLK AND PORTSMOUTH,
Norfolk, Virginia, May 7, 1864.

SIR: I have the honor respectfully to forward by Captain C. C. G. Thornton, 12th Maine volunteers, now acting on my staff, a statement in reply to the communication I had the honor to receive by telegraph.

Captain Thornton was on the Olive Branch, and is subject to examination by the committee.

I have the honor to be, with great respect, your obedient servant,

G. F. SHEPLEY,
Brigadier General, Commanding.

Hon. D. W. GOOCH,
Of Committee on Conduct of the War.

HEADQUARTERS NORFOLK AND PORTSMOUTH,
Norfolk, Virginia, May 7, 1864.

SIR: At my own request having been relieved from duty as military governor of Louisiana, and ordered to report for duty to the commanding general of the army, I left New Orleans, on the evening of the 6th of April, as a passenger in the Olive Branch, a New Orleans and St. Louis passenger steamer *not in the service of the government,* but loaded with male and female passengers and cargo of private parties. The steamer was unarmed, and had no troops and no muskets for protection against guerillas when landing at wood yards and other places.

The boat stopped at Vicksburg, and I went ashore. When I returned to the boat as she was about leaving, I found that a detachment of a portion of the men of two batteries—one Ohio and one Missouri—belonging to the 17th army corps, with the horses, guns, caissons, wagons, tents, and baggage of the two batteries, had been put on board, with orders, as I afterwards learned on inquiring, to report to General Brayman, at Cairo.

The horses occupied all the available space, fore and aft, on the sides of the boilers and machinery, which were on deck. The guns, caissons, baggage wagons, tents, garrison and camp equipage, were piled up together on the bows, leaving only space for the gang plank.

The men had no small arms, so that when the boat landed, as happened in one instance at a wood yard where guerillas had just passed, the pickets thrown out to prevent surprise were necessarily unarmed.

As the boat was approaching, and before it was in sight of Fort Pillow, some females hailed it from the shore, and said the rebels had attacked Fort Pillow, and captured two boats on the river, and would take us if we went on.

The captain of the Olive Branch said they had probably taken the Mollie Able, which was due there about that time from St. Louis.

He turned his boat, saying he would go back to Memphis.

I objected to going back; stopped the boat below the next point; hailed another smaller steamer without passengers which I saw approaching, and ordered it alongside. I ordered the captain of this boat to cast off the coal barges he had in tow, and take me on board with a section of a battery to go to Fort Pillow.

While he was trying to disencumber his boat of the coal barges, another boat, better for the purpose, (the Cheek,) hove in sight. Finding I could get her ready quicker than the other, I had her brought alongside, and went aboard myself with Captain Thornton, of my staff, and Captain Williams, the ranking officer of the batteries.

Before we could get the guns on board, *a steamer with troops* hove in sight *coming down the river* from Fort Pillow.

We could not distinguish at first whether they were Union or rebel soldiers.

I asked Captain Pegram, of the Olive Branch, if the story of the women turned out to be true, and the rebels had the steamer, could his boat sink her. Captain Pegram replied, "Yes, my boat can run right over her." I ordered him to swing out into the stream to be ready for her. When she approached we saw *United States infantry soldiers on board that had just passed the fort.* She kept on going rapidly down with the current, only hailing the Olive Branch: "*All right up there; you can go by. The gunboat is lying off the fort.*"

This steamer was the Liberty. We then proceeded up the river in the Olive Branch. Near Fort Pillow some stragglers or guerillas fired from the shore with musketry, aiming at the pilot-house.

I was then in the pilot-house, and, as we kept on, I observed that one of the two other boats I have mentioned, which followed us at some distance, was compelled to put back. The Olive Branch kept on to report to the gunboat on the station.

An officer came off from the gunboat, in a small boat, and said he did not want any boat to stop; ordered us to go on to Cairo, and tell captain (name not recollected) to send him immediately four hundred (400) rounds of ammunition. There was no firing at the fort at this time.

The Union flag was flying, and after we had passed the fort we could see a "flag of truce" outside the fortifications.

No signal of any kind was made to the boat from the fort, or from the shore

No intimation was given us from the gunboat, which had the right to order a steamer of this description, other than the order to proceed to Cairo, to send down the ammunition.

From the fact that the Liberty had just passed down the river from the fort, with troops on board; from her hailing us *to go by*, and continuing her course down the river without stopping; that no signal was made the Olive Branch from the fort on the shore, and no attack was being made on the fort at the time; that the officer of the gunboat said he did not want any boats to stop, and ordered the captain of the Olive Branch to go on, and have ammunition sent down to him by first boat, I considered, and now consider, that the captain of the Olive Branch was not only justified in going on, but bound to proceed.

The Olive Branch was incapable of rendering any assistance, being entirely defenceless. If any guns could have been placed in position on the boat, they could not have been elevated to reach sharpshooters on the high steep bluff outside the fort.

A very few sharpshooters from the shore near the fort could have prevented any landing, and have taken the boat. We supposed the object of the rebels was rather to seize a boat, to effect a crossing into Arkansas, than to capture the fort. We had no means of knowing or suspecting that so strong a position as Fort Pillow had not been properly garrisoned for defence, when it was in constant communication with General Hurlbut at Memphis.

The Olive Branch had just left Memphis, General Hurlbut's headquarters, where it had been during the previous night. If it had not been for the appearance of the Liberty, I should have attempted a landing at Fort Pillow in the small steamer. If any intimation had been given from the gunboat, or the shore, I should have landed personally from the Olive Branch. The order given to the contrary prevented it.

Coming from New Orleans, and having no knowledge of affairs in that military district, I could not presume that a fort, with uninterrupted water communication above and below, could possibly be without a garrison strong enough to hold it for a few hours.

I write hastily, and omit, from want of time, to state subsequent occurrences at Fort Columbus and Cairo, except to say that, at Fort Columbus, in front of which Buford then was demanding a surrender, I stopped, started to ride out to the lines, met Colonel Lawrence, the commanding officer, coming in from the front to his headquarters. Offered to remain, with the men on board.

Colonel Lawrence said he was in good condition to stand any attack; could communicate with General Brayman; had already taken four hundred (400) infantry and one battery from the L. M. Kennett, which had just preceded us, and left six hundred (600) men, and another, or other batteries, on board, which he did not need. He declined the proffered assistance, as not needed, and immediately on arrival at Cairo I reported all the information in my possession to General Brayman, in command, who was about leaving for Columbus.

Captain Thornton, 12th Maine volunteers, a gallant officer, distinguished for his bravery at Ponchitoula, where he was wounded and left in the hands of the enemy, was on board the Olive Branch, and will take this communication to the committee.

I respectfully ask that he may be thoroughly examined as to all the circumstances.

I am conscious that a full examination will show that I rather exceeded than neglected my duty.

I have the honor to be, with great respect, your obedient servant,

G. F. SHEPLEY,
Brigadier General, Commanding.

Hon. D. W. Gooch,
Of Committee on Conduct of the War

WASHINGTON, D. C., *May* 9, 1864.

Captain Charles C. G. Thornton, sworn and examined.

By the chairman:

Question. What is your rank and position in the army?

Answer. I am a captain, and aid on General George F. Shepley's staff.

Question. Were you with General Shepley when he passed Fort Pillow, about the time of the capture of that place?

Answer. Yes, sir.

Question. Will you state what occurred there, and the reason, if any, why you did not stop there to aid the garrison?

Answer. We were passengers on the boat Olive Branch, which left New Orleans on the 6th of April, without troops. On arriving at Vicksburg, parts of two batteries—a Missouri and an Ohio battery—were put on board. I do not know the exact number of men, but I should think that perhaps there were 120 men with the two batteries. The men had no small-arms whatever—no arms but the guns of their batteries. We stopped at a place to take in wood, where we were told the guerillas had just passed, and we threw out pickets to keep from being surprised. We were unable to arm those men with anything whatever, and merely stationed them so that we should not be surprised, but have an opportunity of getting on board the boat and leave. Upon arriving within three miles—perhaps two and a half miles—of Fort Pillow, some women on shore hailed us and told us that Fort Pillow was captured with two transports or steamers, and motioned to us to return. The captain of the boat turned about for the purpose of returning to Memphis, but General Shepley stopped it. Colonel Sears, the owner of the boat, who was on board, came to me and asked me to go to General Shepley and tell him the importance of our going back to Memphis; that it was dangerous for us to proceed with so many passengers. The boat was a very large one, loaded with passengers, every state-room being occupied by men, women, and children.

Question. How many passengers, non-combatants, do you suppose you had on board?

Answer. Perhaps one hundred and fifty, but that is a mere guess. When Colonel Sears urged me to ask General Shepley to go back to Memphis, I told him I should do nothing of the kind; that if he wished General Shepley to allow the boat to go back, he might see him about it himself. He did so, but General Shepley positively refused to go. He ordered the captain of the Olive Branch to hail a boat which came in sight, and direct her to come alongside. General Shepley then said, "I will have a section of the battery put on this boat, and will go up and reconnoitre." The boat was called the "Hope," I think. There is a point just below where the rebels, if they had a battery, might bring it to bear on us. General Shepley consented to have the Hope go below that point with the boat we were on, in order to have this section of a battery put on board of her. On our way down we met another boat, the "Cheek," which would answer our purpose better, and she was stopped. General Shepley ordered a section of a battery put on board of her, and directed Captain Williams, commanding the battery, and myself, to accompany him up to Fort Pillow to reconnoitre. I suggested to General Shepley, or was on the point of suggesting to him, that perhaps he had better not go himself, but send Captain Williams and myself. The instant I suggested that, he said "No, I will go myself, and personally ascertain the condition of affairs." He asked the captain how many minutes it would take him to get his guns on board. He said he could probably get a couple of guns on in a few minutes.

Just then a steamer, which afterwards proved to be the steamer "Liberty," hove in sight. We supposed at first that she was the Mollie Able, which the captain of our boat said was due at Fort Pillow just about that time, and that she was one of the boats the rebels had captured, if the story of the women was true. When we saw her coming we noticed that she was loaded with troops, whether Union or rebel troops we could not tell. The general said to our captain, "Can you run that boat down?" He said, "If it is the Molliè Able, I can run right over her." When she hove in sight we saw at once that there was no time to put a battery on board the Cheek; General Shepley then ordered the Cheek to move out of the way, and the captain of our boat to swing out, with the intention of running this other boat down if she should prove to be loaded with rebel soldiers. When the boat got nearer, however, we found she had Union troops on board. As she passed us our captain hailed her, and she replied "All right up there; you can go by. There is a gunboat there." We were then satisfied that everything was all right, as she had been allowed to come down by them with so large a body of troops on board.

We went up, and when within perhaps a mile of the place some rebel soldiers fired upon our boat, probably aiming at the pilot-house. I stood on the after part of the deck at the time. The general was in the pilot-house looking out. The shots did not take effect or amount to anything. We went on up, and found no firing at the fort. We stopped at the gunboat, as all boats are required to do which pass. An officer came on board from the gunboat and said to the captain of our boat, "I want you to proceed immediately to Cairo, and send down 400 or 500 rounds of ammunition; and order all boats back that may be coming down; we want no boats here." We talked the matter over, and came to the conclusion that the object of this Fort Pillow affair was not to capture the fort, but to capture more of our boats, if possible, in order to get across the river. That was merely our supposition, as we knew nothing about the battle. There was no firing at the fort at that time, and our boat went on up the river in obedience to the orders of the gunboat, as it had a right to give that order.

We had proceeded but a little way before we discovered a flag of truce at the fort, as it was reported to me; I did not see it myself, but it undoubtedly was there. We passed on a short distance further, and then noticed that our flag at the fort was down; we had seen it flying as we passed the fort. I went to the stern of our boat, and with a glass looked carefully at the fort. After a time I discovered that the gunboat had steamed up a little ways, as I supposed for the purpose of firing upon the right flank of the rebels. We could see a line of fire or smoke in the woods, which we supposed to be from the musketry of the rebels. We then saw a flag raised up on a pole at the fort, I should think ten or twelve feet high. I supposed that our flag had been shot away, and they were raising it again. The guns from the fort at that time were pretty heavy, while the fire of the enemy appeared to be from musketry. I have no doubt now that that was the rebel flag that was raised after the fort was taken.

We proceeded on up to Columbus. Before we arrived there we noticed that there was heavy firing there. On our arrival there we saw a great many troops, and they remarked from the shore that there was hot work there. General Shepley told me to accompany him, and went up to Colonel Lawrence's headquarters, but was told he was at the front. General Shepley ordered two horses to be prepared for us to go to the front, to see Colonel Lawrence. Just as the horses were ready, and we were about starting, Colonel Lawrence came over and rode down to his headquarters. He told us that it was all right; that there had been some skirmishing; that Buford had come there and demanded a surrender of the fort, but he had refused to surrender. General Shepley told him that he had portions of two batteries on hand, and asked him if he wanted them; told him how they came there, and that they were ordered to Cairo as a portion of the 17th corps. Colonel Lawrence said that he had taken 400 troops from the Luther M. Kennett, and, I think, one battery. The Luther M. Kennet had just preceded us as we passed by Fort Pillow. Colonel Lawrence said that he did not need the batteries of General Shepley. General Shepley inquired particularly about the condition of affairs, and told Colonel Lawrence what had occurred at Fort Pillow. After ascertaining that there was nothing to be done by us down there we proceeded to Cairo. On our arrival there General Shepley called upon General Brayman and told him the substance of what occurred; the condition of things as we left, the flag coming down, and the fear that the fort had surrendered. We did not know then that the fort had surrendered, though we know now it had.

The caissons and artillery had been hoisted on our boat by means of what they call a derrick, I think, and were piled up, closely packed all round. It would, therefore, have been impossible for us to have removed those cannon for several hours. It took us several hours to land them at Cairo; and it would have been an utter impossibility for us to have taken those cannon up to Fort Pillow, as we had no infantry to cover our landing; and half a dozen sharpshooters could have undoubtedly captured our boat had we attempted it.

Question. If I understand you, General Shepley had no opportunity to relieve Fort Pillow any way?

Answer. He went on board the boat a mere passenger, with no arms. We did not know any troops were coming on board. Those two portions of batteries, with their guns, were ordered to report at Cairo. The gunboat was lying right by the side of us, and its fire was of no account, and, of course, ours would not have been.

By Mr. Gooch:

Question. Would it have been possible for you to have used your batteries from the boat with any effect upon the rebels?

Answer. No, sir; it would have been an utter impossibility to have done so. If we had gone in and stopped five minutes there, the rebels could have captured us without the least trouble in the world. The question may be asked why we offered assistance at Columbus and not at Fort Pillow. The fort at Columbus is clear in back from the river, and there were infantry troops there to protect our landing. But Colonel Lawrence said he did not expect the fight to occur for some time, even if there was any fight at all, which he did not expect.

Question. At Columbus you could have landed your batteries under the protection of our forces there?

Answer. Yes, sir.

Question. And you could not have done that at Fort Pillow?

Answer. No, sir; for at Fort Pillow we should have been right under the fort, and could have been easily reached. This was all stated to General Brayman, and I was quite surprised when I heard of the testimony in regard to the matter.

RETURNED PRISONERS.

MAY 9, 1864.—Laid on the table and ordered to be printed.

Mr. GOOCH, from the Joint Select Committee on the Conduct of the War, made the following

REPORT.

The Joint Committee on the Conduct and Expenditures of the War submitted the following report, with the accompanying testimony.

On the 4th instant your committee received a communication of that date from the Secretary of War, enclosing the report of Colonel Hoffman, commissary general of prisoners, dated May 3, calling the attention of the committee to the condition of returned Union prisoners, with the request that the committee would immediately proceed to Annapolis and examine with their own eyes the condition of those who have been returned from rebel captivity. The committee resolved that they would comply with the request of the Secretary of War on the first opportunity. The 5th of May was devoted by the committee to concluding their labors upon the investigation of the Fort Pillow massacre. On the 6th of May, however, the committee proceeded to Annapolis and Baltimore, and examined the condition of our returned soldiers, and took the testimony of several of them, together with the testimony of surgeons and other persons in attendance upon the hospitals. That testimony, with the communication of the Secretary of War, and the report of Colonel Hoffman, is herewith transmitted.

The evidence proves, beyond all manner of doubt, a determination on the part of the rebel authorities, deliberately and persistently practiced for a long time past, to subject those of our soldiers who have been so unfortunate as to fall in their hands to a system of treatment which has resulted in reducing many of those who have survived and been permitted to return to us to a condition, both physically and mentally, which no language we can use can adequately describe. Though nearly all the patients now in the Naval Academy hospital at Annapolis, and in the West hospital, in Baltimore, have been under the kindest and most intelligent treatment for about three weeks past, and many of them for a greater length of time, still they present literally the appearance of living skeletons, many of them being nothing but skin and bone; some of them are maimed for life, having been frozen while exposed to the inclemency of the winter season on Belle Isle, being compelled to lie on the bare ground, without tents or blankets, some of them without overcoats or even coats, with but little fire to mitigate the severity of the winds and storms to which they were exposed.

The testimony shows that the general practice of their captors was to rob them, as soon as they were taken prisoners, of all their money, valuables, blankets, and good clothing, for which they received nothing in exchange except, perhaps, some old worn-out rebel clothing hardly better than none at all. Upon their arrival at Richmond they have been confined, without blankets or other covering, in buildings without fire, or upon Belle Isle with, in many cases, no shelter, and in others with nothing but old discarded army tents, so injured by rents and holes as to present but little barrier to the wind and storms; on several occasions, the witnesses say, they have arisen in the morning from their resting-places upon the bare earth, and found several of their comrades frozen to death during the night, and that many others would have met the same fate had they not walked rapidly back and forth, during the hours which should have been devoted to sleep, for the purpose of retaining sufficient warmth to preserve life.

In respect to the food furnished to our men by the rebel authorities, the testimony proves that the ration of each man was totally insufficient in quantity to preserve the health of a child, even had it been of proper quality, which it was not. It consisted usually, at the most, of two small pieces of corn-bread, made in many instances, as the witnesses state, of corn and cobs ground together, and badly prepared and cooked, of, at times, about two ounces of meat, usually of poor quality, and unfit to be eaten, and occasionally a few black worm-eaten beans, or something of that kind. Many of our men were compelled to sell to their guards, and others, for what price they could get, such clothing and blankets as they were permitted to receive of that forwarded for their use by our government, in order to obtain additional food sufficient to sustain life; thus, by endeavoring to avoid one privation, reducing themselves to the same destitute condition in respect to clothing and covering that they were in before they received any from our government. When they became sick and diseased in consequence of this exposure and privation, and were admitted into the hospitals, their treatment was little, if any, improved as to food, though they, doubtless, suffered less from exposure to cold than before. Their food still remained insufficient in quantity and altogether unfit in quality. Their diseases and wounds did not receive the treatment which the commonest dictates of humanity would have prompted. One witness, whom your committee examined, who had lost all the toes of one foot from being frozen while on Belle Isle, states that for days at a time his wounds were not dressed, and that they had not been dressed for four days when he was taken from the hospital and carried on the flag-of-truce boat for Fortress Monroe.

In reference to the condition to which our men were reduced by cold and hunger, your committee would call the attention to the following extracts from the testimony.

One witness testifies:

I had no blankets until our government sent us some.

Question. How did you sleep before you received those blankets?

Answer. We used to get together just as close as we could, and sleep spoon-fashion, so that when one turned over we all had to turn over.

Another witness testifies:

Question. Were you hungry all the time?

Answer. Hungry! I could eat anything in the world that came before us; some of the boys would get boxes from the north with meat of different kinds in them; and, after they had picked the meat off, they would throw the bones away into the spit-boxes, and we would pick the bones out of the spit-boxes and gnaw them over again.

In addition to this insufficient supply of food, clothing, and shelter, our soldiers, while prisoners, have been subjected to the most cruel treatment from those placed over them. They have been abused and shamefully treated on almost every opportunity. Many have been mercilessly shot and killed when they failed to comply with all the demands of their jailers, sometimes for violating rules of which they had not been informed. Crowded in great numbers in buildings, they have been fired at and killed by the sentinels outside when they appeared at the windows for the purpose of obtaining a little fresh air. One man, whose comrade in the service, in battle and in captivity, had been so fortunate as to be among those released from further torments, was shot dead as he was waving with his hand a last adieu to his friend; and other instances of equally unprovoked murder are disclosed by the testimony.

The condition of our returned soldiers as regards personal cleanliness, has been filthy almost beyond description. Their clothes have been so dirty and so covered with vermin, that those who received them have been compelled to destroy their clothing and re-clothe them with new and clean raiment. Their bodies and heads have been so infested with vermin that, in some instances, repeated washings have failed to remove them; and those who have received them in charge have been compelled to cut all the hair from their heads, and make applications to destroy the vermin. Some have been received with no clothing but shirts and drawers and a piece of blanket or other outside covering, entirely destitute of coats, hats, shoes or stockings; and the bodies of those better supplied with clothing have been equally dirty and filthy with the others, many who have been sick and in the hospital having had no opportunity to wash their bodies for weeks and months before they were released from captivity.

Your committee are unable to convey any adequate idea of the sad and deplorable condition of the men they saw in the hospitals they visited; and the testimony they have taken cannot convey to the reader the impressions which your committee there received. The persons we saw, as we were assured by those in charge of them, have greatly improved since they have been received in the hospitals. Yet they are now dying daily, one of them being in the very throes of death as your committee stood by his bed-side and witnessed the sad spectacle there presented. All those whom your committee examined stated that they have been thus reduced and emaciated entirely in consequence of the merciless treatment they received while prisoners from their enemies; and the physicians in charge of them, the men best fitted by their profession and experience to express an opinion upon the subject, all say that they have no doubt that the statements of their patients are entirely correct.

It will be observed from the testimony, that all the witnesses who testify upon that point state that the treatment they received while confined at Columbia, South Carolina, Dalton, Georgia, and other places, was far more humane than that they received at Richmond, where the authorities of the so-called confederacy were congregated, and where the power existed, had the inclination not been wanting, to reform those abuses and secure to the prisoners they held some treatment that would bear a public comparison to that accorded by our authorities to the prisoners in our custody. Your committee, therefore, are constrained to say that they can hardly avoid the conclusion, expressed by so many of our released soldiers, that the inhuman practices herein referred to are the result of a determination on the part of the rebel authorities to reduce our soldiers in their power, by privation of food and clothing, and by exposure, to such a condition that those who may survive shall never recover so as to be able to render any effective service in the field. And your committee accordingly ask that this report, with the accompanying testimony, be printed with the report and testimony in relation to the massacre of Fort Pillow, the one being, in their opinion, no less than the other, the result of a predetermined policy. As regards the assertions of some of the rebel newspapers, that our prisoners have received at their hands the same treatment that their own soldiers in the field have received, they are evidently but the most glaring and unblushing falsehoods. No one can for a moment be deceived by such statements, who will reflect that our soldiers, who, when taken prisoners, have been stout, healthy men, in the prime and vigor of life, yet have died by hundreds under the treatment they have received, although required to perform no duties of the camp or the march; while the rebel soldiers are able to make long and rapid marches, and to offer a stubborn resistance in the field.

Your committee, finding it impossible to describe in words the deplorable condition of these returned prisoners, have caused photographs to be taken of a number of them, and a fair sample to be lithographed and appended to their report, that their exact condition may be known by all who examine it. Some of them have since died.

There is one feature connected with this investigation, to which your committee can refer with pride and satisfaction; and that is the uncomplaining fortitude, the undiminished patriotism exhibited by our brave men under all their privations, even in the hour of death.

Your committee will close their report by quoting the tribute paid these men by the chaplain of the hospital at Annapolis, who has ministered to so many of them in their last moments, who has smoothed their passage to the grave by his kindness and attention, and who has performed the last sad offices over their lifeless remains. He says:

"There is another thing I would wish to state. All the men, without any exception among the thousands that have come to this hospital, have never in a single instance expressed a regret (notwithstanding the privations and sufferings they have endured) that they entered their country's service. They have been the most loyal, devoted and earnest men. Even on the last days of their lives they have said that all they hoped for was just to live and enter the ranks again and meet their foes. It is a most glorious record in reference to the devotion of our men to their country. I do not think their patriotism has ever been equalled in the history of the world."

All of which is respectfully submitted.

B. F. WADE, *Chairman.*

WAR DEPARTMENT,
Washington City, May 4, 1864.

SIR: I have the honor to submit to you a report made to this department by Colonel Hoffman, commissary general of prisoners, in regard to the condition of Union soldiers who have, until within a few days, been prisoners of war at Richmond, and would respectfully request that your committee immediately proceed to Annapolis to take testimony there, and examine with their own eyes the condition of those who have been returned from rebel captivity. The enormity of the crime committed by the rebels towards our prisoners for the last several months is not known or realized by our people, and cannot but fill with horror the civilized world when the facts are fully revealed. There appears to have been a deliberate system of savage and barbarous treatment and starvation, the result of which will be that few, if any, of the prisoners that have been in their hands during the past winter will ever again be in a condition to render any service, or even to enjoy life.

Your obedient servant,

EDWIN M. STANTON,
Secretary of War.

Hon. B. F. WADE,
Chairman of Joint Committee on Conduct of the War.

OFFICE OF COMMISSARY GENERAL OF PRISONERS,
Washington, D. C., May 3, 1864.

SIR: I have the honor to report that, pursuant to your instructions of the 2d instant, I proceeded, yesterday morning, to Annapolis, with a view to see that the paroled prisoners about to arrive there from Richmond were properly received and cared for.

The flag-of-truce boat New York, under the charge of Major Mulford, with thirty-two officers, three hundred and sixty-three enlisted men, and one citizen on board, reached the wharf at the Naval School hospital about ten o'clock. On going on board, I found the officers generally in good health, and much cheered by their happy release from the rebel prisons, and by the prospect of again being with their friends.

The enlisted men who had endured so many privations at Belle Isle and other places were, with few exceptions, in a very sad plight, mentally and physically, having for months been exposed to all the changes of the weather, with no other protection than a very insufficient supply of worthless tents, and with an allowance of food scarcely sufficient to prevent starvation, even if of wholesome quality; but as it was made of coarsely-ground corn, including the husks, and probably at times the cobs, if it did not kill by starvation, it was sure to do it by the disease it created. Some of these poor fellows were wasted to mere skeletons, and had scarcely life enough remaining to appreciate that they were now in the hands of their friends, and among them all there were few who had not become too much broken down and dispirited by their many privations to be able to realize the happy prospect of relief from their sufferings which was before them. With rare exception, every face was sad with care and hunger; there was no brightening of the countenance or lighting up of the eye, to indicate a thought of anything beyond a painful sense of prostration of mind and body. Many faces showed that there was scarcely a ray of intelligence left.

Every preparation had been made for their reception in anticipation of the arrival of the steamer, and immediately upon her being made fast to the wharf the paroled men were landed and taken immediately to the hospital, where, after receiving a warm bath, they were furnished with a suitable supply of new clothing, and received all those other attentions which their sad condition demanded. Of the whole number, there are perhaps fifty to one hundred who, in a week or ten days, will be in a convalescent state, but the others will very slowly regain their lost health.

That our soldiers, when in the hands of the rebels, are starved to death, cannot be denied. Every return of the flag-of-truce boat from City Point brings us too many living and dying witnesses to admit of a doubt of this terrible fact. I am informed that the authorities at Richmond admit the fact, but excuse it on the plea that they give the prisoners the same rations they give their own men. But can this be so? Can an army keep the field, and be active and efficient, on the same fare that kills prisoners of war at a frightful per-centage? I think not; no man can believe it; and while a practice so shocking to humanity is persisted in by the rebel authorities, I would very respectfully urge that retaliatory measures be at once instituted by subjecting the officers we now hold as prisoners of war to a similar treatment.

I took advantage of the opportunity which this visit to Annapolis gave me to make a hasty inspection of Camp Parole, and I am happy to report that I found it in every branch in a most commendable condition. The men all seemed to be cheerful and in fine health, and the police inside and out was excellent. Colonel Root, the commanding officer, deserves much credit for the very satisfactory condition to which he has brought his command.

I have the honor to be, very respectfully, your obedient servant,

W. HOFFMAN,

Colonel 3d Infantry, Commissary General of Prisoners.

Hon. E. M. STANTON,

Secretary of War, Wa hington, D. C.

TESTIMONY.

ANNAPOLIS, MARYLAND,
May 6, 1864.

Howard Leedom, sworn and examined:

By the chairman:

Question. To what company and regiment have you belonged?

Answer. Company G, 52d New York.

Question. How long have you been in the service?

Answer. About seven months.

Question. What is your age?

Answer. Seventeen.

Question. When and where were you taken prisoner?

Answer. At a place called Orange Grove, I think, back of Chancellorsville.

Question. How long ago?

Answer. In November last.

Question. Where were you then carried?

Answer. Right to Richmond.

Question. In what prison were you placed?

Answer. I was put on Belle Isle first, and then I got sick and was taken to the hospital.

Question. Describe how you were treated there, and the cause of your sickness.

Answer. They did not treat me very kindly. I froze my feet on the island.

Question. How came they to be frozen?

Answer. When they took me prisoner they got away the good shoes I had on, and gave me an old pair of shoes, all cut and split open; and when I was on the island, I had just an old tent to lie under.

Question. Did you not have some blankets to put over you?

Answer. No, sir. They took away my blanket, and everything else—my shoes—even a pair of buckskin gloves I had.

Question. Did they give you anything in place of them?

Answer. No, sir; only that pair of shoes I said.

Question. You had stockings?

Answer. Yes, sir.

Question. What kind of a tent did you have?

Answer. The tent was not very good; the rain beat right through it.

Question. How badly were your feet frozen?

Answer. Well, my toes are all off one of my feet now. [The surgeon accompanying the committee here took the dressings off the witness's feet, and exhibited them to the committee. The stumps of the toes were just healing.]

Question. What did they give you to eat?

Answer. They gave us corn-bread, and once in a while a little piece of meat.

Question. How often did they give you meat?

Answer. Maybe once a day; maybe once a week—just as they happened to have it.

Question. Did you get enough to eat, such as it was?

Answer. No, sir; I did not even get enough corn-bread.

Question. How long were you on the island?

Answer. I was on the island only a month, and in the hospital three months.

Question. How long is it since you were exchanged?

Answer. I came here on the 24th of March.

Question. There were others there with you on the island?

Answer. Yes, sir.

Question. How did they fare?

Answer. The same as I did; we all fared alike.

Question. Were any others frozen?

Answer. Yes, sir; plenty of them frozen to death.

Question. Frozen to death?

Answer. Yes, sir.

Question. Were their blankets taken away like yours?

Answer. Yes, sir; they had to lie out in the open ditch. They did not have as good over them as I had.

Question. Did not they have a tent to sleep under?

Answer. No, sir; no tent at all. There was an embankment thrown up, so as to keep them inside like, and they had to lie right down in the ditch there.

Question. With nothing over them?

Answer. If some of them had their blanket, they put that over them; but they had no tent, or anything of that kind.

Question. Nothing to keep off the rain and snow?

Answer. No, sir; nothing at all.

Question. Are you certain that any of them froze to death there?

Answer. Yes, sir, I am.

Question. State about the treatment you received after your feet were frozen, when you were in the hospital.

Answer. Sometimes my feet were dressed there every day; sometimes I went three or four days without dressing—just whether their nurses happened to be busy or not. When I was exchanged, I had not been dressed for four or five days.

Question. Were any of the confederate sick in the hospital with you?

Answer. Not that I know of.

Question. Do you know how they treated their own soldiers that were in the hospital?

Answer. I do not. I suppose they treated them better than they did us, though.

Question. Was your food any better in the hospital than on the island?

Answer. It was when we first went there, but when I came away it was no better.

Washington Collins, sworn and examined.

By Mr. Gooch:

Question. To what company and regiment do you belong?

Answer. Company A, 5th Kentucky infantry regiment.

Question. Where were you taken prisoner?

Answer. I was taken prisoner at the battle of Chickamauga.

Question. Where were you then carried?

Answer. From there to Richmond, as straight through as they could get us through.

Question. State how you were treated after you were taken prisoner.

Answer. We were treated very rough. The eatables we got on the way from the battle-field to Richmond were mouldy crackers, such as you would never try to eat, with one or two exceptions, when we got a little light bread.

Question. Where were you confined at Richmond?

Answer. We were put in tobacco factories, and kept there without clothing or blankets, until our government sent us blankets and clothing, and some provisions.

Question. Were the clothing and blankets which you had when taken prisoners taken from you?

Answer. Yes, sir; our blankets were pretty much all taken from us.

Question. Did you suffer from cold?

Answer. Yes, sir, severely.

Question. Was your money taken from you?

Answer. Those of us that had money, had it pretty much all taken away, or scared out of us.

Question. What kind of food had you after you reached Richmond?

Answer. We got, I should judge, about six ounces of light bread, and in the afternoon about two spoonfuls of black beans—worm-eaten beans.

Question. Was that all you had for the day?

Answer. I think we got, once a day, about two ounces of meat.

Question. What was the character of the meat and bread?

Answer. The character of the meat was pretty tolerably rough. I cannot exactly describe it. I never did eat any beef like some of it; and the first dose of medicine I took since I was in the army, was when I was put in the hospital at Danville. About six or seven weeks ago, before that, I was always a hearty, healthy man.

Question. Have you had any disease or sickness except that occasioned by want of proper food and clothing?

Answer. No, sir; I think not. (The surgeon here remarked, "His disease is the result of starvation, privation, and exposure.")

Question. When were you exchanged?

Answer. We left the 1st of May, I think. I have more of a life-like feeling about me now than I had when I left Richmond.

Question. Do you think you are in a better condition now?

Answer. Yes, sir; I know I am. The authorities did not think it safe for me to start; but I told them if I was going to die, I would rather die on the Chesapeake than die there.

Question. After you grew so very sick, was your food improved any?

Answer. Very little. The last food I received was light diet. When I left the hospital to go on board the flag-of-truce boat, I received about a gill of what they call soup, though in fact it was just nothing; I should say it was only a little starch and water; and then I got a little piece of corn-bread, about that large, (measuriug on his fingers about two inches square,) and we got a piece of meat, once a day, about the same size.

Question. Were the other men treated as you were, so far as you know?

Answer. Yes, sir. I wish to speak of one thing. After this food was issued out, what was called the ward-master would go round in the evening with a little mush made of meal, and give some of us a table-spoonful of it. Say there were 60 or 80 patients, and there would be 6 or 8, maybe 10, of those patients would get a little spoonful of this mush; and then he would come round a little while afterwards and pour a table-spoonful of molasses over it; and just as likely as not, in a few minutes after that he would come round with some vinegar and pour a spoonful of vinegar over that.

Question. Why did he do that?

Answer. He said that was the way it was issued to him.

Question. Did he give any reason for mixing it altogether in that way?

Answer. No, sir; and there were a great many of our own men who treated us as bad as the secesh, because those there acting as nurses, if there was any little delicacy for the sick, would just gobble it up.

Question. Were all of our men suffering for want of food?

Answer. Yes, sir, all of them. In the winter time these secesh got so they would haul up loads of cabbages, all full of lice, and throw them raw into the room for us to eat.

Charles Gallagher, sworn and examined.

By Mr. Odell:

Question. Where are you from?
Answer. From Guernsey county, Ohio.
Question. To what regiment do you belong?
Answer. 40th Ohio.
Question. How long have you been in the service?
Answer. Pretty nearly three years.
Question. Where were you taken prisoner?
Answer. At Chickamauga.
Question. When?
Answer. On the 22d of last September.
Question. State what happened then to you.
Answer. When they took me prisoner they took me right on to Richmond, kept me there awhile, then sent me to Danville and kept me there awhile. I got sick at Danville and was put in the hospital, and then they sent me back to Richmond and paroled me and sent me here.
Question. How did they treat you while you were a prisoner?
Answer. Pretty bad. They gave us corn-bread, and not very much of it; and we had to lie right down on the floor, without any blankets, until a ong while about Christmas. We had just to lie as thick on the floor as we could get.
Question. How were you treated when you were taken sick?
Answer. A little better. We then had a sort of bed to lie on.
Question. Did you have all the food you wanted?
Answer. No, sir.
Question. What kind of food did you get?
Answer. Corn-bread, a little piece of meat, sometimes a little rice-soup, and sometimes a few beans.
Question. How often did you get meat?
Answer. Along through the winter we got a little bit of fresh beef, (perhaps once a day,) and then from about March a little pork.
Question. What was the matter with you when you went to the hospital?
Answer. I got a cough which settled on me, and I had pain in my breast.
Question. Were there any other prisoners at Danville?
Answer. Yes, sir.
Question. Did they suffer at all from want?
Answer. They were pretty hungry.
Question. Did you complain to the authorities that you did not get food enough?
Answer. No, sir; it would not have made any difference. They said there that we got every ounce that was allowed to us.
Question. Did you make your wants known to any one?
Answer. Yes, sir; but they would not give us any more. They would come in and give you a half a loaf of bread, and tell you that was your day's rations; you could take that or nothing.

By the chairman:

Question. Did they give you as much as their own soldiers for rations?
Answer. No, sir; their own soldiers got a great deal more.

By Mr. Odell:

Question. What was your treatment aside from your supply of food? Was it kind?

Answer. No, sir. They just came in and shoved us round; finally, they run us all up from one floor to the second floor, and only let one go down at a time. When he got back they let another go down.

Isaiah G. Booker, sworn and examined.

By Mr. Harding:

Question. How old are you?

Answer. Twenty-one on the 13th of this month.

Question. Where did you enlist?

Answer. Bath, Maine.

Question. How long were you in the army before you were taken prisoner?

Answer. I enlisted on the 5th of September, 1861, and was taken prisoner last July.

Question. Where were you taken prisoner?

Answer. On Morris island, Charleston, South Carolina.

Question. Where were you then sent?

Answer. I was sent to Columbia, South Carolina, where we were kept about two months, and then we were sent to Richmond, put on Belle Isle, and staid there the remainder of the time.

Question. How were you treated at Columbia?

Answer. I was treated a great deal better there than I was at Belle Isle. We got meat twice a day, rice once, and Indian bread once. We got very near as much as we wanted to eat.

Question. How were you treated at Richmond?

Answer. I suffered there terribly with hunger. I could eat anything.

Question. Can you tell us what kind of food you got there?

Answer. Dry Indian bread, and, when I first went there, a very little meat.

Question. When were you taken sick?

Answer. I was taken sick—I was sick with the diarrhœa a fortnight before I went to the hospital, and I was in the hospital a little over a week before I was exchanged. I was released on the 7th of March, and got here the 9th.

Question. How were you treated while in the hospital?

Answer. I was treated there worse than on Belle Isle. We did not get any salt of any account—only a little piece of bread that would hardly keep a chicken alive.

Question. Did you get any rice?

Answer. No, sir.

Question. Any soup?

Answer. Once in a while of mornings I would get a little.

Question. Did the physician come round to see you every day?

Answer. Yes, sir.

Question. Did he give you any medicine?

Answer. He gave me some pills.

Question. What was their manner towards you after you were taken sick and in the hospital? Were they kind, or rough?

Answer. They were neither kind nor rough, but indifferent. The corn-bread I got seemed to burn my very insides. When I would go down to the river of mornings to wash myself, as I put the water to my face it seemed as though I wanted to sup the water, and to sup it, and sup it, and sup it all the time.

Question. Did you make no complaint to the officers on Belle Isle of your food?

Answer. No sir.

Question. Did you ask them for any more?

Answer. No, sir; I knew there was no use. I do not think I spoke to an officer while I was there.

Question. Did you ever tell those who furnished you with the food you did get, of the insufficiency of it?

Answer. Yes, sir.

Question. What answer did they give you?

Answer. That was all we were allowed, they said.

Question. Did you have blankets while you were on Belle Isle?

Answer. I had no blanket until our government sent us some.

Question. How did you sleep before you received those blankets?

Answer. We used to get together just as close as we could, and sleep spoon-fashion, so that when one turned over we all had to turn over.

Question. Did they furnish you any clothing while you were there?

Answer. No, sir; the rebs did not furnish us a bit. It was very warm weather when I was taken prisoner, and I had nothing on me but my pants, shirt, gloves, shoes, stockings, and cap; and I received no more clothing until our government sent us some in December, I think. We had to lie right down on the cold ground.

Question. Did you not have a tent?

Answer. I had none when I first went there. After a while we had one, but it was a very poor affair; the rain would come right through it.

Question. Were you exposed to the dew and rain, and wind and snow?

Answer. Yes, sir.

Question. And before you got the tent you lay in the open air?

Answer. Yes, sir.

Question. How did the others there with you fare; the same as you did?

Answer. Many of them had money, with which they bought things of the guard; but I had no money.

Question. Were there others there who had no money?

Answer. Yes, sir.

Question. Did they fare the same as you?

Answer. Yes, sir.

Question. After you went into the hospital, did you receive the same treatment as their own sick received who were in the hospital with you, or did they have any of their sick in there?

Answer. I think none of their sick were in there. I suffered a great deal with hunger when I was on Belle Isle. When I first went there I had no passage of the bowels for eighteen days, and when I did have one it was just as dry as meal.

Question. Did you have any medicine at that time?

Answer. No, sir; I took no medicine until I went to the hospital. About the middle or last of February (somewhere about there) I took a very severe cold. It seemed to settle all over me. I was as stiff in all my joints as I could be.

Question. Did your strength decrease much before you were taken sick in February?

Answer. Yes, sir; I stood it very well until about the 1st of February. After that I commenced to go down pretty fast. I know that one day I undertook to wash my shirt, and got it about half washed, when I was so weak I had to give it up.

Question. Do you think you had any other disease or sickness than what was caused by exposure and starvation at that time?

Answer. No, sir. When I was taken prisoner I weighed about 170 pounds, I think. I had always been a very hearty, stout man—could eat anything, and stand almost anything.

Isaac H. Lewis, sworn and examined.

By Mr. Julien:

Question. To what company and regiment do you belong?
Answer. Company K, 1st Vermont cavalry.
Question. When were you taken prisoner?
Answer. I was taken prisoner on the 22d of March, on Kilpatrick's raid.
Question. Where were you then carried?
Answer. They carried me to Richmond, and put me in a tobacco house there.
Question. How did they treat you there?
Answer. Well, they did not treat me as well as they might.
Question. What did they give you to eat?
Answer. They gave me corn-bread.
Question. How much and how often?
Answer. Not but very little. They gave me a little twice a day.
Question. Did they give you any meat?
Answer. Once in a while, a little.
Question. What kind of meat?
Answer. Beef.
Question. Could you eat it?
Answer. No, sir.

[The witness here was evidently so weak and exhausted that the committee suspended his examination.]

Mortimer F. Brown, sworn and examined.

By the chairman:

Question. Where are you from, and to what company and regiment do you belong?

Answer. I am from Steubenville, Ohio; I was in the 2d Ohio; Colonel McCook was our colonel when I was taken prisoner.

Question. Where were you taken prisoner?
Answer. At Chickamauga.
Question. Where were you then carried?
Answer. From Chickamauga to Richmond.
Question. How did you fare while in Richmond?

Answer. We lived very scantily, and hardly anything to eat. Some of the boys, in order to get enough to live on, had to trade away what clothing they could to the guard for bread, &c.

Question. What did they allow you to eat?

Answer. When we first went to Richmond our rations were bacon and wheat-bread. We did very well at first, but they went on cutting it down.

Question. How was it finally?

Answer. We received corn-bread once or twice a day—I think it was twice. After we went to Danville we fared a great deal better in regard to rations.

Question. Did you have enough to eat, such as it was?
Answer. I did, at Danville.
Question. How was it at Richmond?

Answer. Well, some had plenty to eat, but, as far as I was concerned, I was hungry most all the time. From the time we left Richmond until we drew our meat at Danville—say ten days—we had with us to eat only what they called Graham bread—nothing but bread and water for those ten days. After we got to Danville it was better. They issued us pork and beef sometimes. There, there would be times when we would be without meat for a couple of days.

Question. What was their bearing and treatment towards you, aside from your food?

Answer. We were treated tolerably kindly until we commenced our tunnelling operations; then they treated us very harshly; then they took the prisoners that had occupied three floors and put them all on two floors, and would only allow from three to six to go to the rear at one time.

Question. What is the matter with you now?

Answer. Nothing at all but scurvy. I am getting along very well now since I got here. The treatment at Danville was a palace alongside of that at Richmond.

Franklin Dinsmore, sworn and examined.

By the chairman:

Question. Where did you enlist?

Answer. At Camp Nelson, Kentucky.

Question. To what State do you belong?

Answer. Eastern Tennessee.

Question. How long have you been in the army?

Answer. I enlisted on the 11th or 12th of last July; I do not remember which day.

Question. To what regiment do you belong?

Answer. Eighth Tennessee cavalry.

Question. Who was your colonel?

Answer. Colonel Strickland.

Question. Where were you taken prisoner?

Answer. At Zollicoffer, near the East Tennessee and Virginia line.

Question. Where were you then carried?

Answer. Right straight on to Richmond. I was taken on the line of the railroad. We were burning bridges there to keep the enemy out.

Question. How did you fare after you got to Richmond?

Answer. They just starved us.

Question. What did they give you to eat?

Answer. For forty-eight hours after we got there they gave us only just what we could breathe; then they gave us a little piece of white bread and just three bites of beef. A man could take it all decently at three bites. That is the way we lived until we went to Danville, and then we had meat enough to make half a dozen bites, with bugs in it.

Question. What brought on your sickness?

Answer. Starvation. I was so starved there that when I was down I could not get up without catching hold of something to pull myself up by.

Question. What did you live in?

Answer. In a brick building, without any fire, or anything to cover us with.

Question. Had you no blankets?

Answer. No, sir; we had not. They even took our coats from us, and part of us had to lie there on the floor in our shirt sleeves.

Question. In the winter?

Answer. Yes, sir.

Question. Did any of the men freeze?

Answer. Yes, sir; many a man just fell dead walking around trying to keep himself warm, or, as he was lying on the floor, died during the night; and if you looked out of a window, a sentinel would shoot you. They shot some five or six of our boys who were looking out. Some of our boys would work for the guards to get more to eat, just to keep them from starving. There would be pieces of cobs in our bread, left there by the grinding machine, half as long as my finger, and the bread itself looked just as if you had taken a parcel of dough and let it bake in the sun. It was all full of cracks where it had dried, and the inside was all raw.

Question. Were you hungry all the time?

Answer. Hungry! I could eat anything in the world that came before us. Some of the boys would get boxes from the north with meat of different kinds in them, and, after they had picked the meat off, they would throw the bones away into the spit-boxes, and we would pick the bones out of the spit-boxes and gnaw them over again.

Question. Did they have any more to give you?

Answer. They had plenty. They were just doing it for their own gratification. They said Seward had put old Beast Butler in there, and they did not care how they treated us.

Question. Did you complain about not having enough?

Answer. Certainly we complained, but they said we had plenty. They cursed us, and said we had a sight more than their men had who were prisoners in our lines.

Question. Do you feel any better now since you have been here?

Answer. A great deal better; like a new man now. I am gaining flesh now.

By Mr. Odell:

Question. What was your occupation before you went into the army?

Answer. I was a farmer.

By Mr. Julian:

Question. Do you know how they treated their own sick?

Answer. No, sir.

By Mr. Odell:

Question. Were other Tennesseeans taken prisoners the same time you were?

Answer. Yes, sir; there were twenty-four of us taken prisoners. The small-pox was very severe among us. Our own men said that they were just trying to kill the Tennesseeans and Kentuckians. Out of the twenty-four, there were ten of us left when they started for Georgia. No man can tell precisely how we were treated and say just how it was.

L. H. Parhan, sworn and examined.

By Mr. Gooch:

Question. From what State are you?

Answer. West Tennessee.

Question. To what regiment do you belong?

Answer. The 3d West Tennessee cavalry.

Question. Where were you taken prisoner?

Answer. In Henry county, West Tennessee.

Question. From there where were you carried?

Answer. From there they marched us on foot, some 350-odd miles, to Decatur.

Question. What were you given to eat?

Answer. Sometimes for twenty-four or thirty hours we would have a little piece of beef and some corn-bread.

Question. Were you a well man when you were taken prisoner?

Answer. Yes, sir; a stout man for a little man. I was very stout.

Question. Were you brought to your present condition by want of food?

Answer. Yes, sir; and sleeping in the cold. They took my money and clothes and everything else away from me, even my pocket-comb and knife, and my finger-ring that my sister gave me. They were taken away when I was captured.

[The witness, who was so weak that he could not raise his head, appeared to be so much exhausted by talking that the committee refrained from further examination. As they were moving away from his bed, he spoke up and said: "I am better now than when I came here. I have some strength now. I hope I shall get better, for I want to see my old father and mother once more."]

James Sweeney, sworn and examined.

By Mr. Gooch:

Question. Where did you reside when you enlisted?
Answer. Haverhill, Massachusetts.
Question. To what company and regiment do you belong?
Answer. Company E, 17th Massachusetts.
Question. When were you taken prisoner?
Answer. First of February.
Question. Where?
Answer. Six miles from Newbern, North Carolina.
Question. Where were you then carried?
Answer. To Richmond.
Question. How were you treated after you were taken prisoner?
Answer. We had no breakfast that day. We started out early in the morning—the 132d New York was with us—without anything to eat. We had nothing to eat all that day, and they made us sleep out all that night without anything to eat. It rained that night; then they marched us the next day thirty miles, to Kingston, without anything to eat, except it was, about twelve o'clock, one of the regular captains, who had some crackers in his haversack, gave us about one each, and some of the boys managed to get an ear of corn from the wagons, but the rest of them were pushed back by the guns of the guard; then we were kept in the streets of Kingston until about nine o'clock, when we had a little pork and three barrels of crackers for about two hundred of us. I got three or four crackers. Then they put us in freight cars that they had carried hogs in, all filthy and dirty, and we were nearly frozen by the time we got to Goldsborough; and near Weldon they camped us in a field all day long, like a spectacle for the people to look at, and when we got to Richmond they put us in a common for a while, and then we were taken to prison. About eleven o'clock that day they brought us some corn-bread. They gave me about three-quarters of a small loaf and a dipper of hard, black beans with worms in them. We were kept there all night. If we went near the window, bullets were fired at us. Two or three hundred men lay on the floor. I was kept between three and four weeks on Belle Isle.
Question. How was it for food there?
Answer. That night they gave us a piece of corn-bread about an inch thick, two or three inches long. Some nights we would have a couple of spoonfuls, maybe, of raw rice or raw beans; other nights they would not give us that. A squad of 100 men of us would have about 20 sticks of wood, and in order to cut that up we would have to pay a man for the use of an axe by giving him a piece of the stick for splitting up the rest. We lay right on the ground in the snow. Twenty of us together would lay with our feet so close to the fire that the soles of our boots would be all drawn, and we would get up in the morning all shivering, and I could not eat what little food I did get.
Question. What is the cause of your sickness?
Answer. Just the food we got there and this exposure. Eating this corn-bread continually gave me the diarrhœa. We would get thirsty and drink that river water. We had little bits of beef sometimes; generally it was tough, more like a piece of India-rubber you would rub pencil-marks out with. What little food we did get was so bad we could not eat it. At first, for five or six days, we could eat it pretty well, but afterwards I could not eat it.

Question. Have you been brought to your present condition by your treatment there?

Answer. Yes, sir; by the want of proper food, and exposure to the cold.

John C. Burcham, sworn and examined.

By Mr. Julian:

Question. Where did you enlist, and in what regiment?

Answer. I enlisted in Indianapolis, in the 75th Indiana regiment, Colonel Robinson.

Question. When were you taken prisoner, and where?

Answer. I was taken prisoner at Chickamauga, on the 20th of September.

Question. Where were you carried then?

Answer. The next day they took us to Atlanta, and then on to Richmond.

Question. What prison were you put in?

Answer. I was on Belle Isle five or six days and nights, and then they put me in a prison over in town.

Question. How did they treat you there?

Answer. Rough, rough, rough.

Question. What did they give you to eat?

Answer. A small bit of bread and a little piece of meat; black beans full of worms. Sometimes meat pretty good, sometimes the meat was so rotten that you could smell it as soon as you got it in the house. We were used rough, I can tell you.

Question. Did they leave you your property?

Answer. They took everything we had before ever we got to Richmond; my hat, blankets, knife. We did not do very well until we got some blankets from our government; afterwards we did better. Before that we slept right on the floor, with nothing over us except a little old blanket one of us had.

Question. What was their manner towards you?

Answer. I call it pretty rough. If a man did not walk just right up to the mark they were down on him, and not a man of us dared to put his head out of the window, for he would be shot if he did. Several were shot just for that.

Question. What is the cause of your sickness?

Answer. Nothing but exposure and the kind of food we had there. I was a tolerably stout man before I got into their hands; after that I was starved nearly to death.

Daniel Gentis, sworn and examined.

By the chairman:

Question. What State are you from?

Answer. Indiana.

Question. When did you enlist, and in what company and regiment?

Answer. I enlisted on the 6th of August, 1861, in company I, 2d New York regiment.

Question. Where were you taken prisoner?

Answer. I was taken prisoner at Stevensville, Virginia; I was there with Colonel Dahlgren, on Kilpatrick's expedition.

Question. Were you taken prisoner at the same time that Colonel Dahlgren was killed?

Answer. I was there when he was killed, but I was taken prisoner the next morning.

Question. What do you know about the manner of his death and the treatment his body received?

Answer. He was shot within a foot and a half or two feet of me. I got wounded that same night. The next morning I was taken prisoner, and as we came along we saw his body, with his clothes all off. He was entirely naked, and he was put into a hole and covered up.

Question. Buried naked in that way?

Answer. Yes, sir; no coffin at all. Afterwards his body was taken up and carried to a slue and washed off, and then sent off to Richmond. A despatch came from Richmond for his body, and it was sent thère.

Question. It has been said they cut off his finger?

Answer. Yes, sir; his little finger was cut off, and his ring taken off.

By Mr. Odell:

Question. How do you know there was a ring on his finger?

Answer. I saw the fellow who had it, and who said he took it off. When they took his body to a slue and washed it off they put on it a shirt and drawers, and then put it in a box and sent it to Richmond.

Question. How far was that from Richmond?

Answer. It was about 40 miles from Richmond, and about 10 miles from West Point.

Question. How were you treated yourself?

Answer. I fared first-rate. I staid at the house of a Dr. Walker, of Virginia, and Dr. Walker told me that a private of the 9th Virginia cavalry took off Colonel Dahlgren's artificial leg, and that General Ewell, I think it was, or some general in the southern army who had but one leg, gave the private $2,000 for it, (confederate currency.) I saw the private who took it, and saw him have the leg.

By the chairman:

Question. How do you know they received a despatch from Richmond to have the body sent there?

Answer. All the information I got about the despatch was from Dr. Walker, who said they were going to take the body to Richmond and bury it where no one could find it.

Question. Did Colonel Dahlgren make any speech or read any papers to his command?

Answer. No, sir; not that I ever heard of. They questioned me a great deal about that. The colonel of the 9th Virginia cavalry questioned me about it. I told him just all I knew about it. I told him I had heard no papers read, nor anything else.

Question. Did you ever hear any of your fellow-soldiers say they ever heard any such thing at all?

Answer. No, sir; and when I started I had no idea where I was going.

Question. Were you in prison at Richmond?

Answer. I was there for four days, but I was at Dr. Walker's pretty nearly a month and a half.

Question. During the four days you were in prison did you see any of our other soldiers in prison there?

Asnwer. Yes, sir.

Question. How did they fare?

Answer. We all fared pretty rough on corn-bread and beans. Those who were in my ward are here now sick in bed.

Question. How happened it that you fell into the hands of Dr. Walker particularly?

Answer. The way it came about was this: In the morning I asked some officers of the regular regiment for a doctor to dress my wound. One of the doctors there said he could not do it. I spoke to a lieutenant and asked him to be kind enough to get some doctor to dress it, and he got this Dr. Walker. The doctor asked me to go to his house, and stay there if I would. I told him "certainly I would go." The colonel of the rebel regiment said that the doctor could take me there, and I staid until Captain Magruder came up there and told Dr. Walker that I had to be sent to Richmond.

Question. Where were you wounded?

Answer. In the knee.

[At this point the committee concluded to examine no more of the patients in the hospital, as most of them were too weak to be examined without becoming too much exhausted, and because the testimony of all amounted to about the same thing. They therefore confined the rest of their investigation to the testimony of the surgeons in charge, and other persons attending upon the patients.]

Surgeon B. A. Van Derkieft, sworn and examined.

By the chairman:

Question. Are you in the service of the United States; and if so, in what capacity?

Answer. I am a surgeon of volunteers in the United States service; in charge of hospital division No. 1, known as the Naval Hospital, Annapolis, and have been here since the 1st of June, 1863.

Question. State what you know in regard to the condition of our exchanged or paroled prisoners who have been brought here, and also your opportunities to know that condition?

Answer. Since I have been here I think that from five to six thousand paroled prisoners have been treated in this hospital as patients. They have generally come here in a very destitute and feeble condition; many of them so low that they die the very day they arrive here.

Question. What is the character of their complaints generally, and what does that character indicate as to the cause?

Answer. Generally they are suffering from debility and chronic diarrhœa, the result, I have no doubt, of exposure, privations, hardship, and ill treatment.

Question. In what respect would hardship and ill treatment superinduce the complaints most prevalent among these paroled prisoners?

Answer. These men, having been very much exposed, and not having had nourishment enough to sustain their strength, are consequently predisposed to be attacked by such diseases as diarrhœa, fever, scurvy, and all catarrhal affections, which, perhaps, in the beginning are very slight, but, on account of want of necessary care, produce, after a while, a very serious disease. For instance, a man exposed to the cold may have a little bronchitis, or perhaps a little inflammation of the lungs, which, under good treatment, would be easily cured—would be considered of no importance whatever; but being continually exposed, and not having the necessary food, the complaint is transformed, after a time, into a very severe disease.

Question. Is it your opinion, as a physician, that the complaints of our returned prisoners are superinduced by want of proper food, or food of sufficient quantity, and from exposure?

Answer. Yes, sir.

Question. What is the general character of the statements our prisoners have made to you in regard to their treatment?

Answer. They complained of want of food, of bad food, and a want of clothing. Very often, though not always, they are robbed, when taken prisoners, of all the good clothes they have on. There is no doubt about that, for men have often arrived here with nothing but their pants and shirts on; no coat, overcoat, no cap, no shoes or stockings, and some of them without having had any opportunities to wash themselves for weeks and months, so that when they arrive here, the scurf on their skin is one-eighth of an inch thick; and we have had several cases of men who have been shot for the slightest offence. There is a man now here who at one time put his hand out of the privy, which was nothing but a window in the wall, to steady himself and keep himself from falling, and he was shot, and we have been obliged to amputate his arm since he arrived here. These men complain that they have had no shelter. We have men here now who say that for five or six months they have been compelled to lay on the sand. I have no doubt about the correctness of their statements, for the condition of their skins shows the statements to be true. Their joints are calloused, and they have callouses on their backs, and some have even had the bones break through the skin. There is one instance in particular that I would mention. One man died in the hospital there one hour before the transfer of prisoners was made, and as an act of humanity the surgeon in charge of the hospital allowed the friends of this man to take him on board the vessel in order to have him buried among his friends. This man was brought here right from the Richmond hospital. He was so much covered with vermin and so dirty that we were not afraid to make the statement that the man had not been washed for six months. Now, as a material circumstance to prove that these men have been badly fed, I will state that we must be very careful in feeding them when they arrive here, for a very light diet is too much for them at first.

Question. You have accompanied us as we have examined some of the patients in the hospital to-day. Do their statements to us, under oath, correspond with the statements which they made when they first arrived here?

Answer. They are quite the same; there is no difference. Every man makes the same statement, and we therefore believe it to be true. All say the same in regard to rations, treatment, exposure and privations. Once in a while I have found a man who pretended to have been treated very well, but by examining closely I find that such men are not very good Union men.

Question. You say that about six thousand paroled prisoners have come under your supervision and treatment?

Answer. Yes, sir.

Question. State generally what their condition has been.

Answer. Very bad, indeed. I cannot find terms sufficient to express what their condition was. I cannot state it properly.

Question. You have already stated that, as a general thing, they have been destitute of clothing.

Answer. Yes, sir; dirty, filthy, covered with vermin, dying. At one time we received three hundred and sixty patients in one day, and fourteen died within twelve hours; and there were six bodies of those who had died on board the transport that brought them up here.

Question. What appeared to be the complaint of which they died?

Answer. Very extreme debility, the result of starvation and exposure—the same as the very weak man you saw here, [L. H. Parham.]

Question. We have observed some very emaciated men here, perfect skeletons, nothing but skin and bone. In your opinion, as a physician, what has reduced these men to that condition?

Answer. Nothing but starvation and exposure.

Question. Can you tell the proportion of the men who have died to the number that have lately arrived from Richmond?

Answer. If time is allowed me I can send the statement to the committee.

Question. Do so, if you please.

Answer. I will do so. I will say that some of these men who have stated they were well treated, I have found out to have been very bad to the Union men.

Question. Are those men you have just mentioned as having been well treated an exception to the general rule?

Answer. Yes, sir; a very striking exception.

Question. Have you ever been in charge of confederate prisoners?

Answer. Yes, sir.

Question. State the course of treatment of our authorities towards them.

Answer. We have never made the slightest difference between our own men and confederate prisoners when their sick and wounded have been in our hands.

Question. You have treated both the same?

Answer. Yes, sir. When any one of their men, wounded or sick, has been a patient in our hands, we have treated him the same as we do our own men.

By Mr. Julian:

Question. Have their sick and wounded been kept separate from ours, or have they been kept together?

Answer. In Washington they were kept separate, but at Antietam, where an hospital was established, in order to have the patients treated where they were injured, the Union and confederate patients were treated together and alike. At Hagerstown almost everybody is secesh. Well, the most I can say is, that some of the secesh ladies there came to me and stated that they were very glad to see that we had treated their men the same as ours.

Question. It is sometimes said, by the rebel newspapers, at least, that they have given the same rations to our prisoners that they give to their own soldiers. Now, I want to ask you, as a medical man, if it is possible, with the amount of food that our prisoners have had, for men to retain their health and vigor, and perform active service in the field?

Answer. I do not believe that the rebels could fight as well, or make such marches as they have done, upon such small rations as our prisoners have received.

Question. Can the health of men be preserved upon such rations as they have given our prisoners?

Answer. No, sir; it cannot, not only on account of quantity, but quality. I have seen some specimens of their rations brought here by our paroled prisoners, and I know what they are.

Question. As a general rule, what is the effect of treating men in that way?

Answer. Just what we hear every day—men dying from starvation and debility. Many of these men—mostly all the wounded men—are suffering from hospital gangrene, which is the result of not having their wounds dressed in time, and having too many crowded in the same apartment. We have had men here whose wounds have been so long neglected that they have had maggots in them by the hundred.

Acting Assistant Surgeon J. H. Longenecker, sworn and examined.

By Mr. Gooch:

Question. What is your position in the United States service?

Answer. Acting assistant surgeon.

Question. How long have you been stationed here?

Answer. Since the 27th of July, 1863.

Question. Will you state what has been the condition of our paroled prisoners, received here from the rebels, during the time you have been stationed here?

Answer. As a general thing, they have been very much debilitated, emaciated, and suffering from disease, such as diarrhœa, scurvy, lung diseases, &c.

Question. In your opinion, as a physician, by what have these diseases been produced?

Answer. By exposure and want of proper food, I think.

Question. Are you able to form any opinion, from the condition of these men, as to the quantity and quality of food which they have received?

Answer. From their appearance and condition, I judge the quality must have been very bad, and the quantity very small, not sufficient to preserve the health.

Question. We have seen and examined several patients here this morning, who are but mere skeletons. They have stated to us, as you are aware, that their suffering arose wholly from the want of proper food and clothing. In your opinion as a medical man, are these statements true?

Answer. I believe that these statements are correct. We have had some men who looked very well. How they managed to preserve their health I am not able to say; but, as a general thing, the men we receive here are very much debilitated, apparently from exposure, and want of sufficient food to keep up life and health.

Question. Are you acquainted with the case of Howard Laedom?

Answer. Yes, sir; I am.

Question. Will you state about that case?

Answer. I did not see the patient until recently, when he was placed in my charge. I found him with all his toes gone from one foot in consequence of exposure. He has suffered from pneumonia, also, produced by exposure, and there have been very many cases of pneumonia here, produced by the same cause, many of whom have died; and we have held post mortem examinations upon many of them, and found ulcers upon their intestines, some of them being ulcerated the whole length of their bowels.

Question. Have you made many post mortem examinations here?

Answer. We have made quite a number of them. We make them whenever we have an opportunity; whenever bodies are not called for or are not likely to be taken away.

Question. Are you enabled, from these post mortem examinations, to determine whether or not these prisoners have had sufficient quantities of proper food?

Answer. Not from that. Those examinations merely indicate the condition in which the prisoners are returned to us.

Question. From all the indications given by the appearance of these men, are you satisfied that their statements, that they have not had sufficient food, both in quantity and quality, are true?

Answer. These statements have been repeated to me very often, and from their condition I believe their statement to be true.

Question. How many paroled prisoners were brought here by the last boat?

Answer. Three hundred and sixty-five, I think.

Question. In your opinion, how many of these men will recover?

Answer. Judging from their present condition, I think that at least one hundred of them will die.

Question. What, in your opinion, will be the primary cause of the death of these men?

Answer. Exposure and want of proper food while prisoners.

Assistant Surgeon William S. Ely, sworn and examined.

By Mr. Harding:

Question. What is your position in the service?

Answer. Assistant surgeon of the United States volunteers and executive officer of hospital division No. 1, or Naval Academy hospital.

Question. Please state the sanitary condition and appearance, &c., of the paroled prisoners received here, together with their declarations as to the cause of their sickness, and your opinion as to the truth of their statements.

Answer. I have been on duty in this hospital since October 3, 1863. Since that time I have been present on the arrival of the steamer New York on five or six different occasions, when bringing altogether some three or four thousand paroled prisoners. I have assisted in unloading these prisoners from the boat, and assigning them to quarters in the hospital. I have found them generally very much reduced physically, and depressed mentally, the direct result, as I think, of the ill-treatment which they have received from the hands of their enemies—whether intentional or not I cannot say. I have frequently seen on the boat bodies of those who have died while being brought here, and I have frequently known them to die while being conveyed from the boat to the hospital ward. Their condition is such (their whole constitution being undermined) that the best of care and medical treatment, and all the sanitary and hygeian measures that we can introduce appear to be useless. Their whole assimilative functions appear to be impaired. Medicines and food appear, in many cases, to have no effect upon them. We have made post mortem examinations repeatedly of cases here, and on all occasions we find the system very much reduced, and in many cases the muscles almost entirely gone—reduced to nothing literally but skin and bone; the blood vitiated and depraved, and an anœmic condiiton of the entire system apparent. The fact that in many cases of post mortems we had discovered no organic disease, justifies us in the conclusion that the fatal result is owing principallly, if not entirely, to a deprivation of food and other articles necessary to support life, and to improper exposure. On all occasions when arriving here, these men have been found in the most filthy condition, it being almost impossible, in many cases, to clean them by repeated washings. The functions of the skin are entirely impaired, and in many cases they are encrusted with dirt, owing, as they say, to being compelled to lie on the sand at Belle island; and the normal function of the skin has not been recovered until the cuticle has been entirely thrown off. Their bodies are covered with vermin, so that it has been found necessary to throw away all the clothing which they had on when they arrived here, and provide them entirely with new clothing. Their hair has been filled with vermin, so that we have been obliged to cut their hair all off, and make applications to kill the vermin in their heads. Many of them state that they have had no opportunity to wash their bodies for six or eight months, and have not done so.

Question. What have been their statements to you in their conversation with you?

Answer. Their reply almost invariably has been, that their condition is the result solely of ill-treatment and starvation; that their rations have consisted of corn-bread and cobs ground with corn, of a few beans at times, and now and then a little piece of poor meat. Occasionally one is heard to say, that in his opinion the rebels are unable to treat them in any better manner; that they have been treated as well as possible; and I have found several who stated that their physicians were kind to them and did all they could, but complained of want of medicines.

Question. Is it your conclusion, as a physician, that the statements of these paroled prisioners, in regard to the treatment they have received, are correct, and that such treatment would produce such conditions of health as you witness among them upon their arrival here?

Answer. Yes, sir; and that in many cases their statements fall short of the truth, as evinced by the results shown in their physical appearance; and these men are in such a condition that even if they recover, we consider them almost entirely unfitted for further active field service—almost as much so, we frequently say, as if they had been shot on the field.

Miss Abbie J. Howe, sworn and examined.

By Mr. Gooch:

Question. From what State are you, and what position do you occupy in this hospital?

Answer. I am from Massachusetts, and am here acting as nurse.

Question. How long have you been here?

Answer. Since the 15th of September, 1863.

Question. Have you had charge of the sick and paroled prisoners who have come here during that time?

Answer. Yes, sir; some of them.

Question. How many of them have you had charge of, should you think?

Answer. I should think I have had charge of at least 250 who have come under my own charge.

Question. Can you describe to us the general condition of those men?

Answer. Almost all of them have had this dreadful cough. I do not think I ever heard the like before; and they have had chronic diarrhœa, very persistent indeed. Many of them have a great craving for things which they ought not to have. One patient who came in here had the scurvy, and he said: "I can eat anything that a dog can eat. Oh, do give me something to eat;" and in their delirium they are crying for "bread, bread," and "mother, mother." One of them called out for "more James river water to drink."

Question. What has been their general complaint in regard to their treatment while prisoners?

Answer. Their chief complaint has been want of food and great exposure. Many of them who had clothes sent them by friends or our government, were obliged to sell everything until they were left as destitute as at first, in order to get more food. I have seen some of their rations, and I would myself rather eat what I have seen given to cattle, than to eat such food as their specimens brought here. One man had the typhoid fever, but was in such haste to get away from the hospital in Richmond in order to get home, that he would not remain there. He had the ravenous appetite which men with typhus fever have; and other men told me that they gave him their rations which they could not eat themselves. This produced a terrible diarrhœa, and he lived but a few days after he arrived here.

Question. What has been the physical condition of these, emaciated or otherwise?

Answer. Just skin and bone. I have never imagined anything before like it.

Question. Have their statements, in relation to their exposure and deprivation of food, corresponded entirely with each other?

Answer. Yes, sir, entirely so, except those who were able, by work, to get extra rations; and those extra rations were not anything like what our men have here, but it gave them as much and as good as their guards had; and they have not only been treated in this way, but they have been ill-used in almost every way. They have told me that when one of them was sitting down, and was told to get up, and was not moving quickly in consequence of his sickness, he was wounded by the rebels in charge. They have often told me that they have been kicked and knocked about when unable to move quickly. I could give a great many instances of ill-treatment and hardships which have been stated to me, but it would take a great deal of time to tell them.

Rev. H. C. Henries, sworn and examined.

By Mr. Odell:

Question. What is your position here?

Answer. Chaplain of the hospital.

Question. How long have you been here?

Answer. I have been on duty since December 7, 1861.

Question. You are familiar with the facts connected with the condition of paroled prisoners arriving here from the south?

Answer. Yes, sir.

Question. Will you state generally what was their condition?

Answer. I think it would be impossible for me to give any adequate description, for I think all language fails to fully express their real condition as they land here. Their appearance is haggard in the extreme; ragged, destitute even of shoes, and very frequently without pants or blouses, or any covering except their drawers and shirts, and perhaps a half a blanket, or something like that; sometimes without hats, and in the most filthy condition that it is possible to conceive of either beast or man being reduced to in any circumstances; unable to give either their names, their residence, regiments, or any facts, in consequence of their mental depression, so that I believe the surgeons have found it quite impossible some times to ascertain their relation to the army. Their statements agree almost universally in regard to their treatment at the hands of the rebels. There have been a very few exceptions, indeed, of those who have stated that perhaps their fare was as good as, under the circumstances, the rebels were able to give them, but the almost universal testimony of these men has been, that they were purposely deprived of the comforts and medical care which could have been afforded them, in order to render them useless to the army in the future. That has been the impression which a great many of them have labored under. They have given their testimony in regard to their condition on Belle Isle. There were three in one room here not long since, who told me that some eight of their comrades died during one or two days, and their bodies were thrown out on the banks that enclosed the ground and left there for eight days unburied, and they were refused the privilege of burying their comrades, until the hogs and the dogs had well-nigh eaten up their bodies. Yesterday, one man told me that he was so starved, and his hunger had become so intolerable, that his eyes appeared to swim in his head, and at times to be almost lost to all consciousness. Others have stated that they have offered to buy dogs at any price for food, of those who came in there; and one actually said that when a man came in there with a dog, and went out without the dog noticing it, they caught him and dressed him and roasted him over the fire, over a gas-light, as best they could, and then ate it; and, as he expressed it, "it was a precious mite to them." Their testimony in regard to the cruelty of the guards and others set over them is to the effect that in one instance two comrades in the army together, who were taken prisoners together, and remained in the prison together, were separated when the prisoners were exchanged. One was returned here and the other left. The one who was left went to the window and waved his hand in adieu to his comrade, and the guard deliberately shot him through the temple, and he fell dead. I mentioned this fact to others of our prisoners here in the hospital, and they said that they knew it to be so. Some of them were there at the time the man was shot.

Question. Do you keep any record of the deaths here?

Answer. I have not kept a record. I have the official notice of the deaths; but inasmuch as the records are kept at the office, and we have had so many other duties crowding upon us—so many deaths here—it has been almost impossible for us to keep any record. I think it is impossible for any description to exaggerate the condition of those men. The condition of those here now is not so bad, as a class, as some we have received heretofore.

By the chairman:

Question. Has the treatment of our prisoners latterly been worse than before, from their testimony?

Answer. I think there has been no very material change of late. I think it has grown worse from the very first; but for a year past, I should judge it could not be made any worse.

Question. Just the same thing we now see here?

Answer. Yes, sir. I would give just another fact in regard to the statements made here by large numbers of our returned prisoners. On Belle Isle, their privies were down from the main camp. From 6 o'clock in the morning until 6 o'clock in the evening they were permitted to go to these sinks or privies, but from 6 at night until 6 in the morning they were refused the privilege of going there, and consequently, so many suffering with diarrhœa, their filth was deposited all through their camp. The wells from which they drew their water were sunk in the sand around through their camp, and you can judge what the effect of that has been. Some of these prisoners, soon after they were put on Belle Isle, not knowing the regulations there, and suffering from chronic diarrhœa, when making the attempt to go down to these privies after 6 o'clock at night, were shot down in cold blood by the guards, without any warning whatever. Several such instances have been stated to me by parties who have arrived here.

By Mr. Odell:

Question. You make these statements from the testimony of prisoners received here?

Answer. Yes, sir; from testimony that I have the most perfect confidence in. Men have stated these things to me in the very last hours of their lives.

By the chairman:

Question. Were they conscious of their condition at the time they made their statements?

Answer. Yes, sir; I think they were perfectly conscious; yet there is one thing which is very remarkable, that is, these men retain their hope of life up to the hour of dying. They do not give up. There is another thing I would wish to state: all the men, without any exception, among the thousands that have come to this hospital, have never, in a single instance, expressed a regret (notwithstanding the privations and sufferings that they have endured) that they entered their country's service. They have been the most loyal, devoted, and earnest men. Even on the last days of their lives they have said that all they hoped for was just to live and enter the ranks again and meet their foes. It is a most glorious record in reference to the devotion of our men to their country. I do not think their patriotism has ever been equalled in the history of the world.

The committee then proceeded, by steamer, from Annapolis to Baltimore, and visited the "West Hospital," and saw the patients there. As they presented the same reduced and debilitated appearance as those they had already seen at Annapolis, and in conversation gave the same account of their treatment at the hands of the rebels, the committee concluded their examination by taking merely the testimony of the surgeon and chaplain of the hospital.

"West Hospital," *Baltimore, Md., May* 6, 1864.

Dr. Wm. G. Knowles, sworn and examined.

By the chairman:

Question. Will you state whether you are in the employment of the government; and if so, in what capacity?

Answer. I am, and have been for nearly three years, a contract physician in the "West Hospital," Baltimore.

Question. Have you received any of the returned Union prisoners, from Richmond, in your hospital?

Answer. We have received those we have here now; no others

Question. How many have you received?

Answer. We have received 105.

Question. When did you receive them?

Answer. Two weeks ago last Tuesday. On the 19th of April.

Question. Will you state the condition those prisoners were in when they were received here?

Answer. They were all very emaciated men, as you have seen here to-day, only more so than they appear to be now. They were very emaciated and feeble, suffering chiefly from diarrhœa, many of them having, in connexion with that, bronchial and similar affections. From the testimony given to me by these men I have no doubt their condition was the result of exposure and—I was about to say starvation; but it was, perhaps, hardly starvation, for they had something to eat; but I will say, a deficient supply of food and of a proper kind of food; and when I say "exposure," perhaps that would not be sufficiently definite. All with whom I have conversed have stated that those who were on Belle Isle were kept there even as late as December with nothing to protect them but such little clothing as was left them by their captors; with no blankets, no overcoats, no tents, nothing to cover them, nothing to protect them; and that their sleeping-place was the ground—the sand.

Question. What would you, as a physician of experience, aside from the statements of these returned prisoners, say was the cause of their condition?

Answer. I should judge it was as they have stated. Diarrhœa is a very common form of disease among them, and from all the circumstances I have every reason to believe that it is owing to exposure and the want of proper nourishment. Some of them tell me that they received nothing but two small pieces of corn-bread a day. Some of them suppose (how true that may be I do not know) that that bread was made of corn ground with the cobs. I have not seen any of it to examine it.

Question. How many have died of the number you have received here?

Answer. Already twenty-nine have died, and you have seen one who is now dying; and five were received here dead, who died on their way from Fortress Monroe to Baltimore.

Question. How many of them were capable of walking into the hospital?

Answer. Only one; the others were brought here from the boat on stretchers, put on the dumb-waiter, and lifted right up to their rooms, and put on their beds. And I would state another thing in regard to these men: when they were received here they were filthy, dirty, and lousy in the extreme, and we had considerable trouble to get them clean. Every man who could possibly stand it we took and placed in a warm bath and held him up while he was washed, and we threw away all their dirty clothing, providing them with that which was clean.

Question. What was the condition of their clothing?

Answer. Very poor, indeed. I should say the clothing was very much worn, although I did not examine it closely, as that was not so much a matter of investigation with us as was their physical condition. Their heads were filled with vermin, so much so that we had to cut off their hair and make applications to destroy the vermin.

Question. What portion of those you have received here do you suppose are finally curable?

Answer. We shall certainly lose one-third of them; and we have been inclined to think that, sooner or later, we should lose one-half of them.

Question. Will the constitutions of those who survive be permanently injured, or will they entirely recover?

Answer. I think the constitutions of the greater part of them will be seriously impaired; that they will never become strong and healthy again.

Question. What account have these men given you as to the comparative condition of those left behind? Did the rebels send the best or the poorest of our prisoners?

Answer. I could not tell that; I have never inquired. But I should presume they must have sent the worst they had.

Question. You have had charge of confederate sick and wounded, have you not?

Answer. Yes, sir; a large number of them. This was the receiving hospital for those from Gettysburg.

Question. What was the treatment they received from us?

Answer. We consider that we treated them with the greatest kindness and humanity; precisely as we treated our own men. That has been our rule of conduct. We gave them the very best the hospital would afford; and not only what properly belonged to the hospital, but delicacies and luxuries of every kind were furnished them by the hospital, and by outside sympathizers, who were permitted to send delicacies to them.

Question. It has been stated in many of the rebel newspapers that our prisoners are treated the same and fed with the same rations as their soldiers in the field. In your judgment, as a physician would it be possible for their soldiers to retain their health and energy if fed as our prisoners have been?

Answer. No, sir; it would be impossible; multitudes of them would have died under such treatment.

Question. I do not know as I desire to question you further. Is there anything more you desire to state?

Answer. I do not know that there is; it is all in a nut-shell.

By Mr. Odell:

Question. Is not the disease as evinced among those men clearly defined as resulting from exposure and privations, and want of proper food and nourishment?

Answer. That is our decided opinion as medical men; the opinion of all of us who have had anything to do with these men.

By Mr. Gooch:

Question. The condition of all these men appears to be about the same. Is there really any difference in their condition except in degree?

Answer. I think that is all. Some men have naturally stronger constitutions than others, and can bear more than others. That is the way I account for the difference.

By Mr. Odell:

Question. Are the minds of any of them affected permanently?

Answer. We have had two or three whose intellect is very feeble; some of them are almost like children in that respect.

Question. Do you think that grows out of the treatment they have received?

Answer. I think the same cause produced that as the other.

By the chairman:

Question. Is not that one of the symptoms attendant upon starvation, that men are likely to become deranged or idiotic?

Answer. Yes, sir; more like derangement than what we call idiocy

By Mr. Gooch:

Question. Can those men whose arms you bared and held up to us—mere skeletons, nothing but skin and bone—can those men recover?

Answer. They may; we think that some of them are in an improving condition. But we have to be extremely cautious how we feed them. If we give them a little excess of food under these circumstances they would be almost certain to be seriously and injuriously affected by it.

Question. It is your opinion, you have stated, that these men have been reduced to this condition by want of food?

Answer. It is; want of food and exposure are the original causes. That has produced diarrhœa and other diseases as a natural consequence, and they have aided the original cause and reduced them to their present condition. I should like the country and the government to know the facts about these men; I do not think they can realize it until the facts are made known to them. I think the rebels have determined upon the policy of starving their prisoners, just as much as the murders at Fort Pillow were a part of their policy.

Rev. J. T. Van Burkalow, sworn and examined.

By the chairman:

Question. What is your connexion with this hospital?

Answer. I am the chaplain of the hospital.

Question. How long have you been acting in that capacity?

Answer. I have been connected with the hospital in that capacity ever since the 20th of October, 1862.

Question. What has been your opportunity of knowing the condition of our returned prisoners?

Answer. I have mingled with them and administered unto them ever since they have been here, night and day. I have written, I suppose, something like a hundred letters for them to their relatives and friends, since they arrived here.

Question. Have you attended them when they were dying?

Answer. Yes, sir.

Question. And conversed with them about their condition, and the manner in which they have been brought to that condition?

Answer. Yes, sir; I have.

Question. Please tell us what you have ascertained from them.

Answer. The general story I have gotten from them was to the effect that when captured, and before they got to Richmond, they would generally be robbed of their clothing, their good United States uniforms, even to their shoes and hats taken from them, and if anything was given to them in place of them, they would receive only old worn-out confederate clothing. Sometimes they were sent to Belle Isle with nothing on but old pants and shirts. They generally had their money taken from them, often with the promise of its return, but that promise was never fulfilled. They were placed on Belle Isle, as I have said, some with nothing on but pants and shirts, some with blouses, but they were seldom allowed to have an overcoat or a blanket. There they remained for weeks, some of them for six or eight weeks, without any tents or any kind of covering.

Question. What time of the year was this?

Answer. All along from September down to December, as a general thing, through the latter part of the fall. There they remained for weeks without any tents, without blankets, and in many instances without coats, exposed to the rain and snow, and all kinds of inclement weather. And where some of them had tents, they were old worn-out army tents, full of holes and rents, so that they are very poor shelters indeed from the storms. I have been told by several of them that several times, upon getting up in the morning, they would find six or eight of their number frozen to death. There are men here now who have had their toes frozen off there. They have said that they have been compelled to get up during the night and walk rapidly back and forth to keep from dying from the cold.

Question. What do they say in regard to the food furnished them?

Answer. They represent that as being very little in quantity, and of the very poorest quality, being but a small piece of corn-bread, about three inches square, made of meal ground very coarsely—some of them suppose made of corn and cobs all ground up together—and that bread was baked and cut up and sent to them in such a manner that a great deal of it would be crumbled off and lost. Sometimes they would get a very small piece of meat, but that meat very poor, and sometimes for days they would receive no meat at all. And sometimes they would receive a very small quantity of what they call rice-water—that is, water with a few grains of rice in it.

Question. You have heard their statements separately?

Answer. Yes, sir.

Question. Do they all agree in the same general statement as to their treatment?

Answer. Yes, sir; they do.

Question. How were they clothed when they arrived here?

Answer. They were clothed very poorly indeed, with old worn-out filthy garments, full of vermin.

Question. What was their condition and apperance as to health when they arrived here?

Answer. They looked like living skeletons—that is about the best description I can give of them—very weak and emaciated.

Question. Have you ever seen men at any time or place so emaciated as these are—so entirely destitute of flesh?

Answer. I think I have a few times, but very rarely; I have known men to become very emaciated by being for weeks affected with chronic diarrhœa, or something of that kind. But the chronic diarrhœa, and liver diseases, and lung affections, which those men now have, I understand to have been superinduced by the treatment to which they have been subjected; their cruel and merciless treatment and exposure to inclement weather without any shelter or sufficient clothing or food, reducing them literally to a state of starvation.

Question. Could any of them walk when they arrived here?

Answer. I think there was but one who could make out to walk; the rest we had to carry into the hospitals on stretchers.

By Mr. Odell:

Question. Did these men make these statements in their dying condition?

Answer. Yes, sir.

By the chairman:

Question. Were the persons who made these statements conscious of approaching dissolution?

Answer. Yes, sir; I know of no particular cases where they spoke of these things when they were right on the borders of death; but they made them before, when they were aware of their condition.

Question. So that you have no reason to doubt that they told the exact truth, or intended to do so?

Answer. None whatever. There has been such a unanimity of testimony on that point, that I cannot entertain the shadow of a doubt.

Question. And their statements were corroborated by their appearance?

Answer. Yes, sir.

Question. You have had under your charge and attention confederate sick and wounded, have you not?

Answer. Yes, sir.

Question. How have they been treated?

Answer. In my judgment they have been treated just as well as any of our own men ever were treated. In fact, they have got better treatment than our men did formerly, for the reason that, in addition to what we have given them —and we have tried to treat them just as we would have them treat our men—

in addition to that, we have allowed the rebel sympathizers of Baltimore to bring them, every day, delicacies in abundance.

Question. Were these rebel sympathizers bountiful to them in that line?

Answer. Yes, sir, very.

Question. What has been the feeling evinced by our returned prisoners, after having received such treatment, in regard to having entered the service? Have they ever expressed any regret that they entered our army?

Answer. As a general thing, they have not. In fact, I have heard but one express a different sentiment. He was a mere youth, not more than 16 or 17 years of age now. His feet were badly frozen. He remarked that he had regretted, even long before he got to Richmond, that he entered the service. But I have heard a number of them declare that if they were so fortunate as to recover their health and strength, they should be glad to return to the service, and still fight for their country.

Question. They then bear their misfortunes bravely and patriotically?

Answer. Yes, sir, they do.

Question. And without complaining of their government?

Answer. Yes, sir, without complaining of their fate, except so far as to blame their merciless enemies.

DEPARTMENT OF THE TENNESSEE, DISTRICT OF MEMPHIS.

Deposition of John Nelson in relation to the capture of Fort Pillow.

EVIDENCE DEPARTMENT,
Provost Marshal's Office.

John Nelson, being duly sworn, deposeth and saith:

At the time of the attack on and capture of Fort Pillow, April 12, 1864, I kept a hotel within the lines at Fort Pillow, and a short distance from the works. Soon after the alarm was given that an attack on the fort was imminent, I entered the works and tendered my services to Major Booth, commanding. The attack began in the morning at about 5½ o'clock, and about one o'clock p. m. a flag of truce approached. During the parley which ensued, and while the firing ceased on both sides, the rebels kept crowding up to the works on the side near Cold creek, and also approached nearer on the south side, thereby gaining advantages pending the conference under the flag of truce. As soon as the flag of truce was withdrawn the attack began, and about five minutes after it began the rebels entered the fort. Our troops were soon overpowered, and broke and fled. A large number of the soldiers, black and white, and also a few citizens, myself among the number, rushed down the bluff towards the river. I concealed myself as well as I could in a position where I could distinctly see all that passed below the bluff, for a considerable distance up and down the river.

A large number, at least one hundred, were hemmed in near the river bank by bodies of the rebels coming from both north and south. Most all of those thus hemmed in were without arms. I saw many soldiers, both white and black, throw up their arms in token of surrender, and call out that they had surrendered. The rebels would reply, "God damn you, why didn't you surrender before?" and shot them down like dogs.

The rebels commenced an indiscriminate slaughter. Many colored soldiers sprang into the river and tried to escape by swimming, but these were invariably shot dead.

A short distance from me, and within view, a number of our wounded had been placed, and near where Major Booth's body lay; and a small red flag indicated that at that place our wounded were placed. The rebels, however as they passed these wounded men, fired right into them and struck them with the buts of their muskets.

The cries for mercy and groans which arose from the poor fellows were heartrending.

Thinking that if I should be discovered, I would be killed, I emerged from my hiding place, and, approaching the nearest rebel, I told him I was a citizen. He said, "You are in bad company, G—d d——n you; out with your greenbacks, or I'll shoot you." I gave him all the money I had, and under his convoy I went up into the fort again.

When I re-entered the fort there was still some shooting going on. I heard a rebel officer tell a soldier not to kill any more of those negroes. He said that they would all be killed, any way, when they were tried.

JOHN NELSON.

Mr. Nelson further states:

After I entered the fort, and after the United States flag had been taken down, the rebels held it up in their hands in the presence of their officers, and thus gave the rebels outside a chance to still continue their slaughter, and I did not notice that any rebel officer forbade the holding of it up. I also further state, to the best of my knowledge and information, that there were not less than three hundred and sixty negroes killed and two hundred whites.

This I give to the best of my knowledge and belief.

JOHN NELSON.

Subscribed and sworn to before me this 2d day of May, A. D. 1864.

J. D. LLOYD,
Captain 11th Infantry, Mo. Vols., and
Ass'nt Provost Marshal, Dist. of Memphis.

Statement of Frank Hogan, corporal in company A, 6th United States heavy artillery, (colored.)

I, Frank Hogan, a corporal in company A, of the 6th United States heavy artillery, (colored,) would, on oath, state the following: That I was in the battle fought at Fort Pillow, Tennessee, on the (12th) twelfth day of April, A. D. (1864,) one thousand eight hundred and sixty-four, and that I was taken prisoner by the enemy, and I saw Captain Carson, and heard some of the enemy ask him if he belonged to a nigger regiment. He told them he did. They asked him how he came here. He told them he was detailed there. Then they told him they would give him a detail, and immediately shot him dead, after being a prisoner without arms. I also saw two lieutenants, whose names I did not know, but who belonged to the (13th) Thirteenth Tennessee cavalry, shot down after having been taken prisoners. I also saw them kill three sick men that were lying helpless in their tents.

I saw them make our men (colored) pull the artillery, whipping them at the same time in the most shameful manner.

I also saw them bury one of our men alive, being only wounded. I heard

Colonel McCullough, Confederate States army, ask his adjutant how many men were killed and wounded. The adjutant told him he had a list of three hundred, and that all the reports were not in yet. Colonel McCullough was commanding a brigade. I also heard a captain, Confederate States army, tell Colonel McCullough, Confederate States army, that ten men were killed out of his own company.

his
FRANK × HOGAN.
mark.

Sworn to and subscribed before me this 30th day of April, 1864, at Fort Pickering, Memphis, Tennessee.

MALCOM F. SMITH,
First Lieutenant and Adjutant 6th U. S. Heavy Artillery, (colored.)

A true copy.

J. H. ODLIN,
Captain and Assistant Adjutant General

Statement of Wilbur H. Gaylord, first sergeant, company B, 6th United States heavy artillery, (colored.)

FORT PICKERING, TENNESSEE, *April* 28, 1864.

I was in the battle fought at Fort Pillow on the 12th day of April, A. D. 1864. The engagement commenced about six and a half o'clock a. m. I was stationed about twenty rods outside the fort with twenty men in a southeast direction, (this was about six and a half o'clock a. m.,) with orders from Major S. F. Booth to hold the position as long as possible without being captured. I staid there with the men about one hour. While there the rebels came within thirty rods and tried to steal horses. They got two horses, and at the same time stuck a rebel flag on the fortifications. While I held this position the white men on my right (13th Tennessee cavalry) retreated to the fort. About ten minutes after this I went with my men to the fort. While going into the fort I saw Lieutenant Barr, 13th Tennessee cavalry, shot down by my side. He was shot through the head. He fell outside the fortifications, about six feet. Ten minutes after getting into the fort Major S. F. Booth was shot at porthole No. 2, while standing directly in the rear of the gun; was shot directly through the heart; expired instantly. I carried him to the bank of the river. As soon as I returned Captain Epeneter, company A, was wounded in the head while standing at porthole No. 4. He immediately went to the hospital, which was below the river bank—about half way down, I should think. Ten men were killed before a flag of truce came in, which was about twelve o'clock m. Five men, who were all dressed alike, came with the flag from the rebels, and Major Bradford, of 13th Tennessee cavalry, who had now assumed command, asked one hour to consider; on the conclusion of which, he returned a decided refusal. The fire on both sides now commenced, and was kept up about half an hour with great fury, when the rebels charged over the works. (I should have said that General Forrest came with the flag.) The enemy was checked and held for a few minutes. As soon as they were fairly on the works, I was wounded with a musket ball through the right ankle. I should think that two hundred rebels passed over the works, and passed by me while I lay there, when one rebel noticed that I was alive, shot at me again and missed me. I told him I was wounded, and that I would surrender, when a Texan ranger stepped up and took me prisoner. Just at this time I saw them shoot down three black men, who were begging for their life, and who had surrendered. The rebels now helped me through porthole No. 4. The ranger who took me captured a colored soldier, whom he sent with me. He also sent a guard. They took me to picket post No. 2. There I was put into an ambulance and taken to a farm-house with one of their dead, who was a chaplain. There I was made to lie out doors all night on account of the houses being filled with their wounded. I bandaged my own wound with my drawers, and a colored man brought water and sat by me so that I could keep my foot wet. Next morning Colonel McCullough came there and sent a squad of men, having pressed all the conveyances he could find to take away his own wounded. Not finding sufficient, nor having negroes enough, they made stretchers from blankets. They could not carry me, and so left me at the farm-house; the man's name was Stone. He got me into the house and into bed. He and his wife were very kind to me. While Colonel McCullough was there he told me Memphis, Tennessee, was probaby in the hands of the rebels. The rear guard of the rebels left there Wednesday about 5 o'clock p. m. The rebels took a young man whose father lived near here, and who had been wounded in the fight, to the woods, and shot three more shots into his back and into his head, and left him until Friday morning, when the citizens took him in. They brought him to the house where I was, and then carried us both to Fort Pillow in an old cart that they fixed up for the occasion, in hopes of getting us on board of a gunboat.

Upon our arrival there a gunboat lay on the opposite bank, but we could not hail her. We laid on the bank. They took the young man back to a house, three-fourths of a mile, but I would not go back. I laid there until a gunboat, the Silver Cloud, took me off, about 2 o'clock a. m., Saturday. They treated me with the utmost kindess on board the boat.

WILBUR H. GAYLORD,
1st Sergeant, Co. B, 6th U. S. Heavy Artillery, 1st Battalion, (colored.)

Sworn to and subscribed before me this 30th day of April, 1864, at Fort Pickering, Memphis, Tennessee.

MALCOM F. SMITH,
1st Lieutenant and Adjutant 6th U. S. Heavy Artillery, (colored.)

A true copy.

J. H. ODLIN,
Captain and A. A. G.

Statement of James Lewis, private, company C, 6th United States heavy artillery, (colored.)

I, James Lewis, private, company C, 6th United States heavy artillery, (colored,) would, on oath, state the following: I was in the battle fought at Fort Pillow, Tennessee, on the 12th day of April, A. D. 1864. The engagement commenced early in the morning and lasted until three o'clock p. m. same day, at which time the enemy carried the fort. The United States troops took refuge under the bank of the river. The officers all being killed or wounded, the men raised the white flag and surrendered, but the rebels kept on firing until most all the men were shot down. I was wounded and knocked down with the but of a musket and left for dead, after being robbed, and they cut the buttons off my jacket. I saw two women shot by the river bank and their bodies thrown into the river after the place was taken. I saw Frank Meek, company B, 6th United States heavy artillery, (colored,) shot after he had surrendered.

his
JAMES + LEWIS.
mark.

Sworn to and subscribed before me this 30th day of April, 1864, at Fort Pickering, Memphis, Tennessee.

MALCOM F. SMITH,
1st Lieutenant and Adjutant 6th U. S. Heavy Artillery, (colored.)

A true copy.

J. H. ODLIN,
Captain and A. A. G.

[This evidence was received after the regular edition was printed.]

P. S. Since the report of the committee was prepared for the press, the following letter from the surgeon in charge of the returned prisoners was received by the chairman of the committee:

WEST'S BUILDINGS HOSPITAL,
Baltimore, Md., May 24, 1864.

DEAR SIR: I have the honor to enclose the photograph of John Breinig, with the desired information written upon it. I am very sorry your committee could not have seen these cases when first received. No one, from these pictures, can form a true estimate of their condition then. Not one in ten was able to stand alone; some of them so covered and eaten by vermin that they nearly resembled cases of small-pox, and so emaciated that they were *really* living skeletons, and hardly *that*, as the result shows, forty out of one hundred and four having died up to this date.

If there has been anything so horrible, so fiendish, as this wholesale starvation, in the history of this satanic rebellion, I have failed to note it. Better the massacres at Lawrence, Fort Pillow, and Plymouth than to be thus starved to death by inches, through long and weary months. I wish I had possessed the power to compel all the northern sympathizers with this rebellion to come in and look upon the work of the *chivalrous* sons of the *hospitable* and sunny south when these skeletons were first received here. A rebel colonel, a prisoner here, who stood with sad face looking on as they were received, finally shook his head and walked away, apparently ashamed that he held any relations to men who could be guilty of such deeds.

Very respectfully, your obedient servant,

A. CHAPEL.

Hon. B. F. WADE,
Chairman of Committee on the Conduct of the War, Senate U. S.

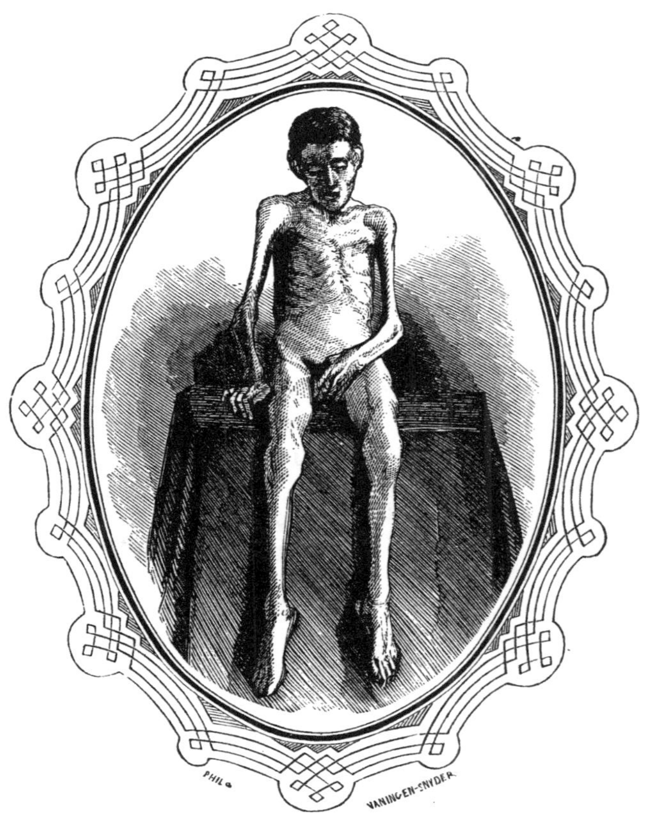
PHIL.
VANINGEN-SNYDER

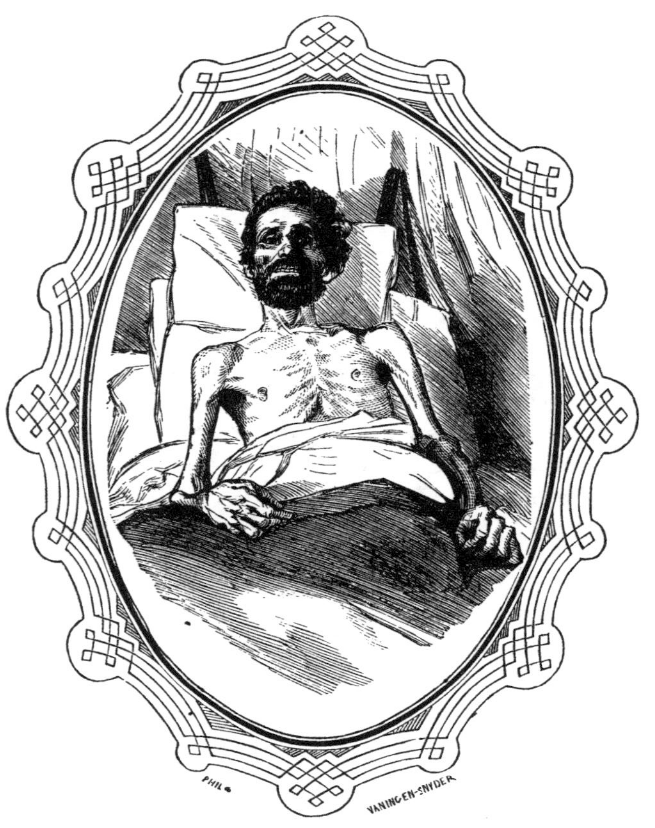
PHIL.
VANINGEN-SNYDER

U. S. GENERAL HOSPITAL, DIV. No. 1,

ANNAPOLIS, MD.

Private FRANCIS W. BEEDLE,

COMPANY M, 8TH MICHIGAN CAVALRY,

Was admitted per Steamer New York, from Richmond, Va., May 2, 1864. Died May 3, 1864, from effects of treatment while in the hands of the enemy.

WEST'S BUILDING HOSPITAL,

BALTIMORE, MD.

Private JOHN BREINIG,

COMPANY G, 4TH KENTUCKY CAVALRY,

Admitted April 18, 1864. Improved a little for two weeks, then gradually failed and died on the 12th instant.

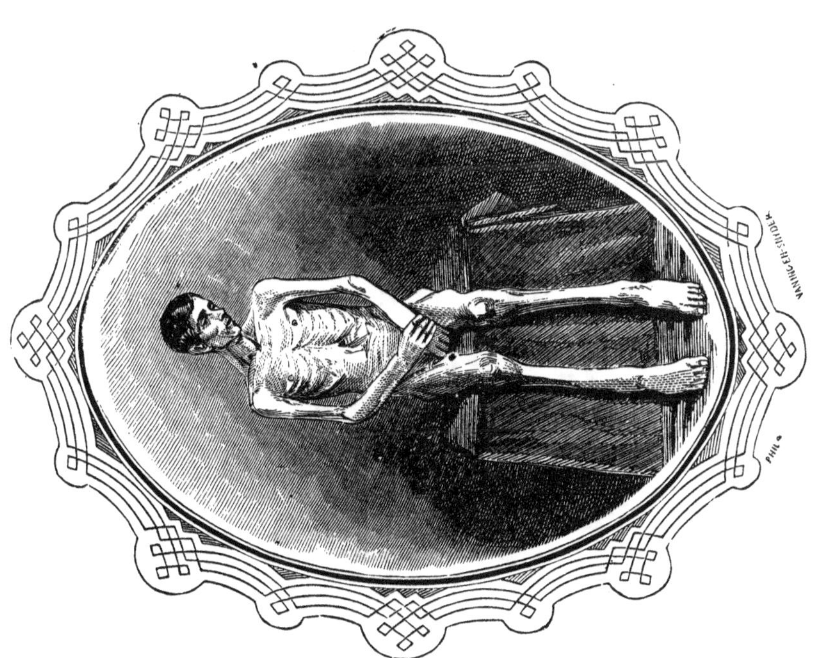

U. S. GENERAL HOS PITAL, DIV.No. 1,
ANNAPOLIS, MD.

Private JOHN Q. ROSE,

COMPANY C, 8TH KENTUCKY VOLUNTEERS,

Admitted per Steamer New York, from Richmond, Va., May 2, 1864. Died May 4, 1864, from effects of treatment while in the hands of the enemy.

U. S. GENERAL HOSPITAL, DIV. No. 1,
ANNAPOLIS, MD.

Private L. H. PARHAM,

COMPANY B, 3D WEST TENNESSEE CAVALRY,

Admitted per Steamer New York, from Richmond, Va., May 2, 1864. Died May 10, 1864, from effects of treatment while in the hands of the enemy.

PHIL
VANINGEN-SNYDER

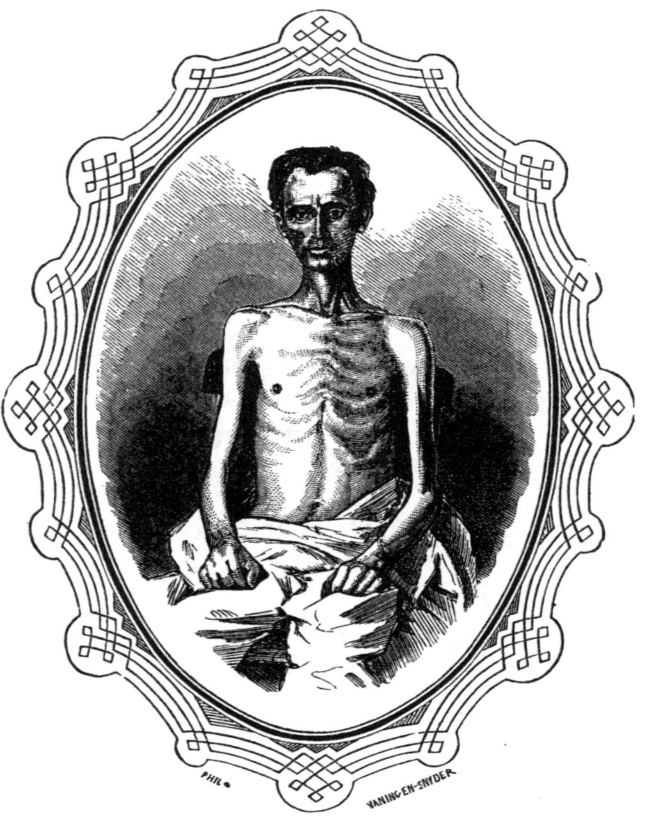
PHIL
VANINGEN-SNYDER

WEST'S BUILDING HOSPITAL,

BALTIMORE, MD.

Private GEORGE H. WIBLE,

COMPANY F, 9TH MARYLAND VOLUNTEERS,

Was admitted from Flag-of-truce boat April 18, 1864. Is slowly improving.

WEST'S BUILDING HOSPITAL,

BALTIMORE, MD.

Private EDWARD CUNNINGHAM,

COMPANY F, 7TH OHIO CAVALRY,

Was admitted from Flag-of-truce boat April 18, 1864. Very little change in his condition since received.

PHIL
VANINGEN-SNYDER

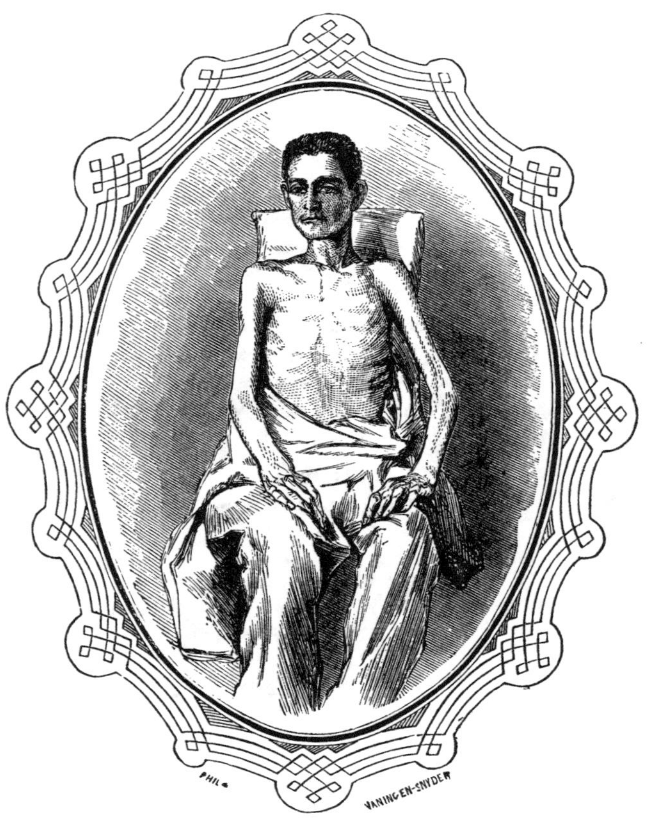
PHIL
VANINGEN-SNYDER

WEST'S BUILDING HOSPITAL,
BALTIMORE, MD.

Private LEWIS KLEIN,

COMPANY A, 14TH NEW YORK CAVALRY,

Admitted from Steamer New York, from Richmond, Va. April 18, 1864. Is improving nicely.

WEST'S BUILDING HOSPITAL,
BALTIMORE, MD.

Private CHARLES R. WOODWORTH,

COMPANY G, 8TH MICHIGAN CAVALRY,

Was admitted from Flag-of-truce boat April 18, 1864. Has improved very much since received.

* 9 7 8 1 4 2 5 5 1 3 6 3 4 *